"Riveting . . . a compelling account of one of the least-known stories in church history [that] unfolds like a good mystery yarn . . . [Stanford] skillfully juggles facts, hints, and possibilities to turn out a fascinating historical detective story . . . a thorough, intelligent, and absorbing tale."
—*Boston Globe*

"Stanford renders the myth itself—how this woman who penetrated the ultimate men's club has been represented, reviled, and revered for more than a millennium—in fascinating detail."   —*Entertainment Weekly*

"Stanford's masterful presentation of the historical evidence makes this the definitive study of an amazing legend that has been a source of fascination for centuries."   —*Publishers Weekly*

"[Stanford] makes a convincing case for leaving the inquiry open . . . His writing is concise and energetic . . . and his approach well thought out. *The Legend of Pope Joan* is a valuable tool for understanding the sexual politics of the Catholic Church—as contentious an issue now as it ever has been—and an extremely engaging read as well."
—*Willamette Week* (Oregon)

"Stanford engagingly relates the legend . . . [His] careful research finds much support for the basic historicity of this widespread myth."
—*Library Journal*

continued on next page . . .

The British press praises *The Legend of Pope Joan*

"Intriguing and colorful history . . . The search for a verdict is fascinating."
—*The Times* (London)

"The story of Pope Joan must be one of the most fascinating enigmas of medieval history . . . In this engaging but scholarly book, [Stanford] traces his quest for the historical Joan . . . He reveals the compulsive power of her story: he approaches the female Pope in rather the same spirit as Thomas Hardy, tiptoeing into the shed on Christmas Eve to see the oxen kneel and 'hoping it might be so.'" —*The Literary Review*

"Peter Stanford, with great skill, takes us back to earlier centuries, and juggles with a succession of delightfully named potentates of the Church, winkling out of fascinating, sometimes hilarious, facts and possibilities . . . Peter Stanford is that rare being, a popular historian with personality and heart." —*Daily Telegraph*

"[Stanford] excavates a figure from a legend, where she was buried to avoid scandal, and powerfully suggests that she may well have actually existed. Step forward, Joan, the only woman pope the Church has ever had . . . Enter Peter Stanford, Joan's champion. His story is beguilingly told as a mixture of thriller and pilgrimage account . . . This is a most entertaining piece of detection and history, which voyages bravely into heretical waters." —*The Independent on Sunday*

"Peter Stanford's ecclesiastical detective story [is] an utter delight . . . [with] careful and wonderfully readable research. [It] continues a tradition of shining light into obscure but fascinating corners of history." —*The Independent*

THE LEGEND OF

Pope Joan

THE LEGEND OF

Pope Joan

IN SEARCH OF THE TRUTH

PETER STANFORD

B

BERKLEY BOOKS, NEW YORK

Originally published in Great Britain in 1998
by William Heinneman under the title *The She-Pope*.

THE LEGEND OF POPE JOAN

A Berkley Book / reprinted by arrangement with
Henry Holt & Company, Inc.

PRINTING HISTORY
Henry Holt & Company edition / January 1999
Berkley trade paperback edition / April 2000

The Penguin Putnam Inc. World Wide Web site address is
http://www.penguinputnam.com

ISBN: 0-425-17347-X

BERKLEY®
Berkley Books are published by The Berkley Publishing Group,
a division of Penguin Putnam Inc.,
375 Hudson Street, New York, New York 10014.
BERKLEY and the "B" design
are trademarks belonging to Penguin Putnam Inc.

PRINTED IN THE UNITED STATES OF AMERICA

10 9 8 7 6 5 4 3 2 1

For Siobhan and Kit

Acknowledgments

Searching out a character that the Church has tried so hard to bury has often been an uphill struggle and would not have been completed without the help and assistance of the following: Simonetta Alder, Sister Lavinia Byrne IBVM, Professor David Canter, Caryl Churchill, Jim and Lena Cross, Audrey and Faith de Candole, Moya Frenz St Leger, Caroline Goodfellow of the Museum of Childhood, Wendy Hefford of the Victoria and Albert Museum, Fiona and Peter Jerreat, Dr Martin Kauffman of the Bodleian Library, Sara Maitland, Dr Rosalind Miles, Professor Gangolf Schrimpf, Ian Skidmore, Bruce Stewart, Michael Walsh, Julie Wheelwright, John Wilkins, Lalla Winkley and her colleagues at Catholic Women's Ordination and David Zak. Carmela Inguanta made good the very large holes in my knowledge of Italian, Jarmilla Vavrova my complete absence of Czech while Maria Locher expanded on my three words of German.

Three people in our own times have worked to unravel the mystery of Pope Joan – the French literary historian Alain Boureau, the venerable Catholic feminist, Joan Morris, who died in 1985, and the Italian historian Cesare D'Onofrio. I am grateful to the last for all his help and to Ivan May for his permission to quote from the writings of his late aunt, Joan Morris, many of which are now stored in the Fawcett Library. The Catholic Central Library in London, a little-known and underused gem, has once again afforded me able and warm assistance. Rosemary and Darroll Pardoe, fellow searchers after Pope Joan, have also been generous with their assistance.

My editors, Tom Weldon and Charlotte Mendelson in London and Marian Wood and Rachel Klauber-Speiden in America, my agent Derek Johns, Lucinda Coxon and my brother Martin Stanford have all offered practical encouragement. And my wife Siobhan has, as ever, been there with support and advice at the crucial moments.

Part One

THE HOLY SHE

Chapter One

'Rome has spoken; the case is concluded'
Saint Augustine of Hippo[1]

In overcrowded cities like London, you get used to living without a view. Save for a favoured few whose homes are cheek by jowl with the great parks, historic churches, or the river, there is seldom anything of interest outside your window unless you are an inveterate curtain twitcher or an aspiring member of Neighbourhood Watch. Holidays, however, are different. You find yourself in strange and intriguing places. You are an outsider with the incentive and the time to find a spot where you can sit back and watch the world go by.

My late-spring sojourn in Rome had been hastily arranged. A friend offered his flat and I wanted to get away. It all seemed perfect, fated even, for those tempted by predestination. But the summer heat had come early and after a couple of over-ambitious rambles around the streets and shrines of this warm nest of the Renaissance, sunstroke threatened and lethargy set in.

The apartment was what estate agents might call ingeniously planned – tiny and claustrophobic. It did, however, have one redeeming feature, enormous floor-to-ceiling windows that over-whelmed the studio room. I would collapse most afternoons into the big, deep, pink armchair in front of this opening, catching whatever breeze was around and pretending to read one of the doorstopper tomes I had brought with me – classically long, potentially enthralling but in my weakened state hardly page-turners. More often than not, I was content to gaze out on the square below.

It could hardly be described as beautiful, in the way that, say, the Piazza Navona is majestically beautiful in its perfect proportions. It had no equivalent of Bernini's Four Rivers Fountain in the centre. Indeed, it was barely a square – more like the confluence of a number of streams where the via dei Querceti widens and flows into several other roads.

The people made it a place. Italians have a marvellous habit of living their lives with great drama on the street. For them this small space was stage enough. The world outside my window was a daily soap opera with the flower seller, the greengrocer and the newspaper vendor interacting with each other. Occasionally they were interrupted by a passing pilgrim or the ironworkers and stone masons who have made this area, at the foot of the Coelian Hill, their quarter. It was a play in a thousand tiny acts, shared intimacies, significant looks, cold shoulders, heated exchanges, wounded exits stage right to the slightly seedy coffee bar, all observed without fear of being spotted from my box in the sky.

The backdrop to this plot was more functional than spectacular. For days I hardly noticed it at all. The architecture of this backwater of Rome, tucked away between the Colosseum, commanding as it does the main traffic artery, and the great cathedral of Saint John Lateran – once the headquarters of Christianity until the popes, on their return from exile in Avignon in the fourteenth century, decided to make the Vatican their base – was nothing to write home about, at least in Roman terms. It has, like every corner of this city, at least half a dozen sites that any other town would celebrate with plaques and signposts, but for Rome they are the 'B' and 'C' list celebrities – the Basilica of Saint Clement, built on the ruins of an earlier pagan temple and emphasising Rome's many histories; the twelfth-century fortress Church of Santi Quattro Coronati; and the Irish College, a seminary with colourful figures and legendary hospitality.

The main visitor routes bypassed what could be seen from my aerial vantage point. The whole area had an insular feel, cut off from the everyday business of Rome two streets away on the main drag of the via San Giovanni in Laterano, bustling between the *centro storico* and the popular housing areas beyond the basilica. This was an enclave within a city, a back garden of trees, wistaria and weeping bushes rambling over the crumbling walls that flanked the streets leading away from the square. Even the traffic, the constant accompaniment to life in Rome, was intermittent. The occasional ancient Fiat, roaring into life with a rattle like cutlery in a tumble-drier, would drown the buzz of conversation, but for the most part what cars, taxis and cycles there were, passed or parked unnoticed.

There were, of course, lulls, intervals in the performance punctuated only by the regular – and I thought in the early hours of the morning remorseless – ringing of the bells of Saint Clement's. And it was in these breaks that my eyes would scan the set. The shuttered windows, the anonymous doorways, the firmly bolted gateways, the back entry to the store-room of the local pizzicheria offered little sustenance to the imagination. So my attention settled on the little shrine – or *edicola* as an Italian friend corrected me when I offered her a guided tour of my panorama – directly opposite my window. It looked more like a sentry box, bolted to the wall, guarding the point where the via dei Santissimi Quattro Coronati began its steep ascent from the square to the church itself. Occasionally funereal carnations would decorate the shrine. I suspected that it was the flower seller finding a home for blooms well past their sell-by date in a budget gesture of devotion. But try as I might, I never witnessed her placing them there behind the locked gates.

I once sat out in the square, among the parked cars, watching the *edicola* in the hope of putting a face to its decorator. To pass the time, I scribbled away with inconsequential thoughts and sketches in my notebook. This seemed to attract an undue amount of attention from those drivers – mainly elegant women – who left their cars double and triple parked. Two or three stood staring nervously at me and then got back in their vehicles and drove off. Might they be the secret *edicola* devotees, I wondered? Italian women are famously pious, and there is often a direct link between the strength and superstition of their faith and the cost of their clothes. Or did they think I looked like a car thief? Perhaps I should have shaved, but I was on holiday.

Finally one woman, her hennaed shoulder-length hair glinting strange shades in the morning sun, revealed the truth. She came over and asked if I was a plain-clothes policeman noting down her registration number to give her a fine. I had a suspicion her hand rummaging in her Gucci bag presaged the offer of a bribe, but when I denied it, she shrugged and said, 'It's what happens today.' And then she walked off. Confused and slightly flushed, I abandoned my vigil soon afterwards.

I couldn't quite get the *edicola* out of my mind and, wandering home one lunch-time a few days later, I spotted a card attached to a garish cocktail of purple and pink carnations. 'My inspiration,' the simple message read. I peered in at the *edicola*. Despite the flaking ochre-coloured walls, its interior was dark. A faded fresco of the Madonna and Child could be made out beyond the greenish grille. As my eyes grew accustomed to the gloom, I saw that it was beautiful without necessarily bringing anything new to its overworked subject. Striking an incongruous note, there was also a ghastly, cloying statuette of Saint Anthony of Padua, clearly a more recent addition. There was something in the neglect and irreverence with which this peeling wayside *edicola* was treated – its sides had that day been plastered by bill stickers advertising *30 Giorni*, ironically a church-operated magazine – that appealed to the melancholy romantic in me. The almost fluorescent colour of the flowers against the pale, sandy-coloured, dirt-encrusted background seemed very poignant. The *edicola* recalled in my mind those overgrown angels and crosses you find in unkempt countryside cemeteries, once loved and tended but today forgotten by all but a handful of devoted souls.

Later still, I was ensconced in my armchair, staring out as I wrote my diary and it occured to me to record this hackneyed pensée. To lift it out of the mire of the commonplace I decided to add a little detail and so searched for any reference to the shrine or indeed the area in the many guidebooks that littered the flat – a reproach, I had already decided, to my lack of sightseeing gusto.

Was the phantom flower donor the only champion of this wayside *edicola*? Evidently yes. Most guides did not even give it a mention. They took you straight from the wonders of Saint Clement's through the Quattro Coronati – with its legend of the Christian stone masons who refused to make a statue of a pagan god and who were martyred for their defiance – and on to Saint John Lateran. However, in one book I happened across an intriguing clue. In her *Companion Guide to Rome*, the English historian Georgina Masson finds herself in the square below my window, looking up the hill to Santi Quattro Coronati.

> Walking up it we pursue exactly the opposite route to that taken in the old days by the papal cavalcade or the 'possesso' on its way to the Lateran; and thereby hangs one or the most fabulous tales of Roman folklore. The papal cavalcade proceeded up the via dei SS Quattro Coronati to this point and then changed over to the via di San Giovanni in Laterano, because in the lower part of the street there was a house known to the Roman populace as that of 'Papessa Giovanna'. Some fragment of a classical relief, showing a woman with her breast bared and a child in her arms, marked the spot; this was removed and the whole house pulled down by order of Pius IV in 1550. How it came to be associated with the fantastic legend, or perhaps even gave rise to it, is not known. But the fact remains that for centuries the Romans told the story of how an Englishwoman called Joan succeeded in being elected as Pope John VIII.[2]

It was at this spot, Masson continued, that Joan, who had hitherto

6

disguised herself as a man, was revealed when she gave birth to a child in the street. 'Both she and it', Masson concludes, 'were killed by the outraged populace and buried by the roadside.'

A fantastic legend indeed. This had certainly not been on the curriculum of my Christian Brothers' school. I was taught that Nicholas Breakspear as Hadrian IV was the only English Pope.[3] A woman pope in an organisation that prides itself, in its clerical reaches at least, on being an all-male club would be a sensation with profound implications for the ongoing debate on women priests. The Catholic church's objection to female ordination is based not on scripture but on tradition. There never have been women priests so there never can be. That argument might be difficult to sustain if once a woman had sat on Saint Peter's throne.

What is more, one of Catholicism's proudest boasts concerning the papacy – that there is an apostolic succession down from Christ to Saint Peter and thence on to his successors, all of them by this token divinely ordained – would be subject to some revision if a woman had been part of that unbroken line. For even if Joan fooled the men around her, she could not have tricked God. He would have known her real identity and gender. Did God want a female pope? And if he did, where does that leave the current Catholic ban on women at the altar?

My mind was racing ahead, shaking off my holiday lethargy. Ms Masson was careful in describing as a legend her account of what might have taken place outside my window. Legends are usually a sliver of fact mixed with a large dollop of fiction. What was real, I wondered, and what fantasy?

A renewed search along the flat's shelves and thereafter in one of Rome's several English bookshops yielded further if inconclusive clues. The *Oxford Dictionary of Popes*[4] did not include its account in the main chronological section. Joan clearly was not someone to be mentioned in the roll-call of honour of popes, though many a male interloper, the 'anti-popes' who had seized the throne by force against the will of the Church, was nevertheless included. Joan was relegated to an appendix. The same details were rehearsed as had been relayed in Masson – though it had her down as 'a native of Mainz in Germany, not England' – and some references were given to various medieval chronicles that told the tale. The tone was sceptical, but ended with a curious tale that Joan had given rise to stories about popes having to undergo a test to prove they were men.

This was beginning to ring a bell. When I was editor of a Catholic newspaper in London, one of our regular columnists, a Welsh priest called Father John Owen, a man with a tendency to speak the truth even when it hurt, had recorded just such a tale as fact.[5] There had been a cardinal whose anointed role it was, when a new pope was selected, to touch the candidate's testicles to make sure he was a man. There had even been a special chair to carry out the procedure. The article had prompted a deluge of rude letters from other priests, usually a sure sign that the author was on to something, but perpetually battered and bruised by such assaults I had never followed it up.

Back in my own chair, I was fascinated. Here was something interesting, a holiday distraction. Where, I wondered, as I looked out of the window, might the little *edicola* fit in? The Madonna and Child, surely, could have no part in this tale of deception and skullduggery. Then another explanation occurred to me, shocking at first, but just possible. Could this be another woman with her infant, a woman by repute the antithesis of Christ's mother, a con-woman with her bastard child at her breast minutes before she was murdered for her treachery, the woman described in Georgina Masson's account? Had Anthony of Padua been added later to give the shrine a veneer of orthodoxy? Was the phantom florist worshipping Our Lady, or the memory of a woman who shocked the church to its foundations? Could the bas-relief that Georgina Masson writes of have survived, or been copied in such a way that both Joan and the Virgin were venerated in a single image? This neglected *edicola* might just have a story to tell after all.

The international headquarters of Catholicism is a place where the outward signs of devotion and belief are often contradicted by what goes on behind closed doors. On one level, Rome – in many of the rituals associated with particular spots – sports almost pagan beliefs in what the old *Penny Catechism* used to deem signs and wonders. The beautiful sixth-century church of Santa Maria in Cosmedin, for instance, gives its blessing to a strange circular mask-like face in the porch known as the 'Bocca della verità'. The mouth is open and visitors are challenged to place their hands inside. Those who have not followed the path of truth risk having their hands bitten off. The church authorities apparently see no harm in this ancient superstition.

And on another more everyday level, there is the strong whiff of hypocrisy that pervades God's business address on earth. During my stay, one priest was planning a court challenge to a hospital's refusal to

8

place him and his partner on a waiting list for *in vitro* fertilisation treatment. Like many couples, they wanted a child. But he had taken a vow of celibacy. His actions prompted shrugs and laughs among the characters outside my window, but no disbelief, and certainly no calls for his resignation.

Only in Rome would this be possible. Hypocrisy in northern Europe revolves around not mentioning things, covering up double standards and double-speak for what those doing it often judge to be positive reasons. In Rome, and more generally in Italy, hypocrisy takes another and more negative form, a devil-may-care attitude. The Romans have even cobbled together their own word for it – *menefregismo*, literally 'I couldn't give a fuck'ism'. It pervades local, regional and national politics. And it affects the way the society functions. The Father who wants to be a father prompts only thoughts of 'good for him if he can get away with it'.

Here in Rome then, only in Rome, could the story of Pope Joan seem possible. Only here might a woman in drag have pulled off the ultimate scam.

Behind its castellated walls the Vatican Museum contains a dizzying array of treasures. Michelangelo's *Last Judgement* in the Sistine Chapel, the 'Raphael Rooms' decorated by the master of the Italian Renaissance, priceless tapestries, early maps, even horse-drawn carriages all attract a constant procession of awestruck admirers. The Catholic church is custodian to one of the greatest, largest and most eclectic collections of art, artefacts and *objets* in the world.

With their knack for organisation and compartmentalising every aspect of human existence, the Vatican authorities offer four well-signposted routes around their vast exhibition hall of a museum. Even those who opt for the most arduous option see only a fraction of what is on display. Tucked away in antechambers and dusty corners are exhibits that have been left in a kind of limbo, technically within the fold of the museum but outside the boundaries of the authorised version. They are unexplained and often unlit, glimpsed only by those who lose their way or else show extraordinary cussedness and independence of spirit in refusing to be regimented on ready-made route marches.

It was for just such a musty corner that I was heading with my new-found purposefulness. A bit of digging had identified the Gabinetto delle Maschere ('Mask Room') as containing the infamous 'ball-feeling' chair. In the entrance hall of the museum, various closures were announced, but there was no mention of the Gabinetto, nor of the larger Galleria delle Statue which leads to it. So I took a deep breath and scaled the long, gently sloping and circular ramp that rises up from street level to the ticket desks. I paid my money and followed the signs, through a courtyard and past a gaggle of Korean nuns whose passive stares refused to meet my eyes. These were the only women allowed any sort of official role in the contemporary Catholic church and even then as a kind of superior line in laity. Nuns have never had any claim on clerical status. What would they make, I wondered as I galloped up some steps, across another courtyard and through the sculpture gallery to the Gabinetto, of the idea of a woman pope?

My path was blocked by a 'No Entry' sign and a chain. A smart young man in an expensive suit with a badge identifying him as a Vatican Museum employee was standing nearby. I explained – with just a hint of hyperbole – that I had come all the way from London to see one item in the Gabinetto and wondered if it were possible, for a few moments only, for him to let me in. It was, after all, only a matter of unhooking the chain.

He appeared genuinely sympathetic to my predicament, but patiently explained that it was much more complicated than I imagined. He led me to a more senior colleague – in the Vatican Museum seniority is designated by a uniform and a surly attitude. The room was closed, he proclaimed, because of a shortage of staff. He directed me to the Information Desk on street level to make my representations.

As I retraced my steps, I caught sight of myself in one of the security mirrors, pushing past smiling, relaxed holiday-makers, a frown of impatience imprinted on my forehead, a man possessed. Not for the last time in the months ahead, I wondered what on earth I was doing looking into the riddle of Pope Joan, playing ecclesiastical detective in the manner of Ellis Peters's Brother Cadwael. The pink armchair that had been my holiday home suddenly beckoned.

The Information Desk attendant was wholly unimpressed that I had once edited a Catholic newspaper in London. Whether it was the editing, the paper or those weak-kneed, liberal-minded, quasi-Protestant English Catholics he objected to, I could not fathom. 'Are you a student of art?' The attendant put it in a neutral tone, taking a pad out of his desk. It was going to take a white lie.

A second, younger, man was summoned by telephone to accompany me. I assumed that we were off to the Mask Room. But no, we arrived via two lifts in the administration block. At least it avoided the stairs again. I was handed over to a mustachioed man in a uniform behind a desk. He asked me how long I needed. 'Five minutes.' I was trying to be accommodating. He disappeared. Five minutes passed. I began to worry that I was having my allotted time here in the waiting room.

On the stroke of five, he returned with a middle-aged woman. She had another form for me to fill in. 'Art student' I carefully inscribed in capitals. Again it acted as an absolution. Then she disappeared. Finally another young man in short sleeves appeared in the room. He was to accompany me, he explained, but first he needed to find his jacket. Old-world courtesies are important here. Nakedness, even of arms, is only tolerated in the exhibits.

Finally we set off, back to the main ticket hall and through the galleries. Half-way there, I was handed over to another guardian. 'No staff,' he explained apologetically as he undid the chain on the Mask Room. 'Never open.' I resisted pointing out that a time-and-motion study could easily yield at least half a dozen potential guardians, all of them currently underemployed with form-filling and five-minute absences.

The Gabinetto delle Maschere was being used as an informal store-room, bits of lighting equipment, scaffolding and scraps of black paper everywhere, covering what is its principal attraction, a mosaic floor, taken from Hadrian's Villa at nearby Tivoli. It includes masks in its design. Hence the name of the room. With eyes downcast to take in this marvel of antiquity, you could easily miss the huge commode-like chair in aubergine marble which sits in the window recess. It carries no explanatory note, only a thick coat of dust.

It's a strange object. There is, for a start, something curious about its proportions. The seat is very high and has cut into it a keyhole shape, the stem open to the front. On closer examination it could be an elderly, rather grand commode, once used by popes, perhaps, but now an embarrassing reminder of their humanity. However, the chair back is at a curious reclining angle, far too relaxed, it would seem, for any practical bodily movement. And the legs, too, are unusual – two slabs of marble down either side, ending in a flourish in the shape of a lion's claws, but leaving the centre, under the keyhole, open and uncluttered.

Variously known as the *sedia stercoraria* – which translates as the 'dung chair' – or, rather more understandably, as the 'pierced chair', this then was the object used to test the sex of newly installed popes before they were handed the keys of Saint Peter. Any candidate chosen by his peers to occupy the papal throne was required, before his election could be verified, to sit on this elaborate seat while a young cardinal took advantage of its design to touch his testicles.

There was only one way of testing this theory against the object before my eyes. My guardian angel had wandered off, leaving me all alone in the Mask Room. The chair wasn't behind railings and had, from the patterns in the dust, recently been used as an impromptu cupboard. It was almost inviting weary passers-by to sit down. With a glance behind me, I plonked myself down. It felt like a desecration. The Vatican Museum has the aura of a church and all my childhood training revolved around not touching anything in God's house. Pulse racing, white-faced, I leant back and back and back. As I'd thought, this could not be a commode. The angle of the back was more like a deck-chair. But the keyhole shape, I noticed as I brought my spine vertical, was in precisely the right place for the test.

I slid off with a nervous jolt and tried to rake and rearrange the dust patterns with the pages of my notebook to cover my sacrilege before the attendant returned. When he reappeared I was studiously buried in scribbling. With a smile, I hurried off, tripping over the disengaged chain as I made for the exit before a thunderbolt struck.

The story of checking the pope's masculinity may be a fantastic and much-ridiculed legend, I thought, but it stood up to the scrutiny of a casual investigation. In my mind I was already on to the next stage – finding an eyewitness to this bizarre test. For that I would need a library.

There were more check-points to pass before I could keep my appointment with Father Leonard Boyle, the Irish Dominican who runs the Vatican Library. Since the Vatican functions – like Monaco, San Marino and Andorra – as a miniature sovereign state, you have to show your passport before you can enter the hub of the Catholic church via the Porta Sant'Anna. No one had mentioned this to me, however, and when I presented myself there several days later, it was only a British Museum reader's card that saved me from deportation.

Offices in Rome tend to be huge with high ceilings to keep them cool in the height of the summer. Father Boyle's was no exception and dwarfed its resident. A slight man in his late fifties, his clerical garb was smart and exact. He had the air of a doctor working his way through a list of patients as he collected me from the reception room. I recounted my past career and my present interest in documentary evidence of strange tests on new popes and the history of Pope Joan. I had half expected to be shown the door for even breathing her name, but Father Boyle rested back in his chair, the faintest trace of a smile on his face.

As he considered his response, the phone rang and he disappeared behind his monumental desk to deal with the arrangements for a group of pilgrims who wanted to see round the library. He was all charm and affability in conversation with the caller. I began to feel hopeful. The Catholic clergy contains many troubled, tortured and difficult individuals, hiding behind its power structures, but occasionally you meet wonderful, charming men, at ease with their vocation and channelling their energy into their chosen field with good humour and exceptional learning. Father Boyle might just be one of this endangered species.

Once he'd finished his call, Father Boyle sauntered almost casually across his office and dropped a bombshell. I had happened upon the Vatican's unofficial expert on Pope Joan. Some thirty years previously, he explained, when as a young priest he had been based with his fellow Irish Dominicans at the ancient basilica of Saint Clement near my holiday flat, his enthusiasm for history had set him off researching – among the many other legends connected with the area, he stressed – the woman he jokingly referred to as 'the local hero'.

The church – and he delved into an adjoining stock-room to produce his booklet on Saint Clement's[6] – is on the route of the *possesso* mentioned by Georgina Masson. 'I even used to annoy the then rector', he recalled with a conspiratorial laugh, 'by trying to persuade him to put a plaque up to her in the street outside, just to pull his leg.'

A Donegal man, Father Boyle has spent nearly four decades in Rome, the last eleven in charge of the Vatican Library and its priceless collections of 150,000 volumes of manuscripts. One of the perks of the job, he said, was that it had given him a chance, in increasingly rare quieter moments, to follow up some of his youthful passions. Like Pope Joan.

He began listing some of the medieval manuscripts that referred to Joan. While I recognised a few from my initial reading, Father Boyle appeared to be talking about a Domesday Book's worth of sources. Before my eyes Pope Joan was transformed from potentially the creation of one long-forgotten writer of malicious fairy-tales into a regular feature of medieval literature about the papacy.

As if reading my mind, Father Boyle made his position clear. 'The most interesting part of the legend', he said, resting back against his desk, 'is not whether it is true or not. Of course it's not.' He must have sensed that I was crestfallen. 'But where did those medieval chroniclers get the story from? That's where the real detective work needs to be done. More to the point, if they all copied each other, where did the first person get it from?'

He was several steps ahead of me, but his enthusiasm was contagious. The next few days – and possibly weeks – unfolded. In a library. For Father Boyle, it was a manuscript mystery, a question of sources. The task – not an easy one, he freely acknowledged – was to search out the source of an ancient Chinese whisper.

First I needed to be quite sure that he felt there was no truth in the story. 'Elements in it are true,' he conceded. 'For instance, it's quite true that popes were in the habit of stopping off at San Clemente on their way from the Vatican to the Lateran. They passed that way. If it was the middle of the day they would stop for lunch and if it was evening, they might stay the night. That this happened in the early Middle Ages can be proved. But the whole story of Pope Joan – no.'

'Weren't you ever tempted to take your research further?' I ventured, knowing the answer. He gestured at the heaps of papers waiting for his attention all around him as if to say 'one day, perhaps'. On cue, the telephone interrupted our conversation again.

'Another thing you should be looking at', he continued when he put down the receiver, 'is the role of Bernard Guy, the arch-inquisitor.' Father Boyle had, it seemed, allocated me the task of tracking down Pope Joan. I noted the name. 'He was the role model, I've been told, for Umberto Eco's hero in *The Name of the Rose*.'[7] Guy, Father Boyle said, was a tough historian who dedicated himself to separating the wheat from the chaff when it came to legends, yet he left the story of Joan 'a bit in the air'. 'He repeats her legend and adds the words "as it is said". He doesn't say it's true, but then he doesn't dismiss it.'

There were other parts of the riddle that needed probing. Like the role of his own order, the Dominicans, in promoting the story of Pope Joan. 'It was largely Dominican writers who were involved. Martin of Poland was a Dominican and a very distinguished lawyer. So if it was a trick, why would he have written about her?' Another name to note. I was twitching to get on.

In the library itself, the card index revealed a plethora of references to Joan. They were half-way through computerisation, Father Boyle explained, as he took me on a short tour of the facilities. Oblivious to my very un-Roman desire to sit down straight away and go through the sources, he led me to the coffee bar that he had established for users of the library.

My cappuccino downed with unseemly haste, I was about to take my leave when I managed to articulate a thought that had been niggling away for some time now. Wasn't the story embarrassing for the Vatican, I asked. Should he be helping me and, more to the point, should I be contemplating researching such a tale?

'Nicely embarrassing.' He grinned. 'No one gets in the least worked up about it.' And then he considered. 'It's not even embarrassing. These stories are just taken as part of it all. It is flattering that the Church has so much woven around it.'

Chapter Two

'When could they say, till now, that talked of Rome,
That her wide walls encompassed but one man?
Now is it Rome indeed and room enough,
When there is in it but one only man.'
William Shakespeare, *Julius Caesar*

I quickly discovered that, whatever gloss Father Boyle put on it, the standard response of the Catholic church to talk of Pope Joan has been to damn it as a Protestant forgery. The scenario is simple. After the Reformation, dedicated followers of Luther, Calvin and Henry VIII tampered with ancient manuscripts and inserted fictitious references to a woman pope so as to make the papacy look foolish and hence belittle its claim to universal, God-given authority. These references were often so cunningly disguised that subsequent generations of readers could not tell the original from the interpolations and hence assumed that for much of the Middle Ages, Joan's existence was a truth universally acknowledged.

The She-Pope's story is recorded by some 500 chroniclers[1] of the papacy and matters Catholic, writing from early medieval times until the end of the seventeenth century. Among the phalanx of authors who testify unambiguously to her existence are papal servants, several bishops and some of the most distinguished and respected medieval chroniclers, writers whose accounts are the bedrock of current historical and church orthodoxy about their period. Yet in the matter of Joan, it is suggested that those manuscripts which date back to before the Reformation were subsequently altered.

At first glance, this official version is plausible. Joan's literary heyday – between 1200 and 1600 – belongs largely to the age before the mass production of books. What texts do still exist are often in later versions, opening the door to the possibility that the originals may have been amended to include references to Joan. If my investigation was not to be stillborn, my time in the library would have to show that this explanation did not stand up to scrutiny.

The first printed texts appeared in the middle of the fifteenth century with Johann Gutenberg of Mainz, credited as the earliest European to use movable type, closely followed by William Caxton. Before that –

and indeed with all but a handful of the most popular books for some 200 years afterwards – texts were handwritten. Each new copy had to be transcribed word for word on to parchment. In the early medieval period – up to 1200 – the scribes were mostly monks and nuns, and more often male religious than female. They were the only group with both the time to spend laboriously producing, illuminating and illustrating manuscripts, and the learning – literacy remained the domain of a privileged few – to master the complexities of the task.

The great monasteries had libraries that grew to become treasure houses of texts. Monks from smaller foundations would visit, write out a new version of one of the books they found in the library and travel back with the result of their labours to their own house. Then others would visit them for the same purpose, passing the text down a chain. It was a torturously slow process, made slightly less taxing by having its own language of abbreviations. 'PP', for example, stood for pope.

However, mistakes in transcription would inevitably creep in. Often, too, there was the temptation to add interpolations to the original as a means of showing superior learning or adapting it to local circumstances. In that way a text could be altered over the years as amended copies were made of already amended copies of an unseen – and too often lost, given the turbulence of the times – original.

It is not surprising that in the pre-1200 period there was not a great range of texts. Most were on religious and ecclesiastical themes: versions of the Bible, lives of pontiffs and emperors, accounts of papal or ecclesiastical happenings, hagiographies of venerable saints who sent the devil packing.

However, in the post-1200 era, the monopoly of the monasteries on books was broken, allowing a greater experimentation with formats, subjects and styles. A new generation of professional scribes and artists grew up in towns, many of them educated by monks and some of them graduates of the newly-founded ecclesiastical universities of Paris, Bologna and Oxford. These lay craftsmen were the first flourishing of the book trade. Their customers were the university libraries, whose demand for illustrated books could not be satisfied by the monasteries. Increasingly, too, the rich and powerful wanted manuscripts to celebrate their own families and achievements. 'Books of Hours' were among the most popular manifestations of this trade, collections of prayers and readings handwritten to the orders of a particular nobleman or his lady.

The greater part of these early manuscripts and books, however, is composed of ecclesiastical chronicles, written by monks and clerics, circulated and copied many times over. Most monasteries where writing was undertaken would keep a chronicle of local events, but the bigger institutions specialised in overviews of church history.

For the time when Joan is said to have held the papal throne, and for almost four hundred years afterwards, these vast, all-embracing accounts are historians' principal source of insight. This was after all the Dark Ages, so named because of the lack of information about what happened. Hovering indistinct but not undetected in the gloom of this shadowy landscape is the figure of Pope Joan.

If Pope Joan can be counted as having an early champion, a biographer in today's terms, it was the Dominican Martin Polonus – or Martin of Poland as Father Boyle had referred to him. Any attempt to trace a kind of family tree back through the various versions of her life inevitably ends up at him. Many subsequent writers reproduce his details and phrases verbatim.

Martin and Joan were not contemporaries. His chronicle first appeared in 1265, almost 400 years after the dates he gave for her reign. It was as if a current-day biographer were writing about the reign of Elizabeth I or the achievements of Sir Walter Raleigh.

Martin was a senior churchman at a time when the papacy was at the height of its powers and much of the turmoil, gloom and insecurity that characterised the Dark Ages had lifted. His writings celebrated that church hegemony. He was one of the most esteemed chroniclers of an age of outstanding scribes, with a reputation for seriousness and scholarship. His writings have endured because, unlike his rivals, he seldom fell victim to embroidering fanciful notions on to the facts that he was reporting.

Born in Troppeau, Poland, in the early years of the thirteenth century, he joined the Dominican order as a young man and was sent to Rome, where he rose steadily through the ranks, reaching the exalted post of papal chaplain under Clement IV (1265–8). His legal skills were well used in the Church's already burgeoning bureaucracy, but his passion was history and so he took up the popular medieval cleric's pastime of compiling chronicles.

Given the favour he enjoyed under several popes, and his access to all papal documents, his writings have come to be regarded by later generations as the quasi-official line of the Vatican. In his own time, too, they attracted admiration. Most of the major monastic libraries would have kept a copy of his chronicles. The first *Chronicon*

Pontificum et Imperatum ended in 1265. He subsequently amended this detailed and by all accounts dispassionate account of popes and emperors to extend its reach until 1277.

Soon afterwards, he was named Archbishop of Gneisen in Poland by Pope Nicholas III (1277–80). It was a curious appointment since Martin Polonus had already reached the ripe old age – by the standards of his contemporaries – of seventy. Perhaps it was homesickness that made him accept, or just obedience to the pope. On the long journey to his new diocese, he took ill and died in Bologna, in central Italy.

His *Chronicon Pontificum et Imperatum*, however, outlived him. In both the first and the updated versions, popes are listed on the left side of the page, with emperors on the right. The originals of both editions of the chronicle are now lost, but a fourteenth-century copy, held in Berlin's Staatsbibliothek, is thought to be the oldest still in existence[2]. It tells the following story after an account of the death of Pope Leo IV in 855:

> After the aforesaid Leo, John, an Englishman by descent, who came from Mainz, held the see two years, five months and four days, and the pontificate was vacant one month. He died at Rome. He, it is asserted, was a woman. And having been in youth taken by her lover to Athens in man's clothes, she made such progress in various sciences that there was nobody equal to her. So that afterwards lecturing on the Trivium at Rome she had great masters for her disciples and hearers. And for as much as she was in great esteem in the city, both for her life and her learning, she was unanimously elected pope. But when pope she became pregnant by the person with whom she was intimate. But not knowing the time of her delivery, while going from Saint Peter's to the Lateran, taken in labour, she brought forth a child between the Colosseum and Saint Clement's Church. And afterwards dying, she was, it is said, buried in that place. And because the Lord Pope always turns aside from that way, there are some who are fully persuaded that it is done in detestation of the fact. Nor is she put in the Catalogue of the Holy Popes, as well on account of her female sex as on account of the foul nature of the transaction.

Alongside the account quoted above, the Berlin manuscript contains an additional page. It is of a later date than the rest of the text and makes no attempt to integrate itself. The addenda retells the same story but embellishes it with new and shocking details: that Joan's lover was a secretary-deacon, that the street where she was disgraced was forthwith known as the 'Vicus Papissa' – Georgina Masson's description of the thoroughfare outside the window of my Roman flat – and that she was not killed after her deception was revealed but rather deposed and banished to a convent where she lived in penance to see her son become Bishop of Ostia, a coastal town at the mouth of the Tiber near Rome.

This effort at embroidering on the 'facts' as Martin Polonus recorded them was the first of many down the ages that added details to the skeleton of the story, names, places, emotions, motivations. It was Martin Polonus's basic text, however, that subsequently became the standard by which the story of Pope Joan was judged true or false. Supporters of the She-Pope tried to prove its authenticity, explaining away the gaps in some surviving versions of it as the work of Catholic librarians anxious to cover up an embarrassing tale, while detractors argued that talk of a female pontiff in drag had been added later by Protestants who tampered with originals held in various libraries around Europe in a concerted attempt to discredit the papacy. It brings to mind a picture of libraries as the battleground of the Reformation.

This 'official' version of history which rejects Joan's pontificate as a Protestant plot depends on the idea that Martin Polonus's was the first chronicle to mention it. This 'school' has channelled most of its energy into proving that all remaining early copies of the manuscript have been tampered with. Yet, as my trawl through the various mentions of Joan on the card index was showing, Martin Polonus was not the first to talk of the She-Pope. He can certainly claim to have furnished the most detail, but the family tree has deeper roots.

The German historian, Frederick Spanheim, a Protestant professor of philosophy at the University of Leyden at the end of the seventeenth century, tracked down some 500 references to Joan in manuscripts many of which have subsequently been lost. Given his denominational background and the climate of the times, Spanheim may well have taken pleasure in the discomfiture his study caused the Vatican. His *de Papa Foemina*, first published in 1691 in Latin, was so much in demand in French translation as *Histoire de la Papesse Jeanne* that there were three separate reprintings before 1736.[3]

Yet however popular his writings, and however much they pandered to anti-papal sentiments, they cannot be dismissed as lightweight; his scholarship was careful and precise, with lists showing every reference had been double-checked. Spanheim ascribed the first recorded

20

references to Joan to Anastasius, the papal librarian and her contemporary, and to a monk called Rudulphus, five years later. Neither original source still exists and both have to be discounted today through lack of corroboration. Some sceptics have suggested that Rudulphus did not live until the eleventh century,[4] though it could be that Spanheim was referring to a now lost document from Rudulphius of Fulda.

Spanheim's quotes from Anastasius are likewise open to question, since they cannot now be traced back to the originals that he examined. Anastasius was papal librarian in the ninth century, with many of the same responsibilities as Father Boyle. He is a key figure in the riddle of Pope Joan, principally because it was part of his official responsibilities to update the Church's own, official *Liber Pontificalis* – or *Book of Popes* – with details of contemporary incumbents in the latter part of the ninth century. The various versions of this text are the principal and indeed often the only source of information for historians of the papacy in the Dark Ages.

The earliest version of Anastasius's chronicle that survives today is a 1602 edition, published in Mainz after the Reformation. It contains references to Joan's story but at that time her tale was well enough known from other sources to make forgery or interpolation on the ninth-century original a possibility.

Though Spanheim has him down as endorsing the history of the She-Pope, another possibility is that Anastasius was the historian responsible for the 400-year gap between Joan's life and Martin of Poland's account. For if he had decided – or been ordered – to remove all trace of her deception from the *Liber Pontificalis*, then the centuries of official silence are more easily understood. The details of Joan's reign would have been expunged from the authorised version and could live on only in the oral tradition and unofficial texts.

This theory fits better with the Anastasius known to later historians.[5] He was a decidedly unsavoury character who tried in 855 – the year, according to Martin of Poland's record, when Joan died – to seize the papal throne. Though he had the backing of the Emperor Louis II, grandson of Charlemagne, Anastasius was blocked by a popular revolt in Rome in favour of Benedict III. He was neither well liked nor well respected. His reputation was as a schemer and hedonist, with little time for piety and less still for the moral constraints of Christianity.

With Benedict on Saint Peter's throne, Anastasius was excommunicated but later rehabilitated by Benedict's successor, Nicholas I (858–67) and subsequently put in charge of the papal library by

Hadrian II (867–72). There he is said to have shown a talent for rewriting history to his own and his master's advantage. As J. N. D. Kelly comments in his *Oxford Dictionary of Popes*,[6] Anastasius 'did not hesitate to get rid of documents incriminating himself'.

Did he also delete any mention of Joan from the papal chronicle? Out of loyalty to the popes who rehabilitated him he might have felt he had no choice. The precedents for such lack of scruple among more godly figures than Anastasius are strong. His contemporary and another still studied chronicler, Hincmar, Archbishop of Rheims (845–82), frequently suppressed information damaging to the Church in his letters and other writings. Even the theologian and monk Alcuin of York, right-hand man to Charlemagne, was not above being economical with the truth. In one of his letters he owns up to destroying a report on Pope Leo III (795–816), detailing his adultery and his corrupt administration of church offices.[7]

And if Anastasius did delete Joan on orders from above, then perhaps he recorded this act of omission in a diary or a letter and it is to that that Spanheim referred. But with Anastasius there is surely another factor to be taken into account – his enormous sense of grudge and disappointment. The nephew of Arsenius, an immensely powerful figure in Rome who purchased for himself the title of Bishop of Orte, Anastasius came to regard the papacy as his birthright, the appropriate setting for his undoubted intelligence and good connections. His failure to hold the papal throne for more than three days and his immediate and subsequent consignment to the ranks of 'anti-pope' must have rankled, particularly compared with the success of an upstart foreigner from Mainz who turned out to be a woman. There is no evidence for this, but the possibility that such a crucial and malevolent figure corrupted the records of the papacy in the centuries after Joan's death to make her disappear cannot be discounted.

Seeing Anastasius as central to the riddle of Pope Joan, some later writers have presented him as her sworn enemy, others as the father of her misbegotten child. Noting that Joan and Anastasius shared a knowledge of Greek, historian Joan Morris has speculated rather unconvincingly that he may have been her lover: 'Anastasius fits the picture perfectly. He was a few years older than Joan, he was of a Germanic family, so that he may well have studied at Fulda for a while'.[8]

Morris's reference to Fulda raises an important question about Pope

Joan's origins. Martin Polonus had already cleared up any confusion in my mind as to whether Joan came from England or Germany. She was, he wrote 'of English' descent, but came from Mainz in Germany. Along with Inghilhem and Fulda, Mainz was one of the principal centres of Christianity in Germany in the Dark Ages and a base for English missionaries who came in the eighth and ninth centuries to bring the word of God to the pagan people of this region. In the connection with the English missionaries lay, I was sure, the possibility of an explanation for the description of Joan as 'of English descent'. It simply needed further investigation.

But another confusion had now appeared: between Mainz, mentioned by Martin Polonus as Joan's birthplace, and Fulda, the town most associated with her by the historians who have subsequently championed her cause. The two are less than 100 miles apart – though in the ninth century this would have counted as some distance – and were closely linked, with Inghilhem, as the cultural centres of Charlemagne's empire.

Each of the three had its distinct but inter-connected role, as can be seen in the life of Saint Boniface, known to this day as the 'Apostle of the Germans' who in the eighth century led the English efforts to convert the Germans. At Inghilhem he would visit the palace of Charlemagne, while Mainz was Boniface's own administrative centre, where he chose to establish his cathedral. He was later appointed Archbishop of Mainz by the Pope. At Fulda, by contrast, he founded a monastery and would retreat there for periods of prayer, reflection and study. The library at Fulda's monastery was one of the most celebrated in Europe and the town had a reputation as a centre of scholarship across the continent. After Boniface's death, the ongoing link between Fulda and Mainz was reinforced with the head of the monastery also serving as Archbishop of Mainz. Hrabanus Mauras in the ninth century went from one post to the second, while Rabanus, in the tenth century, held both simultaneously.

The young Joan, according to both Martin Polonus and many of the chroniclers quoted by Spanheim, was an outstandingly bright child. Fulda, with its books and air of scholarship, would have acted as a magnet to her and her parents who, by all accounts, sought to encourage her to exercise her mind. Though born in Mainz, Joan would have visited Fulda, spent time there in its rarified atmosphere, though once she reached the age of twelve the doors of its monastery and any further access to education would have closed on her as a woman.

If the *Liber Pontificalis* omitted Joan, others between 855 and Martin of Poland 410 years later dared to break the silence. Foremost among them was the theologian Marianus Scotus who had close links with both Fulda and Mainz. An Irish monk with a taste for severe hardship characteristic of the times, he lived between 1028 and 1082. As a twenty-four-year-old he entered a monastery in Ireland – then renowned for its ascetic Christian scholarship and learning, rather than the often unthinking and showy piety with which it is sometimes popularly associated today. Like many Irish monks of the period, he later travelled to Germany as a missionary with the aim of converting the pagan peoples. His chosen method of evangelisation was to retire to an abbey cell, first at Fulda and later at Mainz, where he was walled in and lived as a recluse. He converted by example and by the power of his prayers.

Marianus gives the impression in his writings that Joan's story was still remembered in Fulda and Mainz. *Historiographi*, his chronicle, which is fiercely loyal to the papacy in the face of the claims of its secular detractors, tells of the year 854: 'Leo the Pope died in the kalends of August. After him succeeded Joan the woman who sat two years, five months and four days.'[9]

The duration he quotes is identical to that later mentioned by Martin Polonus. So if Martin Polonus's credibility can be brought into question by the Catholic authorities, then Marianus Scotus may likewise be sidelined. The earliest version of his work still in existence to mention Joan comes from 1559, allowing plenty of time either for forgers or for a more measured rewrite in the light of versions of Martin of Poland's chronicle then circulating. Furthermore, since an earlier edition of Marianus Scotus, held in the British Museum, contains no reference to Joan, his worth as a witness for the defence of the She-Pope is questionable.

The brevity of Marianus Scotus's remarks on Joan have also led many doubters to suspect a trick, but it should be borne in mind that these chroniclers would not have repeated the story with any relish. It was, they imply and Martin Polonus states, a black mark in the history of the papacy, one which should be acknowledged briskly and honestly rather than covered up.

Marianus Scotus did not mention Joan having a child. The first reference to that came in the chronicle of Sigebert, a Benedictine monk from the Abbey of Gembloux in Belgium. A contemporary of Marianus, he outlived him by many years and Sigebert's list of popes continues through to 1112 when he died. Indeed, given that Sigebert spent part of his life at Metz – close to Mainz – he may well have encountered Marianus, if only through a wall.

Deemed by the medievalist Joseph Strayer 'one of the most prolific, multi-faceted and important authors of the eleventh century',[10] Sigebert headed an abbey with a reputation for scholarship and a library of international importance. He may have been consulting some texts now lost but then available in that library when he wrote in his *Chronographia* of Pope John: 'It is rumoured that this John was a woman and that only a single person knew about it who was her lover, and caused her to become pregnant and she gave birth to a child whilst pope, for which reason she is not counted among the popes and is not given a number.' This account, however, is not in all the early editions of Sigebert's writings,[11] and where it is, it is often in the margin. It cannot therefore be taken as an unimpeachable source.

In a sixteenth-century edition, Sigebert records a prophetess of Moguntia, another name for Mainz, who succeeded in persuading her archbishop to ordain her to the priesthood. This may or may not be an alternative reference to Joan, though the lack of disguise of her womanhood could rule this out. Equally – if one bears in mind the distorting effect of transferring oral history down the generations into written testaments – it may be that the story of this earlier 'prophetess' was transformed into the tale of Pope Joan.

Sigebert casts one other beam of light – albeit through a glass darkly – on the She-Pope with a reference to the Bishop of Ostia. Martin Polonus later was to claim that Joan's son went on to be Bishop of Ostia. Sigebert reports that it was a particular privilege of the bishops of Ostia – from the third century until an unspecified date – to crown popes. In recounting the tale of a pope many of his contemporaries would have preferred to forget, Martin Polonus's mention of the see of Ostia therefore takes on a special significance. It is rather like mentioning a friend's name to get yourself an introduction to a powerful man or woman. The friend's name acts as a sign that you are bona fide. The mention of Ostia symbolically gives added weight to accounts of Pope Joan.

Sigebert was the first of a run of chroniclers, some of them very considerable figures, who tell of Pope Joan. All come one after the other in quick succession and all were writing before Martin Polonus. The connections between them and the degree to which one influenced the other is impossible to judge at so great a distance and with so little supporting material. Yet while questions can be raised about the dating of various of the editions that contain these chroniclers' records, overall their effect is to reduce the time slip between the dates given for Pope Joan and Martin Polonus's first mention of her.

Otto of Freising was one of the most important of this group, a man of his time with interests in both the secular and ecclesiastical domains. He has been described as 'the greatest medieval historical thinker'.[12] Grandson of the Holy Roman Emperor Henry IV (1050–1106) and a Crusader in the army of his half-brother Conrad in 1147, Otto was also a Cistercian monk, a scholar and Bishop of Freising in Germany until his death in 1158. His treatise *The History of Two Cities* mentions 'Pope John VII, a woman', but puts her back at the start of the eighth century. The original version of this work – completed, it is thought, between 1143 and 1146 – has been lost, and surviving copies containing mentions of Joan were completed after the time of Martin Polonus.[13]

Godfrey of Viterbo, an Italian chronicler, in his *Pantheon* of 1191 maintains the dominant view on dates – between Leo IV and Benedict III – but urges that 'the popess Joan is not counted' on account of her deception. His book is dedicated to Pope Urban III (1185–7) whom he served as chaplain and secretary. It may have been taboo to praise Joan in such company, but Godfrey's example would suggest it was not taboo to mention her. Again, though, there are no originals of Godfrey's chronicle.[14]

Gervase of Tilbury, an English writer who spent much of his life in France, adds another element to the picture, building up to the narrative presented by Martin Polonus. In his *Otiis Imperialibus* of 1211 – of which an original copy is available – Gervase states under his entry for the year 849: 'John the English, Pope, was a woman and gave birth between the Colosseum and Saint Clement.'[15]

Sigebert's reference to a child is now fleshed out, though some opponents of the story of the She-Pope have raised question marks over the veracity of Gervase's observations. With the next figure in this chain of information, however, there can be no doubting historical accuracy. The French Dominican Jean de Mailly wrote his *Chronica universalis* in 1225. Original copies survive with the following entry for 1099:

It is known of a certain pope, or rather popess who was female. She pretended to be a man. By her intellect she became a curial secretary, then a cardinal and went on to become pope. One day, while she was getting off her horse, she gave birth to a child. Immediately the Roman justices tied the feet to the tail of the horse, but meanwhile the people stoned her for half a league. At the point where she died and was buried, it was written: *Petre, Pater Patrum, Papisse Prodito Partum* (O Peter, father of fathers, betray the child-bearing of the woman pope).[16]

The Roman historian Cesare D'Onofrio believes that it was de Mailly who created the story of Joan and who was later copied – though he moved the dates – by Martin Polonus.[17] De Mailly lived in Metz near the German border with France and is principally remembered as a hagiographer of saints. He was largely responsible, too, for the *Chronica Universalis Mettensis* of 1250 which repeats word for word his earlier account of Joan.[18]

In this latter chronicle, Joan's papacy is again put at 1099, but explained away against the more conventional record by stating that Paschal II, who according to the official roll of honour ascended to the papal throne in that year, did not actually begin his reign until 1106, leaving seven years for Joan. If Martin Polonus knew of de Mailly's writings – and there is no evidence that he did, de Mailly being a comparatively minor scribe – he evidently decided that he had most of the details regarding timing and length of service wrong.

The French Dominican Stephen de Bourbon acknowledged de Mailly as the source for his *De diversis materiis praedicabilibus*, written shortly before his death in 1261. De Bourbon moves the date forward a year and expresses his outrage.

But an occurrence of wonderful audacity or rather insanity happened around 1100, as is related in chronicles. A certain woman, learned and well-versed in the notary's art, assuming male clothing and pretending to be a man, came to Rome. Through her diligence as well as her learning in letters, she was appointed as a curial secretary. Afterwards, under the devil's direction, she was made a cardinal and finally pope. Having become pregnant she gave birth while mounting (a horse). But when Roman justice was informed of it, she was dragged outside the city, bound by her feet to the hooves of a horse, and for half a league she was stoned by people. And where she died, there she was buried, and upon a stone placed above her, this line was written: *Parce, Pater Patrum, Papisse Prodere Partum* (Forbear, father of fathers, to betray the child-bearing of the female pope). Behold how such rash presumptiousness leads to so vile an end.[19]

Though he claimed de Mailly as his source, de Bourbon was already changing details – most notably the tombstone inscription – either through the shortcomings of his copying or for some grander design now lost. This account is notable, too, in that it explicitly links Joan to the devil for the first time. In the fearful, introspective and image-laden world of medieval Christianity, Satan was an omnipresent figure, looming larger even than God. All who offended the Church in any way – be they pagans who resisted attempts to convert them, Jews who bankrolled Christian expansionism and then demanded their money back, Moslems who invaded Spain, Knights Templar who grew too independent or Cathars and Waldensians who objected to the worldly goods of Rome – were damned as cohorts of the devil, demonised and cast out into darkness.[20]

The devil crops up again in the account of Joan, dated 1261, by an anonymous Dominican of Erfurt, near to Joan's alleged birthplace in Germany. Returning the story of the She-Pope to the Dark Ages, the writer of *Chronica Minor* gives a new slant on the inscription mentioned by de Mailly and de Bourbon.

> There was another false pope, whose name and year are unknown. For she was a woman, as is acknowledged by the Romans, and of refined appearance, great learning and hypocritically of high conduct. She disguised herself in the clothes of a man, and eventually was elected to the papacy. While pope, she became pregnant, and when she was carrying, a demon openly published the fact to all in the public court by crying this verse to the pope: *Papa, Pater Patrum, Papisse Pandito Partum* (O Pope, father of fathers, disclose the child-bearing of the woman pope).[21]

It is an odd turn-about for the story, since the demon is not in league with Joan and she appears to be its enemy. However, the account does demonstrate that the phrase beginning *Papa, Pater Patrum* was a minor riddle within the wider riddle of Joan's existence. A final twist was given by another German chronicle – the *Flores Temporum* – written by an anonymous author or authors around 1290. This came after Martin Polonus's first chronicle in 1265 and copied his basic narrative, but inserted an episode with a woman possessed by the devil.

She (Pope Joan) was made pregnant . . . At this time a demoniac was questioned on oath as to the time the demon would depart. The devil responded in verse: *Papa, Pater Patrum, Pandito Partum. Et tibi tunc edam, de corpore quando recedam* (O Pope, father of fathers, disclose the child-bearing of the woman pope. And then I will make known to you the time I will depart from the body).[22]

Again the story was changing shape, fitting more easily into the existing fears and conventions of the devil-obsessed medieval period. But behind such tampering, the riddle of Joan had clearly developed a fascination. The Dominicans – as Father Boyle had already suggested, and as revealed by this run-through of the main figures in the literary drama taken from the library shelves – played a crucial part in promoting the tale.

Though hedged with question marks over provenance – and confused by the existence only of later editions of earlier works which cannot therefore be verified against the Protestant forgers so demonised by a later generation of official Catholic scholars – there is enough manuscript evidence from all over Europe and from a variety of otherwise respected sources to suggest that Joan was more than a whim of the Dominican Martin Polonus. He may have given her story the stamp of authenticity and authority, but others, no less venerable, had written of her earlier.

While the Vatican Library contained manuscripts which sketched the outline of Joan's story, it was nearer to home that I found conclusive proof that she was not, as has constantly been alleged, the creation of post-Reformation Protestant forgers. The standard contention of the Church down the ages that the She-Pope had been invented and inserted into old history books by zealots anxious to do down the Church of Rome can conclusively be shown to be bunkum.

There are a handful of libraries around the world that stand head and shoulders above the rest. The Vatican is one. The British Museum Library is another. Paris's Bibliothèque Nationale is a third. One step down are the great collections. Among their number is Oxford's Bodleian Library. Its medieval manuscripts can be counted in tens of thousands – not hundreds of thousands as is the case with Father Boyle's library – but among its collection is a rare copy of Martin Polonus's chronicle.

The Duke Humfrey Library is on the second floor of the Old Bodleian and has been there since 1488, when it was established in

29

memory of Duke Humfrey of Gloucester, the younger brother of Henry V and a Renaissance man who handed over his collection of books to the newly-founded School of Divinity at the university. A creaking wooden staircase leads up to the enquiries desk where two ancient manuscripts – as arranged in advance by post – were waiting. My real interest was Martin Polonus's *Chronicon Summorum Pontificum et Imperatorum Romanorum*, known to the Bodleian simply as Manuscript 452. But a helpful librarian had directed me to another text on Pope Joan held at the Bodleian, a seventeenth-century French work.

I was issued with a foam reading mat – two triangles lying on a rectangle so you don't strain the spines of these venerable old manuscripts – and directed to the seating area. Scholars bent over their manuscripts in the prayerful silence of medieval monks. I found a place under an extraordinary portrait of a Bishop of Lincoln. He appeared every inch a woman down to his pursed lips. But perhaps my quest for Pope Joan was beginning to make me to look askance at everyone in ecclesiastical garb.

Since my French is marginally better than my shaky Latin, I opted for the younger of the two volumes first.[23] Written by hand in the second half of the seventeenth century, it rehearses the usual account of Pope Joan and then stands up and knocks down arguments for and against. The library label announced that the manuscript was 'very neatly written' – which I assumed to mean easy to decipher. As I quickly found out, you can be neat without being clear. The brown ink had seeped through the thin parchment and marked the next page, so the echo of already-read words disguised their successors.

Having for three-quarters of the text reviewed in a brusque sort of way the various writers who had chronicled Joan, the anonymous author suddenly revealed his or her hand and returned to the damning line first taken in the introduction on this 'inept and malicious fable'. Quite how so many documentary sources could be dismissed so lightly the writer never bothered to address. This was polemics, and legitimate doubts were swept aside with confident talk of a Protestant plot and of the wantonness of women.

With the main business of reducing Joan to a fairy-story thereby concluded, the last quarter of this book consisted of an index, mainly of writers already known to me, who had mentioned the She-Pope in their outpourings but also, strangely, of some, plucked at random from the annals of history, who should have. If the story had been true, the argument went, then the following might have been expected to mention her ... Since they did not, she could not have existed, two negatives making a positive.

The high rhetoric of the whole piece was its most revealing feature. Evidently Joan had been a subject of fevered debate in the seventeenth century between clerics – given the sermon-like feel of the text, my instinct was that its author was a man or woman of the cloth – and those who would damn the Church.

The Bodleian cannot be specific about the origin of its copy of Martin Polonus.[24] It is believed to be English and was given to the library by the dean and canons of Windsor in 1612. However, it can be clear on the date – fourteenth century, before the Reformation. I had imagined that establishing the vintage of ancient books, rather like finding out if the Turin Shroud is Christ's burial wrap, was done by carbon-dating techniques. The librarians at Duke Humfrey greeted my assumption with polite mirth. Why bother with gadgets when their own expertise was sufficient? Between them they could spot every style of script and illustration and date it to within a couple of decades. After all, they pointed out, you would not mistake a Degas for a Hockney, or a letter written by your grandparents at the start of this century for one written today.

So with the Martin Polonus manuscript, they would start with the date of the final entry – the last pontiff mentioned is John XXII who in 1316 became the second of the Avignon popes – and work forward from that point in time. The style of the script – high Gothic, with arches, pointed minims and adornments – is as distinctive to the trained eye as the Gothic façade of Chartres Cathedral is to an architectural historian. The decorated letters, at the start of each section, give further clues. Their colouring and shape have their own chronology as in the parallel world of art history.

If, then, as the Bodleian has established, the references to Joan in Martin Polonus are from the fourteenth century, and not later additions in the margins or on a fly-sheet, then the allegation that Protestant forgers were responsible for the story of Joan can be conclusively proved false.

Inside a worm-eaten leather binding attached to a wooden backing were the sheets of parchment. Early pages began with coloured capitals written in a big flowing hand. Later a modest letter would start the litany of popes on the left-hand page, and a similarly discreet flourish the emperors on the right. The hand was small and scrawling with grand swirls, the ink after all these years a pale brown.

On folio 31 was John VIII, nestling in his/her usual place between Leo IV and Benedict III. It took a few minutes to get used to the handwriting. The first three or four words were a struggle, but then they came more easily. Like getting the hang of reading music, suddenly your eye is in and you are tripping along. *Joannes 8. Cognomento Anglicis natione Maguntinus* (John VII, known as the English, born in Moguntia). Before moving on to the version quoted earlier from the Berlin copy, this edition of Polonus told that John VIII was the first since Saint Ambrose to write so many prefaces to masses. A fourth-century bishop of Milan, Ambrose was a great preacher and hymn-writer. The compliment to John/Joan was a significant one but was followed by an explanation that, since John had been a woman, these prefaces were no longer used. So there it was in the text, well before the Reformation and its allegedly cunning raids on libraries.

The strangest touch was a note in the margin – scribbled in black in a different hand with a large arrow at some later date by an astonished reader – *ffemina fuit pp*. In the shorthand language of medieval manuscripts, double 'F' signifies a capital and for 'pp' read '*papa*'. So 'the Pope was a Woman'. Perhaps it was a would-be Protestant forger, surprised to find Joan's femininity already in the text, but making doubly sure that no one missed this damning incident in the history of the papacy. Or was it a seminarian, poring over the manuscript in all seriousness as part of his studies when he came upon this remarkable reference. He had been as taken aback as I was when I discovered her on my Roman holiday. Unable to contain himself, but forbidden in the seminary library to speak, he had scribbled a note in the margin and passed it to his friend sitting alongside.

The main text states that this John VIII could not be included in the catalogue of popes on account of her sex. And so the next John listed – in 872 – is referred to again as John VIII, but the same interfering hand in black has crossed this out and put instead IX. And each John thereafter has been tampered with in like fashion.

Perhaps I have a pessimistic and suspicious turn of mind, but it was hard to believe that the time-honoured retort of the Catholic church to the story of Pope Joan – that it was a Reformation forgery – could so easily be dismissed. What, I asked the librarians, if a seventeenth-century forger had set out to imitate the written and illustrative style of the fourteenth century in producing a new version of Martin Polonus with the story of Joan in the main text? The answer was simple. They would not have had the expertise. The detailed knowledge of styles and dates that is today available in abundance at the Duke Humfrey is a decidedly modern development. As late as the nineteenth century, for instance, the Bodleian was buying manuscripts that were deemed by experts to be fourteenth century, only for subsequent experts to find out that they came from Anglo-Saxon times. Any later attempt to reproduce the Gothic style of the fourteenth century would be spotted, I was reassured. It would be as unmistakable and over-the-top as a Victorian copy of a medieval building.

Here, then, was the conclusive evidence which gave the lie to any talk of post-Reformation forgers inventing Joan. What had not been changed in the fourteenth-century manuscript was the central assertion that there was a Pope Joan who ruled for two years, five months and four days before she gave birth to a child and was killed. Well before the Reformation Joan was accepted as fact. True or false, the story of Pope Joan had a source other than malicious forgery.

I was hooked, but there was one other matter arising from my trip to Rome that I had to clear up. Was there any evidence that the strange seat I had seen in Rome and read about in skimpy guidebooks was what it was alleged to be?

Bernardino Coreo, a Milanese writer and historian offers an eyewitness account of the coronation of Pope Alexander VI in 1492 in his *Patria Historia* of 1503. He concludes: 'Finally, when the usual solemnities of the "sancta sanctorum" ended and the touching of testicles was done, I returned to the palace.'[25] Alexander VI was, of course, the most notorious of the Borgia popes and a certain irony is added to Coreo's account by the fact that the pontiff's four grown-up sons were in the audience when their father was so rudely frisked.

Another eyewitness was the Welsh late-medieval chronicler, Adam of Usk, an Oxford-educated cleric who travelled across the continent to Rome and in 1404 witnessed the election of Innocent VII. He recounts Innocent's triumphal procession through the streets of Rome from the Vatican to the Lateran:

Then, after turning aside out of abhorrence of Pope Joan whose image with her son stands near Saint Clement's, the pope, dismounting from his horse, enters the Lateran for his enthrone-ment. And there he is seated in a chair of porphyry, which is pierced beneath for this purpose, that one of the younger cardinals may make proof of his sex; and then while a *Te Deum* is chanted, he is borne to the high altar.[26]

As late as September 1644 the Swedish writer Lawrence Banck is recording a similar spectacle at the elevation of Innocent X.[27] Bartolomeo Platina, keeper of the Vatican library under Pope Sixtus IV (1471–84), is another who mentions the ceremony in his *Lives of the Popes*. Moreover, this venerable and well-placed scholar links it explicitly with Pope Joan. He includes his reference at the end of an entry on Pope John VIII who reigned, according to Platina, in the middle of the ninth century. John was a woman, this insider records, who disguised herself as a man and tricked her way to the papal throne. Once she was discovered, the practice of touching the testicles was introduced as part of the enthronement ceremony to ensure that no such treachery should ever be allowed again.[28]

Chapter Three

'Men have had every advantage of us in telling their own story. Education has been theirs in so much higher a degree; the pen has been in their hands.'

Jane Austen, *Persuasion* (1818)

The key question as I took Pope Joan to my heart was one of timing. Until an exact time-scale for the events of her life could be sorted out, everything else remained a jumble of references and interpretations. If we take the date most often quoted – AD 853 to 855 – as the span of Joan's pontificate, then the first written record which comes in the eleventh century with Marianus Scotus follows after a silence of two centuries. And, as I had already discovered in my trawl through medieval manuscripts, Marianus Scotus is not an unimpeachable source. If we wait for one who unambiguously deserves the accolade – Martin Polonus and the Bodleian version of his book of popes and emperors – then there is a time slip of some 400 years. Even Jean de Mailly only narrows that gap by fifty years.

Down the ages, this interlude has been the most telling evidence in the hands of those who have prosecuted Joan as an historical fantasy. Forget talk of Protestant plotters, they say, and explain these centuries of silence.[1] Joan may have been much remembered, they argue, but hers is a story no more real than Saint George, patron of England, or Saint Christopher, guardian of motorists, both likewise celebrated in folklore but, according to recent research, without historical substance.[2]

Faced by this well-rehearsed onslaught, witnesses for the defence have too often substituted invention for hard fact. Such an approach may entertain the jury but has not as yet succeeded in swinging it. In 1843, for example, in his best-selling tract *A Woman in the Chair of Saint Peter*, the Dutch historian, Professor N. C. Kist, claimed that in 855, after the revelation of Joan's treachery and her subsequent death, Rome issued an edict instructing every God-fearing man and woman never to mention her name again.[3] It was only in the thirteenth century, Kist went on, that a counter-order was signed reversing this obliteration of the past and giving the green light to a new generation of chroniclers who until then had been kept well-buttoned. Kist's theory did offer a practical answer to the time gap, but not one that stands up to scrutiny.

His interpretation of events presupposes a quasi-inquisitorial dictatorship in Rome centuries before the Inquisition was set up. Arguably, Kist's account is the very reverse of what would have been possible. In the ninth century the powers of the papacy, its capacity to impose its will on the faithful, let alone the gossipy corridors of power, were weak and discredited by scandal after scandal. An order of silence would have had little effect and, if it had any, probably the opposite of what was intended. Only in the thirteenth century, following Innocent III (1198–1216) with his knack for giving practical expression to his aspirations to universal authority and control, could such a blanket ban be attempted with any hope of success. And even then the odds were against it. The Vatican, as John Cornwell remarked in his investigation of the strange death of Pope John Paul I, is alternately 'a court, a palace of gossipy eunuchs' and 'a village of washerwomen – they get down in the river, wash clothes, punch them, dance on them, squeezing out all the old dirt'.[4]

Kist's case is further weakened by his speculative and – in the absence of anything but circumstantial evidence – frivolous suggestion that Joan was in fact Leo IV's widow, elevated to the papacy as a mark of respect for her dead husband.

Yes, it was possible for popes to have a widow. Hadn't Saint Peter himself, according to the gospels, had a wife?[5] In those long-distant days of the ninth century, marriage was still regarded as an honourable state for priests. Only with the Council of Trent in 1545 did men have a straight and exclusive choice between a vocation to marriage and one to the priesthood. But Kist – like many of the Joanites and, I was beginning to suspect, myself – was an incurable romantic. If my investigation was to progress, I would have to resist rather more forcefully than he had inventing facts to sustain what he wanted to be true.

One of the problems with any attempt to evaluate the legend of Pope Joan is that it has attracted so many writers and historians with over-active imaginations, the 'strange but true' brigade who today fashion theory after theory about UFOs or the layout of the pyramids.

The fall-back of harder-hearted, less fanciful defenders of Joan has been to dwell on the fact that this was the Dark Ages, a period of political turmoil, illness, famine and marauding armies across Europe, when for many life hung by a thread. There was little time for scholarship or keeping records for posterity. Moreover, the argument goes, if the lack of a contemporaneous written record is taken as sufficient in itself to damn any story or character, Jesus himself is in trouble. The gospels are the words of God in the words of man and were written up to seventy years after Christ's crucifixion. In the intervening period they remained part of the oral tradition and even once committed to paper were thereafter much rewritten and reordered to suit the tastes and influences of the day, a process that continues in our own time.

By this measurement, Joan's story remained in the oral tradition much longer and therefore may well have been so amended as to lose anything but an outline resemblance to what it was originally describing. It would, of course, seem stronger if that initial gap, at best 200 years, could be reduced. That was the aim of a remarkable feminist historian, Joan Morris, who died in 1987.

The daughter of a Plymouth Brethren father who late in life renounced all belief and never darkened the door of a church again until his funeral, and the niece of Phyllis Morris, the woman credited as the model for Cruella de Ville in *101 Dalmatians*,[6] Joan Morris spent her early years as an artist, decorating churches. However, the greater part of her life was dedicated to investigating the role of women in the early church. She published one well-received book, *The Lady Was a Bishop* in 1973, examining in minute detail the quasi-episcopal role of some abbesses as late as the high medieval period.[7]

The steely academic discipline that characterised this work gave way in the last fifteen years of her life to a more quixotic quest – the search for Pope Joan. By now a tertiary or auxiliary nun of the Milan-based Order of Saint Paul, she was determined to bridge the gap between 855 and Martin Polonus. Her interim findings appeared in a privately published pamphlet in 1985 and made a considerable, though disputed and incomplete, contribution to the ongoing debate.[8] By the time of her death two years later, she had failed to make any further progress. She left this world, according to her nephew and literary executor Ivan May, 'a disappointed dissident, but still, just, a Catholic'. Her work has been largely neglected.[9]

May allowed me access to those of Joan Morris's papers still in his safe-keeping. Others I found in the subterranean Fawcett Library at London's Guildhall University, a neglected though fascinating collection of suffragist literature dating back to the early years of the twentieth century.

*

Joan Morris had focused on the most obvious source for information about the papacy in the Dark Ages – the few surviving medieval pontificals or 'pope books', some officially sanctioned and some not. These are versions of the lists of pontiffs which began to appear around the eighth century and which were once in the charge of Anastasius the librarian. Searching through the various versions of these tomes, Morris hit upon one particular example, an eleventh-century pontifical, *Parisinus Lat. 5140* in the Bibliothèque Nationale in Paris.

Pope Joan is not mentioned in the text. Yet there is much confusion between Leo IV and his 'official' successor-but-one, Nicholas I. Notably absent is any section on the intervening pope, Benedict III. Present instead is an account of an unnamed pope, assumed by most historians to be Benedict but identified by Morris as potentially Joan. She was convinced she had detected a complex conspiracy that, when unravelled, assigned Joan a new position in the papal roll of honour, after Benedict III but before Nicholas I, rather than between Leo IV and Benedict as is usually alleged.

The eleventh-century pontifical, Morris suggested, had been distorted by a forger. In the manuscript, the life of Leo IV comes abruptly to a close a quarter of the way down folio – or page – 131. So abruptly that the last line is unfinished and stops half-way through a word – *cum orbiecles et in cir* . . . – part of a list of gifts in gold and silver which Leo had given to churches. On folio 132 – the facing page – the text restarts a third of the way down on what is clearly the life of an entirely different pope. But which one? The word 'Benedictus' has been written in the margin, in red ink and in a different hand from that used in the main account of this unnamed pope. And then it has been crossed out. Above the text, the same amender has also written 'Nicolaus', again in red, though the 'l' strangely is in black.

The most likely scenario is that a phantom scribbler came across the gap when reading through the manuscript and decided to add some words of guidance. He or she would seem to have assumed that since the account came after Leo it must be Benedict and so wrote in his name. But then on reading on, he or she discovered that Benedict's burial by the unnamed subject of this entry is referred to in the narrative. Logic then suggested that it was Nicholas, officially his successor. So that name was written in, misspelt.

The mystery deepens when, on closer examination, the story told begins to conflict with some of the details known about Nicholas.

Indeed, there are distinct overtones of parts of Joan's story as it was later recorded by writers like Martin Polonus. What is more, there is an emotional charge to the tale which hints that there might be more to this unnamed pope than meets the eye, in particular a veiled sexual chemistry with the men he meets. Could the She-Pope have been the successor to Benedict and the predecessor of Nicholas? Based on her work on the Paris manuscript, this was Morris's most iconoclastic suggestion.

The unnamed pope in the document is described as having been a serious child, little given to play and directed by his father into the liberal arts. Overcoming subsequent opposition from his parents, he is later ordained to the subdiaconate by Pope Sergius II (844–7) and becomes a great favourite of Sergius's successor, Leo IV, who promotes him to the full diaconate. The clergy, nobles and people soon recognise in this anonymous pope 'outstanding graces' and, following the death of Leo and the elevation of Benedict to the papal throne, he comes to play a central part in the administration. Benedict cannot bear to be without him, it is written, and consults him on every matter from proclamations to arbitrations. On the death of Benedict, his beloved right-hand man joins the other deacons in carrying the corpse of the pontiff into Saint Peter's and it is he alone who lays the dead pope to rest in his tomb.

Could this description of the unnamed pope be applied to Pope Joan as she was later portrayed by Martin Polonus? Pope Joan, it was said by the chroniclers, excelled in the liberal arts and was a special favourite of Pope Leo, outstanding among her contemporaries and the trusted assistant of the pontiff. And there is enough uncertainty in the dates given by the various chroniclers to make Joan Morris's thesis a possibility, though the vast majority of the medieval writers are explicit in positioning her after Leo.

Morris made great play out of a particular section in the account in *Parisinus Lat. 5140* detailing a meeting between the Emperor Louis II, heir to Charlemagne's lands, and the unnamed pope. On hearing of the death of Benedict, the document recounts, Louis hurried to Rome to offer his condolences. The people of the city and their clergy met in the Church of Saint Dionysius, where after a period of debate they were 'illuminated by a sudden light' and unanimously elected the unnamed deacon as pope. Such references to divine intervention are not uncommon in such 'pope books' and no special significance should be attached to this one.

The chosen one, however, took fright and sought refuge in Saint Peter's, declaring himself unworthy to govern but giving no reason. Again, these were details, Morris emphasised, that fitted with the story of Joan as it was later told. Her reluctance to accept the papal throne would be understandable if she feared detection, as would her failure to reveal the reason behind her hesitation.

The crowd, however, the manuscript goes on, insisted and accompanied him to the Lateran Palace where they placed him on the apostolic chair and acclaimed him their spiritual overlord. A formal coronation then took place in Saint Peter's in the presence of the Emperor. Much stress is placed on the brilliant conversational powers of the unnamed pope and the spell they cast on Louis II. After a splendid dinner, the Emperor retired to his camp outside the city at a place called Quintus. There, at a later though unspecified date, the Pope, along with senior advisers and supporters, journeyed to visit him. When Louis II saw the Pope approaching, according to this account, he went out to meet him, greeted him warmly and led him and his horse by the reins to the camp, where a sumptuous banquet was prepared. Afterwards, Louis lavished the Pope – described as 'beautiful to behold' and 'decorous in bearing' – with many gifts.

Morris then contrasted this account with what history taught of Nicholas I. He was indeed a confidant of his three predecessors as Pope but had a very difficult and turbulent relationship with Louis II. The Emperor at one stage invaded Italy and ransacked Rome to punish Nicholas. For his part, Nicholas was so conscious of the dignity and authority of the papacy – condemning those like the archbishops of Ravenna and Rheims who disagreed with him – that it is hard to imagine him either doubting his powers to hold the position or going out of his way to visit a temporal sovereign. Harder still to reconcile is the picture of Nicholas allowing Louis to lead his horse by its reins. It was at the time the gesture of a gentleman towards a lady rider.

Moreover, the unnamed pope is portrayed as something of a saintly mystic – 'intent on fasting and in the function of Divine Worship, generous to the poor, protector of the orphans, supporter of widows'. Even allowing for the hyperbole of ecclesiastical chroniclers, there has to be a doubt that this could be the same proud, grand and belligerent Nicholas.[10]

Morris's detective work offers an intriguing possibility. The whole tone of the passages she quoted, particularly those concerning the relationship between the unnamed Pope and the Emperor, seem to rule

40

out any reference to Nicholas. Yet there is no firm evidence that it is Joan. The possibility is certainly there but it falls short of proof.

Morris was exploiting a negative, filling a vacuum with speculation. However, she was also showing that the official record cannot definitively be said to rule out Joan. Morris found a gap where the She-Pope might fit. And she added an irony. While the Catholic church habitually talks of Protestant forgers in relation to Joan, Morris pointed the finger back at the Vatican as a nest of forgers.

For all her hopes of repositioning Joan after Benedict, Morris was no nearer to building an unanswerable case by the time of her own death. In seeking to add weight to what she realised was an unproven theory about the significance of the echoing silence at the heart of *Parisinus Lat. 5140*, she sought out later versions of the same account to see what other generations of historians had made of the curious hiatus. The chronicle *Vatican Lat. 3764* used the identical text but extended later into the eleventh century. Once in the possession of the Cave Monastery near Salerno in the south of Italy, the chronicle arrived in Rome in 1593 and became the basis for most subsequent printed versions of the lives of earlier popes.

Where the Paris manuscript ended abruptly mid-sentence while recounting Leo IV's generosity to churches, the Vatican version completed the list. Instead of then summing up with the number of ordinations carried out during Leo's reign – as was the custom in the accounts given of other popes in the book – there was a curious story about two Roman political leaders which had little or no bearing on Leo. Gratian and Daniel became embroiled in a complicated row about a plot to seize power in the city. Daniel was found guilty of slander, the Vatican chronicle stated, and then Leo IV died. The *non sequitur* suggests a stop-gap but again there is no way of proving it.

The Vatican text then continued with a very short life of Benedict, before taking up the account of the unnamed pope from the Paris script, under the heading Nicholas. The nineteenth-century French scholar Louis Duchesne, in his three-volume study of the 'pope books' published in 1886, highlighted a marked change of style around this section of the Vatican manuscript, though he offered no explanation for it.[11]

If a later writer was trying to make good the space, why include what appears to be a filler on Gratian and Daniel and then truncate Benedict so much? It makes no sense. If you have three-quarters of a page to fill, you would simply conclude the life of Leo as quickly as possible, then insert an account of Benedict, before transforming the details of the unnamed pope into the story of Nicholas. The comparison between the two chronicles suggests that whatever apparently had been torn out of the Paris version was either lost for ever with no chance of recreating it or considered so sensitive that it could not be reinstated in the later text. The first option is unlikely. There would have been other sources to pad out stories of Benedict and Nicholas. If not, a few paragraphs of hagiography would have sufficed. The recourse to Gratian and Daniel suggested that Rome at least believed there was something here to be ashamed of.

Thanks to Morris's labour, the impression of an historical conspiracy gains impetus. Unable to find further evidence, she then made a leap of faith and declared herself for Joan. However much I wanted to jump with her, I could not share her certainty that she had found the key to unlock the riddle of the She-Pope.

As Morris demonstrates, it can be hard to draw a line between fact and fiction with the She-Pope. Women in particular seem to have fallen victim to the process of mixing a remarkable life story with fiction. Women are, feminist historians have argued, more accustomed to having ideas and stereotypes projected on to them (usually by men) and therefore have, in the historical field, suffered more from the attentions of myth makers who want to reduce their real significance in a man's world and reposition them in traditional feminine roles.

Cleopatra, the French essayist Theophile Gautier wrote in 1845, 'is a person . . . whom dreamers find always at the end of their dreams'.[12] The Egyptian queen has been reinvented in fictional form twice over – once in the propaganda of her enemies as a stereotypical temptress using her feminine wiles to trick men and much later as a screen goddess. The truth was both duller and more interesting. She was, evidence from coins of the time suggest, no great beauty, and was never in love with Mark Antony. Rather, she was, her most recent biographer Lucy Hughes-Hallett writes, an adept politician and strategist, more than a match for any man, who battled to protect her own territory and influence against the Roman Empire. To relegate her to the role of a conniving bimbo with romantic obsessions, who took her life in a fit of passion, does her an enormous disservice.[13]

Likewise Joan of Arc, the seventeen-year-old peasant girl who intervened in 1429 in the struggle between Lancastrian England and

Valois France, has been submerged under successive waves of patriotism, Catholic piety and feminism.[14] In similar fashion the Victorians exploited Grace Darling, the lighthouse-keeper's daughter who saved shipwrecked passengers off Lindisfarne in 1838. She became a national heroine but in the process her story was amended, her poor background exaggerated and her less attractive characteristics airbrushed out as her face became a feature of tea-sets, dinner-services and soap-dishes. In the porcelain version she was younger, prettier, more feminine, a romantic, doe-eyed teenage waif who could never have wielded oars. And indeed there may have been some truth, however unintentional, in this suggestion since eyewitness accounts report that it was Grace's father who did the rowing with her merely assisting, though subsequently he was written out and it became a solo act of bravery on her part.[15]

Fact and fiction, reality and myth. The word myth, often employed in the context of Pope Joan, is much abused in our own times. It is taken to mean something that is not true – 'only a myth'. Yet in the classical world and in various religions and popular cultures for centuries thereafter, myths had a much more positive purpose – to illustrate a truth through events which may be partially true but also substantially embellished. Mythology was never meant simply to describe historically verifiable events. It had a broader purpose – to build on events or human experience to draw out realities that are perhaps too elusive to be discussed or even faced in a logical and coherent fashion. At its most abstract, mythology has been defined as an ancient form of psychology.

With Pope Joan it was not a black-and-white question – true or false, reality or myth? Rather, she was potentially at the centre of a myth in the old-fashioned sense – an historical character built up for a whole series of purposes in different periods. While this is a distraction and an obstacle for the investigator trying to ascertain whether Pope Joan ever existed, it could not, I reflected, be regarded as a wholly negative process. Without it Joan might have disappeared over the historical horizon altogether.

Chapter Four

'It's bad enough to be a girl, anyway, when I like boys' games and work and manners! I can't get over my disappointment in not being a boy; and it's worse than ever now, for I'm dying to go and fight with papa and I can only stay at home and knit, like a poky old woman.'

Louisa May Alcott, *Little Women*[1]

Most of the chroniclers refer to the female pope as John or Joan 'the English'. The majority follow Martin Polonus's explanation that such a title comes not from her birthplace – Germany – but on account of her parentage. There have been voices of dissent. Felix Haemerlein, writing at the end of the fifteenth century, suggested that she had been educated in England.[2] The anonymous *Flores Temporum*, written shortly after Martin Polonus's chronicle, substitutes Margantius (Margam) for Maguntinus (Mainz) and directs the reader's attention to the Cistercian Abbey of Margam, south of Port Talbot, in Wales.[3] There are two problems with this approach – Wales, as any man of Harlech will tell you, is not England, and Margam Abbey was not founded until 1147, two centuries after Joan's papacy.

The mainstream suggestion is that her mother and father were among (or followers of) the English missionaries who joined the drive spearheaded by Saints Boniface and Lioba in the eighth century to bring Christianity to the pagan Teutonic peoples.

Rome is so much the bejewelled orb at the centre of the Christian universe – or has traditionally presented itself as such – that my image has always been of the word of God spreading out from the Italian peninsula over Europe like the ripples in a pond. And indeed, generations of Christians have been encouraged to think that. But in Ireland they know better. And in England, too, there is a strong case for seeing powerful cross-currents rather than concentric circles.

'Along with the Irish, the English monks were the great cultural transmitters of the eighth and ninth centuries,' writes Paul Johnson in his *History of Christianity*.[4] The British Isles were at the time the heart of Christian Europe and of most missionary activity.

The Irish to this day celebrate their role in exporting Christianity and more particularly learning to continental Europe. Those who followed in the monastic tradition of Saint Patrick carried from the

44

fifth century onwards their own distinct, simple and scholarly Celtic Christianity to Britain and the European mainland. Patrick took up and developed ideas of monasticism that had first appeared in the third century with the desert fathers – nomadic, isolated, ascetic and often shadowy figures who starved themselves into sanctity.

Patrick's approach took root not only among the lower orders but also with princes and local nobility. More significantly for Pope Joan, it involved men and women as co-workers, shoulder-to-shoulder before God. Fathers would grant their sons and daughters lands and fishing rights upon which to found monasteries, some for men, some for women, and some with separate communities of men and women under one roof. In the great empty landscape of Ireland these rudimentary dry-stone houses became treasuries of knowledge, scholarship and a unique form of spirituality.

It was Saint Columbannus, born around 540, who led the drive to spread such austere but enlightened practices from Ireland to Britain and mainland Europe. Columbannus set sail in 575, kitted out like his fellow monks in long white habits, carrying curved staffs and hand-produced liturgical books in waterproof leather bags. Around their necks, we are told, they had water-bottles and pouches containing holy relics and consecrated wafers. Strange though they must have appeared when they landed in Brittany, by the time of Columbannus's death in 615 the Celtic monks and nuns had spread across England, Scotland, France, Italy and the Alps to forty monasteries. Each had its library and – unlike earlier establishments on the continent – its share of lands to sustain the monastic community and those in its care.

The down-to-earth approach of these men and women, their willingness to share the drudgery of peasant people, and their flexibility in accommodating existing pagan beliefs was key to their lives. But Rome grew worried. The Celts' dislike of hierarchy, their scorn for ecclesiastical titles, their concentration on a one-to-one relationship with God all threatened those who saw the Church as a powerful and grandiose structure intervening between sinful humanity and a distant God. The Celts' willingness to work with women stood in direct contrast to the prevailing ideas in Rome.

The arrival of Augustine in Kent in 597, despatched by Pope Gregory the Great to convert the Angles and Saxons of southern and eastern Britain to the 'official' version of Christianity, brought Roman and Celtic approaches head to head. The mixing of the two, in 664 at the Synod of Whitby hosted by one of the symbols of Celtic sexual

45

equality, the great abbess Hilda, saw the independent-minded Celts subjugated to Roman influences.

Whatever the fine words at Whitby, Roman practices and Celtic traditions could not coexist. So, as if in answer to Pope Gregory's prayers, Benedict of Nursia had developed in the early part of the sixth century a monastic rule that survives to this day and which sought to reconcile the best of Celtic simplicity and scholarship with the overriding needs of a growing and hierarchical Church. It was Benedict's common-sense approach which would have shaped the monastic tradition in which Joan grew up and from which, the chroniclers tell, she felt excluded at the age twelve.

By the end of the ninth century Benedict's rule was well established and fairly universally followed. It charted a middle course between the severity of the Celts and the style of Rome. Monks and nuns had beds and decent clothing – simple but warm. Each was given a pen and writing tablets, shoes and blankets. Otherwise all property was held in common and there were regular searches to ensure that the rule was not ignored. Harsh but not barbaric, discipline was ever present. Breaking the rules was punished with withdrawal of holy communion, 'the punishment of the lash' and as a last resort expulsion.[5]

Benedict, however, followed the prevailing attitude in Rome towards the role of women and abandoned much of the Celtic tradition that had seen men and women working side by side. Benedict's own attitude is betrayed by his treatment of his sister, Scholastica. Like him, she consecrated her life to God from an early age, but, unlike him, was not admitted to a monastery. It is thought she remained at the family home and built her own life of prayer and contemplation.

Benedict would have approved of such an arrangement. He believed that women and men had to be kept absolutely apart. When Scholastica was on her deathbed, Benedict refused her plea to be allowed into his monastery so they could spend her last hours together. Only when a fierce thunderstorm broke out was he convinced that God wished him to make an exception and Scholastica was let in.

Under Benedict's system, then, the opportunities of advancement for women were severely curtailed. Female monastic houses were by and large the poor relation of their male counterparts, though still centres of scholarship in their own right. Yet in spite of the obstacles, some women did still manage to achieve positions of prominence. Of these perhaps the most relevant to Pope Joan's history is Lioba.

British monasticism retained strong Celtic influences for many decades after the Synod of Whitby and it was against this backdrop that it unleashed in the eighth century a powerful missionary push on northern Europe with Saint Boniface at the helm. Born in Devon around 675, Boniface spent his early adult life as a monk first at Exeter and later at Nursling, near Southampton.[6] Primarily a scholar, but drawn to teaching and evangelising, he compiled the first ever Latin grammar written in England. However, when he was forty he felt called by God to abandon all he knew and undertake the perilous journey across the English Channel to the unknown lands of Europe where he believed heathen people were awaiting conversion. His mission took him to Hesse, Bavaria and Westphalia.

Such was his success that three times he was summoned to Rome to be rewarded and made a bishop. A prodigious writer of letters, Boniface worked ceaselessly and with great effect, latterly backed by Pepin the Short, King of the Franks and father of Charlemagne. At the age of seventy he turned his attention to modern-day Holland where, at Dokkum, he and his companions were set upon by heathen Frieslanders and killed.

As his work had grown in scope and spread, Boniface had called on monks and nuns from his native Wessex to join the crusade. Among those who answered his appeal was his cousin Lioba, at the head of a party of thirty nuns sent by Abbess Tetta of Wimborne. While Boniface was celebrated and fêted by the ecclesiastical authorities, Lioba remained a shadowy figure, literate and hard-working but out of the limelight. According to later hagiographies 'the Scriptures were never out of her hand'.[7] Her most influential contact was with Hildegard, wife of Charlemagne. The two became great friends in Lioba's old age.

Fulda in Germany was Boniface's favourite monastery, his spiritual home. For Lioba, too, the place had a special significance, though she lived with her nuns on a hill outside the town. Fulda shone above all others in its day, the centre of historiography east of the Rhine and a treasury of ancient texts and chronicles. Such monasteries were akin to universities, and it was monks who ensured that many of the ancient texts still with us today did not disappear into the chasm that was the Dark Ages. At Fulda vital texts by Tacitus, Suetonius, Ammanianus and Servius were preserved by a group of extremely capable monks. There were original works produced too – Hrabanus Mauras, a Fulda monk who went on to be Archbishop of Mainz, compiled one of the first encyclopaedias of knowledge.

It was at Fulda that Boniface and Lioba were buried side by side. In

Germany, they were named saints by popular acclaim – before Pope Gregory IX in 1234 made such titles the exclusive property of the Vatican – and it is in Germany that their memory is still held sacred, while in their birthplace they are largely forgotten. Boniface is today popularly known as the Apostle of Germany.

If any trace of Joan or her ancestors could be found in England, logic suggested that there might be some clues in the launching pad for so many of these expeditions to Germany, Wimborne Minster. It was from there after all that Lioba set out, and moreover in the annals of Fulda, Joan's first home, there are clear traces of its debt to Wimborne. In a life of Lioba written by the monk Rudolphius of Fulda between 800 and 850,[8] there are detailed references back to Wimborne.

Despite Father Boyle's comforting words back in the Vatican Library, many of the standard Catholic textbooks decried all attempts to resurrect the historical figure of Pope Joan as tantamount to heresy and the work of the devil. Their admonitions flashed across my mind as I drove down to Dorset one summer morning to search Wimborne for evidence.

As I slipped and slid along the fast lane of the motorway in driving rain, a large black hearse pulled out behind me as if from nowhere, its headlights, sidelights and fog lights on full beam. It was inches from my tail, going at an unseemly speed, one big dazzle in the driving mirror. I tried to accelerate to lose it, but it just sped up. When I attempted the opposite tactic and veered into the slow lane it followed suit. And it was then, gazing ahead into the darkness and gloom, pursued by a blaze that threatened to engulf me, that the words of all the Catholic opponents of Joan's memory came back to me. What if this was the devil come to get me, God's punishment for unearthing Joan's skeleton and the shameful chapter that went with it? Perhaps I have should let sleeping female popes lie.

Then, as quickly as this modern horseman of the apocalypse had come, it disappeared. The hearse pulled off at the signpost for Southampton and the sun reassuringly peeped through the clouds. Light had replaced darkness in the oldest biblical cliché of all.

Wimborne, called Wimborne Minster on my road map, stands a little way inland from the seaside resort of Bournemouth. It was founded in Anglo-Saxon times by Saint Cuthburga on the site of an earlier Roman settlement. Cuthburga was the sister of King Ine of Wessex and was married off for some complex dynastic motive to King

48

Aldfrith of Northumbria. It was clearly an unusual marriage and there is more than one story about how husband and wife got on. Some say that Cuthburga had already decided out of religious conviction to remain a virgin and that the King granted her wish, after a decent interval, to retire to a convent. Others say that she bore him a son, Osred – who ultimately succeeded his father – before withdrawing conjugal rights and decamping for the convent. And there is another version that presents Cuthburga as trapped in an unhappy marriage and finding solace and escape in the veil.

Whichever version is true, the queen went to Barking Abbey in Essex where she studied under Saint Hildelith and remained in seclusion until her estranged husband died. She was then free to do as she wanted and, with a grant of land from her brother and the able assistance of her sister Cwenburga, she founded between 702 and 705 a monastery dedicated to prayer and learning at Wimborne. It is believed to have been the first of its kind in Dorset.

Like many Anglo-Saxon foundations, Wimborne was a double monastery, made up of communities of both men and women. The two lived separately, each in their own building behind battlemented walls, and met only for daily mass. But it was Cuthburga, like Hilda of Whitby before her, who was in charge. Like their Celtic counterparts, there were still a handful of women who were permitted – usually on account of their great wealth or royal connections – to hold positions of authority in the early medieval church with quasi-episcopal jurisdiction over the lands of their monastic foundation.[9] The practice, though, was in decline and Wimborne was one of the last bastions of this enlightened approach.

An austere woman, dedicated in her prayer and fasting, Cuthburga ran this growing community until her death in 727, when she was succeeded first by her sister Cwenburga and three years later – on Cwenburga's death – by the Abbess Tetta. Tetta was the sister of King Aetherlheard who had followed Ine as ruler of the West Saxons. It was under Tetta's guidance that Wimborne became a missionary centre, launching pad for Lioba. Several of the letters Lioba wrote home can still be seen in the local Dorchester Museum.

Wandering around Wimborne Minster today – the Anglo-Saxon foundation, I discovered, had been all but obliterated by invading Danes in the tenth century – the age of ecclesiastical sexual equality is as hard to picture as the monastery and abbey that once stood there. But they did and women did once exercise real power until Rome,

Benedict and his rule stamped out the last vestiges of an earlier system. The result has been a thousand years when women have been denied any position of authority in the Catholic church. To think back before that time is like trying to conjure up an age when intelligent men thought the world was square and you could fall off the edge. We know it happened, but it is almost beyond our conditioned modern consciousnesses to make the leap.

Two transcendant glimpses forced their way through the clouds over Wimborne. First and most obviously it offered me one explanation as to why this German-born woman was called 'Joan the English' by chroniclers. Her parents were either among the English helpers from Wimborne who joined the nuns and monks in Germany, or possibly one of them was a Wimborne religious who fell in love and married.

Second and more intriguingly Wimborne stands, as the early feminist ecclesiastical historian, Lina Eckenstein, wrote in 1896, 'last in line of well-authenticated monastic foundations made by women during the Anglo-Saxon period. Others no doubt existed at this time and we find among them some of the centres most influential in enabling Anglo-Saxons to attain a high degree of culture within a hundred years of their conversion to Christianity.'[10]

The example of the scholarly, mixed community at Wimborne – passed on by parents to a daughter hungry for knowledge and with great potential – gave Joan an alternative vision to the prevailing Benedictine rule with its relegation of women. Wimborne showed that women could hold positions of power in the Church if they first had mastered worldly attributes. Days of some form of equality of opportunity might have passed, but only just.

Thanks to her parents, Joan seems very likely to have heard of them, been inspired and calculated that at the age of twelve her trip to Athens, dressed as a man, might furnish her with the knowledge that would in its turn lead to the sort of advancement that had come to Cuthburga, Cwenburga and Tetta by accident of birth and place. Even if she had to deceive to get there, Joan could see from these women that her sex need not be a disclaimer to leadership in the Church.

As with most of Joan's history, those infuriating conditional tenses and perhapses have to be included, for there are precious few records of anything to do with Wimborne in her period, and certainly nothing that lists the brave souls who accompanied those missionaries who set out from the comfort and security of Wimborne for the English Channel and thereafter an unknown and reputedly barbarian land.

Chapter Five

'When you meet a human being, the first distinction you make is "male or female?" and you are accustomed to make the distinction with unhesitating certainty.'

Sigmund Freud, *Feminity*[1]

The stories of Cuthburga, Tetta and Hilda, passed on by parents or their fellow missionaries, need not have been alone in inspiring the young Joan to believe that her sex was not an impediment to achieving a position of power and influence in the Church. Today's Christianity – particularly that led from Rome – has a tendency to present an authorised version of its own history which excludes Joan, as it excludes the contribution of many other women who in the early centuries stood side by side with men in spreading the word, in enduring subsequent persecutions and even at the altar. 'Christian memory', according Elizabeth Schussler Fiorenza, Professor of Theology at Harvard Divinity School, 'has cut out the women in early Christianity, who have shaped early Christianity, who have shaped the Christian story and who are not remembered.'[2]

Burying the history of women's contributions is not, of course, an exclusively Christian failing. Pliny the Elder tells us in his *Natural History* that information was intentionally hidden regarding the work of women doctors, for, according to the opinion of his day, women should be quiet and as inconspicuous as possible so that after they were dead no one would know that they had lived.[3] But Christianity has undeniably surpassed its rivals in the roll-call of women pioneers it has misplaced in the mists of time. When, for example, was the last time a sermon was preached on the role of Joanna, the wife of one of King Herod's stewards mentioned in the New Testament as lending crucial support to Jesus and his followers?[4] Or Chloe, Lydia, the mother of Mark, Nymopha, Prisca and Aquila, all of whom played host to the fledgeling Christian communities in the Acts of the Apostles and the writings of Saint Paul?

Such were their revolutionary status and hatred of hierarchy and ostentation that for the first two centuries Christians tended to meet not with great show in churches and chapels but in private homes. Women – many of them well-born converts – were prominent among those who gave encouragement to the new religion by playing host to it within their houses.

By the third century, a process of institutionalisation had begun to transform such house churches with their diverse and shared leadership into a more rigid and pyramidal structure of bishops and priests, dioceses and parishes. Furthermore, because Christianity sought acceptance and respectability – and achieved it in 313 when the Emperor Constantine legalised what had hitherto been an outlawed cult – it had to bow to prevailing cultural expectations, including prejudices about a woman's proper sphere. In Greco-Roman society – as to some extent in Mediterranean and Latin societies today – women ruled the home and the family, but the public exercise of leadership was left to their men.

The early women leaders of Christianity therefore found themselves largely cast to one side by a new generation of male chiefs. But not entirely. Contemporary research has highlighted inscriptions from mid-fifth-century tombstones in southern Italy and Calabria to show that women were *presbiteras* or priests. A letter written by Pope Gelasius I (492–6) to his fellow believers in southern Italy confirms such evidence. 'We have heard', he wrote, 'that divine affairs have come to such a low state that women are encouraged to officiate at sacred altars and all matters reserved for the male sex.'[5]

Women priests were not the norm, this letter makes plain, but they existed. To judge from the fifteen or so tombstones testifying to the existence of *presbiteras* that have now been uncovered by researchers in southern France, Turkey and former Yugoslavia, they may have been widespread. Yet in the face of such evidence, Rome attempts to shrug off its own history with a casual assertion that *presbitera* is an ambiguous word. It can also mean wife of a priest.

Such an explanation of course offers no response to Pope Gelasius's letter but there Rome changes tack and emphasises that he was condemning the practice. Condemnation does not, though, mean it did not happen. It is as if Rome cannot bear to take seriously the research work into women priests in the early church lest it gets drawn into a debate it knows ultimately it cannot win. Academic endeavour is suppressed in the light of modern ecclesiastical prejudices. Precedents, whatever their exact legal status, are denied. The echoes of Pope Joan are deafening.

Mary Ann Rossi, based at the Women's Research Center of the University of Wisconsin and one of the leading lights in this field of historical and archaeological exploration, finds that the complete absence of depictions of women – save for the Virgin – in most churches and church buildings arouses her suspicions that there was once and indeed still is a cover-up.[6] The fact that there are so few representations of women in the treasury of church art, rather than convincing her of the lowly status of her sex, only makes her curious. She is one of many writers and scholars to have studied a celebrated mosaic, on view to the public right under the Vatican's nose.

The Church of Santa Prassede lies in the shadow of the great basilica of Santa Maria Maggiore in Rome – called, with an unattractive military ring, Saint Mary Major by the English. Santa Prassede with columns taken from pagan temples stands on the site of what is thought to be a house where the early Christians worshipped in private. The first church on the site is recorded at the end of the fourth century and the current building was originally erected in the ninth century.

It contains mosaics that date back to the fifth century. One portrays four female figures against a gold background. Three have the traditional round halos reserved for the sainted dead. One has a square variation that signifies she was still alive when the mosaic was completed. The three are readily identifiable – the Virgin Mary along with Saints Prassede and her sister Pudentiana, daughters of a first-century Roman senator and early convert reputed to have played host to Saint Peter when he came to Rome in AD 64. Around the head and shoulders of the fourth figure are the words Theodora Episcopa – 'Bishop Theodora' – though the 'a' of Theodora has been partially but not very successfully erased by scratches made to the tile of the mosaic. Another example perhaps of the poor workmanship of those ubiquitous forgers, but his or her efforts were all in vain for the offending words are repeated in an inscription on a marble slab on one of the columns outside the chapel housing the mosaic.

Here, unlike in the case of the *presbiteras*, there is no suggestion that Theodora was illegally enthroned as a bishop. But again Rome has a ready answer. And again it is not very convincing. Theodora, we are told, was the mother of Pope Paschal I (817–24), a patron of the rebuilding of a church on this site. But why is she called a bishop? There is no evidence that popes bestowed courtesy titles on their mothers and certainly not those titles officially reserved for men. Furthermore, why has someone tried to deface the feminine ending to her name? It is not, after all, the only mention of a woman bishop in

Rome. In the Vatican Library, under Father Boyle's stewardship, there is a manuscript taken from an epitaph from the cemetery of the Basilica of Saint Valentine in Rome. It refers to an inscription about a 'femina episcopa'.[7]

There are other surviving fragments of evidence within Rome itself that further challenge the official Catholic line that women priests have never existed and never will. Below the streets of the Italian capital is a city of the dead, a maze of 1800-year-old burial chambers known as the catacombs. In the first centuries after Jesus's death Rome was drunk on the blood of the Christian martyrs. The men and women who died side by side in arenas like the Colosseum were buried side by side in the catacombs. This labyrinth of tunnels and subterranean chapels was also a place of shelter when the persecutions were at their height, a sanctuary in which to celebrate the Eucharist in private. Different areas were named after individual saints and decorated to recall both biblical themes and the heroic witness of those who had given their lives for their faith.

In the Catacomb of Saint Priscilla, excavated at the end of the last century, the gallery of wall paintings includes such standard themes as Moses striking the rock, the visit of the three kings to the manger and Abraham preparing to offer his son Isaac in sacrifice to Yahweh. And there is an early third-century fresco showing seven figures standing round a table with their hands upraised, concelebrating what appears to be a simple Eucharist with bread and wine. Though the colours are faded and the rich red background has down the ages submerged much of the detail, it is undeniable that at least one, and possibly all, the figures are women. The Pontifical Commission on Sacred Archaeology acknowledges that there is a veiled woman present in the picture, but stresses that it is a man who is actually breaking the bread.[8] Researchers, however, have studied this male figure and pointed out that his garb – in terms of style and skirt length – is that of a woman, not a man. The fact that all seven have their hands raised – a gesture that is to this day reserved for priests at the Eucharist – appears to indicate that all were of equivalent status.

Such evidence, it seems, will always be hotly contested by Rome. Since it bases its objections to women priests not on scripture or the words of Christ but rather on tradition, it is no surprise that researchers attempt to discover a hidden history that undermines its position. It may have taken ecclesiastical detectives 1500 years or more to rediscover the evidence of women as ordained ministers and leaders in Christianity, but in Joan's time, 400 years after these tombstones tell of *presbiteras* and just a few decades after Pope Paschal was associated with the Church of Santa Prassede, the trail may not yet have gone cold.

In an age of widespread illiteracy and a dearth of writing materials, information was passed by word of mouth, from mother to daughter, from neighbour to neighbour, from traveller to the towns he visited and, in the case of the Church, by missionaries and itinerant preachers like the Dominican order. Official declarations from the Pope could reach the far-flung outposts of Christianity only at the speed of the fastest mule, while the historical evidence collected in monastic treasure houses was inaccessible to all but a privileged few.

With this random and often localised information non-technology, myths, folklore and plain rumour – depicted by Shakespeare in *Henry IV, Part II* as a character in garments 'painted full of tongues' – quickly grew up. A favourite in the fifth century and later in the early medieval period were the 'infancy gospels' which centred on Jesus's childhood. These were widely spread by preachers and word of mouth, though seldom in writing. The few traces that exist to this day are strange medieval illustrations of Jesus sliding down sunbeams. In general these tales presented an unattractive picture of Jesus as a bully and a brute. In one story that has survived Jesus turns his playmates into pigs and puts them in the oven. His mother Mary has to rescue them. The echoes of anti-Semitism are clear, but beyond that, at such a distance, the exact source of these infancy gospels and their real or imagined significance is impossible to ascertain.[9]

What they do show, though, is that the ecclesiastical authorities, despite having the keys to libraries and access to stores of documents, were often powerless to control or even shape the flow of stories and legends. If they did they would hardly have encouraged stories that depicted the Messiah as a spiteful little boy. So, however much an increasingly male-dominated church may have wanted to eradicate the memory of Hilda, Cuthburga and their like, it was not so easily achieved. In Joan's time, they were too recent to ignore, and indeed, though the practice of having women in charge of double monasteries was in decline, some abbesses still exercised episcopal powers. At Quedlinburg in Saxony such a practice continued right up to 1539.[10]

The young Joan, growing up at Fulda under the tutelage of her parents and eager for knowledge, could have assimilated a picture of a church where women had until recently been leaders but where now they were beginning to be marginalised. Moreover, the library at Fulda may well have contained texts that are now lost to us after its subsequent destruction in the Thirty Years War in the seventeenth century. Described in all the chronicles as fiercely intelligent, Joan may have decided that this was a temporary set-back and that all she had to do was find a way round the current block until greater tolerance was restored.

A clear distinction has to be entered here between Joan's era and the high Middle Ages when the anti-woman movement in the upper echelons of the Christian church reached the peak of its hysteria with Thomas Aquinas deeming the female sex 'misbegotten men', arguing that women were inferior by nature and therefore incapable of leadership.[11]

Such ideas were of course current in the Joan's time. As early as the fourth century learned fathers like Saint John Chrysostom (347–407) had been writing of women: 'The whole of her bodily beauty is nothing less than phlegm, blood, bile, rheum and the fluid of digested food. If you consider what is stored up behind those lovely eyes, the angle of the nose, the mouth and cheeks, you will agree that the well-proportioned body is merely a whitened sepulchre.'[12] And a few years later, one of the most influential Christian writers of all time, Saint Augustine (354–430), declared in his *Confessions*: 'By the sex of her body, she womankind is submissive to the masculine sex. This is analogous to the way in which the impulse for action is subordinate to the rational mind's prudent concern that the act is right.'[13]

At a popular level, Augustine's teaching fed into ideas about women and the basic flaws of their bodies. Menstrual blood was believed to turn wine sour, make crops barren, rust iron and infect dog bites with poison. With such a destructive power, the idea of women handling the body and blood of Christ as the priest and chief celebrant of the Eucharist was out of the question.

Yet even in the ninth century such views had not taken on the terrifying power that they would later assume. The young Joan may still have legitimately harboured hopes that her Church would return to its earlier practice of offering some avenues of opportunity for women.

Potentially the greatest influence on the young Joan, available and some contemporary historians argue actively promoted at her time, was the example of virtuous, God-fearing and saintly women who followed their vocation in the Church by dressing up as men. Saints' tales were one of the standard tools at the time for teaching a largely illiterate faithful about Godly virtues. Pope Gregory the Great (590–604) had picked up an already existing trend of hagiography in Christianity and promoted it as a way of inspiring believers and new converts to live in imitation of hallowed figures. No matter that most of the stories were exaggerated or even fabricated, or that tales of wrestling with the devil were beyond the daily experiences of their hearers, the company of saints became the role models of Christianity. Their examples were well-known and often quoted by even uneducated souls. The trade in their relics, believed to hold miraculous powers, was booming in centres of pilgrimage and country fairs alike.

Pelagia was one such saint. She was an actress living in Antioch in the fourth century, 'celebrated for her beauty, her wealth and the disorder of her life' as Alban Butler piously reports in his *Lives of Saints*.[14] A synod was called in her city and she was drawn to hear Bishop Nonnus of Edessa preach. His words so moved her that she asked him to baptise her, which he duly did. However, when news that this notorious woman had converted reached the streets of Antioch there was uproar. Dressed as a man, Pelagia escaped the outcry and made her way to Jerusalem where she lived in a cave on the Mount of Olives as a hermit, known and revered by local people as Pelagius, the 'beardless monk'. It was only when she died and was buried that her gender was discovered. But such deception did not stand in the way of her acclamation as a saint.

Though today the Vatican has a complex and long-winded process for declaring saints which would inevitably exclude Pelagia should her case now be submitted for scrutiny, in the early church it was the people – not the bureaucrats – who bestowed the honour, another example of the more democratic, spontaneous atmosphere which once prevailed in Christianity. And because Pelagia was unusual, her legend spread sufficiently for it to have lived on well past her death and down to our own age where it is still honoured in Greece.

Precisely the same problems that face the detective searching for Pope Joan confront the young Catholic wondering whether to make Pelagia – or any of these early Christians – his or her confirmation saint. Their legends have been much embellished over the ages. Trying to identify the kernel of truth in them is difficult. Some history books can be trusted, standard works like Eusebius's *Ecclesiastical History*.[15] If the saint is mentioned there, he or she continues to remain on the 'A' list in the Catholic canon. Others, without such an unimpeachable protector, face relegation and recategorisation.

The nineteenth-century Belgian historian Father Hippolyte Delehaye dedicated his life to studying tales of saintly virtue and uncovering their origins.[16] He argued that Pelagia's story fell into the category of romance, fashioned by later generations from a story or character in the oral tradition. 'The author chooses and ponders his subject,' Delehaye wrote in *The Legends of the Saints*, 'and brings his abilities and imagination to bear on the work of art he has conceived. If his theme is the character and doings of an historical person, or the events of an historical period, the result is an historical romance or novel . . . If the writer's aim is to depict the life and spirit of a saint honoured by the Church by means of a series of happenings that are partly real and partly imaginary, then the work may be called a hagiographical romance.'

The Pelagia who inspired the story may have been another fourth-century woman from Antioch who, unlike her namesake, was a virgin and martyr at the age of fifteen. She is mentioned in the writings of Saint John Chrysostom and Saint Ambrose – both of whom fall into the category of unimpeachable sources – and continues to be accorded full honours by the Church with a feast day on 8 October. On to the brave but – in the context of the bloody persecution of the early church – commonplace story of the modest Pelagia, Delehaye claims, was added the tale of the wanton Pelagia who cross-dressed to achieve earthly peace and eternal reward. The inspiration for this synthesis, Delehaye suggested, was a story mentioned by the same Saint John Chrysostom in his sixty-seventh homily on Saint Matthew's gospel. There he talks of an unnamed actress from Antioch who renounced her wicked ways, donned a hair shirt and lived as a recluse. 'We know from outstanding examples', Delehaye concluded, 'that historical tradition about local saints soon disappears when a legend begins to develop, and that hagiographers are not afraid of making alterations which render their subjects practically unrecognisable.'

Delehaye took Pelagia's story as the starting point of whole series of 'imaginary' stories about women saints who took on the garb of men. In the fifth century, there were Saints Apollinaris and Euphrosyne, both high-born Egyptians. Apollinaris dressed as a man, called herself Dorotheus and lived as a hermit monk in the desert where she earned fame by curing her sister. Her true identity and sex remained hidden, even from the sister, until her death. Euphrosyne wanted to avoid an arranged marriage, so disguised herself as a young monk, Smaragdus, and entered a monastery. Her holiness began to attract pilgrims, one of whom was her father who did not recognise her. Only on her deathbed did she summon him and tell him the truth.

There was one variation on the theme of cross-dressing concerning Saints Eugenia and Marina that centred on the manner of the revelation of their deceit. Eugenia, the daughter of a third-century Roman governor of Alexandria, ran away from home, dressed up as a man and entered a monastery. Later she was accused of adultery with a woman visitor to the monastery. She was tried and sentenced to death. From prison she summoned her father and revealed herself to him as female and his lost daughter. He pardoned her and was guided by her example to convert to Christianity.

Marina who lived in the fourth century was the daughter of a widower father who decided he wanted to enter a monastery. Since he did not want to leave her behind, he pretended she was a boy and passed her off as such until his death when she was seventeen. Marina's task was to drive the monastery's cart into the local town to collect supplies. One day the monk was accused of getting the local innkeeper's daughter pregnant. Unable to defend herself against such charges without revealing her gender, Marina was thrown out of the monastery and lived as a beggar at the gates with the child she was alleged to have fathered. After many years the abbot took pity and admitted them both into the fold. Soon after, Marina died and the monks learned her secret.

A second variation had saints like the sixth-century Brigid – honoured to this day in her native Ireland as second only to Patrick – avoiding an unsuitable marriage that would distract them from matters spiritual by miraculously growing a beard, being rejected by her suitor as ugly and thrown out by her father. Uncumber and Wilgefortis were other 'bearded saints'. The latter was the child of a non-Christian ruler of Portugal and his Christian wife. Wilgefortis, whose feast is still marked on 20 July in Portugal, was a pious girl who decided to remain a virgin. Her father had other plans for her – marriage to the King of Sicily. In despair, she prayed for divine assistance and sprouted a beard and moustache. Her marriage failed and her father had her crucified as a punishment. The same story is told of Saint Uncumber in England, where she is the patron saint of married women who wanted to get rid of their husbands.

Buried in the uncertain early days of Christianity, there is even a story told in the mysterious Gospel of the Egyptians – today found in the Nag Hammadi Library – that Jesus promised to save Mary by making her a man. Whether he is referring to Mary his mother, the allegedly wanton Mary Magdalen or Mary of Bethany, racy sister of homely Martha, is unclear.

Whether or not this, or any, or all of the tales of cross-dressing saints are fact or – as Delehaye alleged – fiction can perhaps be judged by their similarity to better-documented cases in later centuries of women who chose to dress as men and often to remain celibate in order to achieve advancement or professional fulfilment in the world. The parallels that can be drawn between these saints and such women suggests that Delehaye was too dismissive. The saints fit in with a well-established pattern.

Emma Edmonds fought as Franklin Thompson in the US Civil War. She ran away from home to escape an unhappy match and an abusive father, as she later recounted in *Nurse and Spy in the Union Army* (1865). When she once returned in her disguise, only the animals recognised her. Christian Davies, born in Dublin 1667, was left all alone in the world when her husband and the father of her three sons disappeared. So, disguised as a man, she enlisted in the army, in order to find him. Some thirteen years later they were reunited, but only after surgeons had discovered her true identity when they were dressing a wound after the Battle of Ramilles. Or Dr James Miranda Barry, a woman who disguised herself as a man in order to gain admittance to the then exclusively male Edinburgh Medical School in 1812 and who spent the rest of her life as a respected male doctor, her true sex only being discovered after she died.[17]

Julie Wheelwright, who has studied these later cross-dressers in her book *Amazons and Military Maids*, endorses the line leading back from them to the transvestite saints of the early Church, famed for their piety and saintliness, and even to Joan herself in her rise to the top post in the Church.

What was interesting about the women I studied and what applies to these saints and even Joan was that they were always known as the best men in their field. They could perform these fantastic feats. And I think these women saw their over-achievement as a guarantee of their safety from discovery. Certainly they were regarded as a bit eccentric, a bit peculiar or as having odd habits, but that was the end of the story. No one thought to question them about their gender.[18]

60

Wheelwright considers that the chastity demanded of the monks may even have made the religious life a more attractive option for women cross-dressers than the army or navy were later. 'As a woman in disguise as a man it would be very difficult to have a heterosexual relationship. A lot of the women that I looked at were trying so hard to be men and to internalise their masculinity that to have a heterosexual relationship would be a very schizophrenic situation. Therefore to be a monk, where sex is technically out of the question, would have an obvious appeal.'

Joan, studying as a young girl in the great libraries at Fulda and mixing with missionaries and travelling preachers, would have had access to the stories of the cross-dressing saints. No one denies that they were current in the Dark Ages. Marina's name, for instance, appears in an English litany of the seventh century. Whether she believed the details or not, they would have given Joan an idea as to how to achieve advancement.

The extent of their influence should not be underestimated. Catherine of Siena, one of the most enduring and 'officially' celebrated figures in the fourteenth-century Church, with her high-profile attempts to reconcile popes and emperors, her spiritual raptures and her unlikely band of followers (or 'Caterinati'), named Euphrosyne as her role model. The inspiration is clear and accepted – Catherine, like Euphrosyne, faced being forced into marriage against her will but escaped into a female religious order in 1367. If Euphrosyne could inspire, in her flight from marriage, Catherine, one of the few women saints to be accorded by the Vatican the posthumous title of 'Doctor of the Church', why could she not also inspire Joan in her escape from female stereotypes?[19]

Various scholars have attached differing interpretations to the clutch of cross-dressing saints. Some have suggested that the cult of Saint Pelagia is evidence that the Christian Church continued to worship pagan goddesses by disguising them as saints. The Romans took over Greek gods and renamed them and the Christians did much the same, borrowing even such central players in the New Testament drama as the devil from other religions. Pelagia, according to the German scholar Herman Usener in the nineteenth century, is Aphrodite, the goddess of the sea and of erotic pleasure and animal fertility.[20] On Cyprus, at least, Aphrodite was worshipped in rituals where women in men's clothing offered sacrifices to the goddess. Among the many aliases under which Aphrodite is known is Pelagia. Such a process is not unlike current practices in Latin America where mass-going Catholics also participate in animist cults like Candombole in Brazil, Voodoo in Haiti or Santoria in Cuba where Christian saints are dressed up as pagan fertility symbols or demons.

Another theory, articulated by the American historian and psychoanalyst John Anson, has it that these stories are 'monastic fantasies.'[21] He notes the universal maleness of the chroniclers who recorded the tales – and who may indeed have been responsible for inventing them and projecting them on to the lives of otherwise dull saints. Anson theorised that celibate scribes were letting rip with their dreams of uncovering a woman disguised as a man within their own monastery and then having secret sexual liaisons with them. 'What finally comes into view', Anson wrote,

> is the guilty desire that underlies the whole dreamwork; for instead of an overture rejected, a sexual act is committed and laid to the blame of the saint, who undergoes punishment as a kind of surrogate. Thus, quite simply, the secret longing for a woman in a monastery is brilliantly concealed by disguising the woman as a man and making her appear guilty of the very temptation to which monks are most subject; finally, after she has been punished for their desires, their guilt is compensated by turning her into a saint with universal remorse and sanctimonious worship.

Marjorie Garber, in her celebrated study of cross-dressing *Vested Interests*, takes Anson's theory one step further.[22] This group of stories about transvestite saints reflects, she claims,

> an anxiety about the question of paternity which, in the case of the Catholic Church, is in fact a foundational mystery. For twelfth-century monasticism the story of the cross-dressed 'father' might well, as Anson suggests, bear the brunt of a celibate clergy's repressed and conflicted desires, but it also points toward other kinds of conflict, social, theological as well as sexual. The identity of the father was the mystery – and the certainty – on which the faith was based. These 'local' stories of other mysterious paternities, with their transvestite under- and overtones reanimate the conundrum of divine fatherhood in the context of a world-turned-upside-down. A crisis of belief is here displaced onto the axis of gender.

Garber's theory tells us something of the confused thinking on gender in the twelfth century when Pope Joan's history began to be retold. But a more intriguing variation on the theme of the cross-dressing saints is provided by Vern Bullough of the department of history at California State University. He is an expert witness whose research has given him special insight into both Pope Joan and those senior clerics who later promoted her story so assiduously.

Bullough examines the cases of Pelagia and her like in *Sex, Society and History*[23] and argues that throughout Christian history, rising to a crescendo in the medieval period, it was fairly common to express women's inferiority by describing them as men turned inside out. 'One reads in popular literature, that women who spread their legs very far would have their organs fall out and become men.' In most medieval literature, he points out, the ovaries are called the female testes. To counterbalance this medieval dislike of weak, child-bearing women, Bullough suggests, female cross-dressers 'were tolerated and even encouraged, since they were striving to become more male-like and therefore better persons. Male transvestites, on the other hand, were discouraged not only because they lost status but also because during the formation of western attitudes most writers could only find one possible explanation for a man's adopting woman's guise, namely, a desire to have easier access to women for sexual purposes.'

So though Christianity in theory frowned upon transvestism – 'a woman must not wear men's clothes nor a man put on a woman's dress; anyone who does this is detestable to Yahweh your God' (Deuteronomy 22:5) – in practice it encouraged able women by pushing the example of the cross-dressing saints. At some level, capable women who wanted to get on and win the respect of the ecclesiastical authorities were encouraged to try to appear to be men.

Unsurprisingly, Bullough cannot provide direct proof of such learned fathers of the Church telling women to dress as men, but he has assembled a mass of circumstantial evidence. The woman saint, he stresses, tends to don male attire at a point of crisis in her life. Her actions then mark a break with the past. Some even burn their clothes or visualise themselves as males. Saint Perpetua, a third-century martyr in Carthage, had a dream while in prison waiting to be thrown to the lions. In the dream she was borne into the amphitheatre of death, stripped of her clothes and changed into a man in order to meet the challenge ahead. By such examples, Bullough argues, women were encouraged to visualise themselves as attaining the merits of the higher sex.

In the fourth century Saint Jerome, a noted misogynist, endorsed such a trend when he wrote: 'Long as woman is for birth and children, she is different from man as body is from soul. But when she wishes to serve Christ more than the world, then she will cease to be a woman and will be called man.'[24] Saint Ambrose in the same century was another who apparently gave such a development his blessing: 'She who does not believe is a woman and should be designated by the name of her sex, whereas she who believes progresses to perfect manhood, to the measure of the adulthood in Christ. She then dispenses with the name of her sex, the seductiveness of youth, the garrulousness of old age.'[25]

Chapter Six

'Dressed as I am in jeans and a sweater, I have no idea to which sex the policemen will suppose me to belong, and must prepare my responses for either decision. I feel their silent appraisal down the corridor as I approach them, and as they search my sling bag I listen hard for a "Sir" or a "Ma'am" to decide my course of conduct.'

Jan Morris, *Conundrum; An Extraordinary Narrative of Transsexualism*[1]

It would have taken Pope Joan's parents weeks, possibly months to travel from Wimborne and the south coast of England to join up with their fellow missionaries at Fulda. I did it in a few hours. For them the journey would have been on a rickety boat across the North Sea, a long foot-slog to the abbey town north-east of current-day Frankfurt, with the constant risk of attack by hostile forces or bandits. I slid out to Heathrow airport on the Tube early one summer morning, caught a plane to Frankfurt's glistening and enormous airport, then took two trains to Fulda – total journey no more than four hours. The only threat I encountered was my own fear of flying.

As I walked out of Fulda station on to the town's main thoroughfare, lined by chain stores, banks and pavement cafés, that impression of being an unbridgeable ocean apart from the ninth century was reinforced. There couldn't be a trace of Joan in this utilitarian swath of concrete and paving slabs, aluminium windows and municipal frippery. No remnant of the world she once inhabited could be left after 1100 years, I remarked to Maria, my translator for the day. She smiled enigmatically and strode purposefully ahead. Fulda, she explained comfortingly, had three very different parts – the real town, which we were now crossing, the administration town away to the north, and the church town, our destination.

By the time we reached the huge piazza in front of the cathedral the journey backwards in time had begun. It was now the 1600s, in the shadow of a great, bulbous baroque façade. My expert witness on this stage of Joan's life was waiting on the steps. Professor Gangolf Schrimpf taught philosophy at Fulda's thriving seminary. There were fifty students at present, he told me, forty from the diocese of Fulda alone. He spoke the figure with pride. This place obviously had some sort of secret, I remarked. In most western countries, the entire

Catholic church doesn't manage fifty new priests each year. Vocations are falling so quickly that parishes are without priests and Catholics are going without access to the mass and the sacraments. The professor grinned. Perhaps Fulda was a little special, he conceded. But then he was biased. A lay man in his fifties, he was the sort of easygoing, learned but unpompous teacher whose excitement at knowledge was infectious. He managed, where all previous seminary professors had failed, to make the prospect of six years' study for the priesthood seem like an attractive intellectual option, its other drawbacks notwithstanding.

Might the memory of Pope Joan play a part in the allure of Fulda's seminary, I ventured tentatively? 'Her story is not so well known. I have heard it,' he admitted with the air of one of the *cognoscenti*, 'but Fulda is above all a place where Boniface and Lioba are remembered.' Boniface's tomb was in the cathedral behind us, he said, while Lioba had been laid to rest high on a hill above the town at the Church of Saint Peter. He gestured vaguely beyond the roof-tops. 'Boniface and Lioba were cousins and wanted to be buried in the same grave in the monastery. But the monastery here was closed for women and if women pilgrims had wanted to see her grave, they couldn't. So she was moved to Saint Peter's.' It was an arrangement that Benedict would have approved, given his treatment of his sister Scholastica. And the remains of the monastery? 'Gone. They built three churches here' – he pointed again to the cathedral behind him – 'each on the ruins of the previous one. And then in 1803 the monastery closed.'

It was Abbot Sturmi who founded the Benedictine Abbey at Fulda around 744, getting the approval of Rome and independence from the local bishop in 751. But it is Boniface's name that is most associated with the foundation. After his burial there in 755, plans took shape to transform the simple 40-metre-long building into something grander. The Ratger-Basilika was consecrated in 819, half-way between the era of Boniface and that of Joan. It was in the environs of this great abbey church, with its monastery, school and cloisters that she grew up. Then, in the late seventeenth century, the old abbey was torn down, its Saxon origins obliterated by a twin-towered baroque basilica with the monastery and cloister clustered around a courtyard at the rear.

Was there anything left that dated back to Joan's time? 'Nothing in the cathedral, though there is a model of the old abbey in the Town Museum. There are fragments of Saxon walls here and there.' And what of the manuscripts that made up Fulda's once unsurpassed library? 'Not unsurpassed,' the professor corrected gently, 'but it was certainly the most important east of the Rhine. Sadly the entire library was destroyed in the Thirty Years War in the seventeenth century. Everything was lost, though today we are assembling copies of some of the manuscripts that once were here.'

I was about to lose heart and hurry back to the station, when the professor added almost as an afterthought: 'the only building from that time is' – and he swung round and gestured to a turreted and gabled chapel, perched precariously above the piazza – 'Saint Michael's, which was once the chapel to the monastery.'

I was keen to start there, but was persuaded to save the best till last. In the company of Professor Schrimpf we were to follow in the footsteps of the day-trippers who have made Fulda a centre of pilgrimage down the ages and begin with Boniface himself. Our illustrious guide led the way to the saint's grave which lies under the main altar of the cathedral.

The tomb, the professor explained, as we stood admiring its carved marble front, used to be the centre of the monastery and once it stood at the point where the public on one side of the grille and the enclosed monks on the other brushed shoulders. Recent scientific investigations have shown that the bones contained in it match the saint's dates. Furthermore, they demonstrate signs of the arthritis and other ailments that he was recorded as having suffered from.

This tomb, without its fancy frontice, would have been a feature of Joan's young life, a site of veneration, a place of prayer for her, as for the handful of people alongside us now, silently seeking Boniface's intercession and irritated by our whispers. At last I was getting a sense of Joan's footsteps, standing in her shadow. The faithful kneeling before icons and images, searching through prayer for a way of understanding the mundane and the extraordinary, the good and evil forces that shape lives has been a common experience right back to earliest times. Timeless rituals addressed to a multitude of gods unite their participants in every age in a mutual bemusement and a mutual hope. Where Joan may once have prostrated herself before the saint whose exploits would have dominated her childhood, searching for help as she struggled with the conflict between her sex and her desire to get an education, I now settled down for a few minutes on my knees to ask for enlightenment in the various stumbling blocks in my own life and a clue as to the outcome of my investigation.

Despite his professed love for the town and the reverence with which his memory is still honoured there, Boniface spent little time in Fulda. It was only after he had met his untimely end at the hands of the pagan Frieslanders in Holland that he spent any time in the abbey. Yet his image adorns most of the ecclesiastical buildings in Fulda, usually with a book in his hands in memory of the legend, the professor explained, that he tried to defend himself against the blows of his murderers with the Bible.

Boniface too gave me a clue to Fulda's real significance in Joan's story. Once a year, Professor Schrimpf said, all the German bishops gathered at the saint's tomb to pray and reflect. They met in the 'Boniface Room' in the adjoining former monastery building, now housing the seminary and diocesan offices, to hammer out policy. 'It is because Boniface was the Apostle of Germany. He is a tradition of Catholics in Germany. He is still seen as a sign of unity, a focus, and Fulda is his place.'

On reflection, the professor admitted that there had been highs and lows in such a reverent attitude to Boniface – 'it really all started again in the nineteenth century in the time of Bismarck and his *Kulturkampf* – but the place of Fulda was clear. As the professor put it: 'It has always been more of a symbol of German Catholicism than a centre.' If Pope Joan was either a wholly invented story or a real episode subsequently amended to hit at the Catholic church, locating her in Fulda gives an extra bite to the subversion. For here, in the heartland of German Catholicism, was born and developed the ultimate subversive, the woman who would be pope.

Yet if the intention was to use Fulda's reputation against the Catholic church, why not call her 'Joan of Fulda'? Instead she was always Joan 'the English'. And what of the clear and historical links between Fulda and England? These had not been made up by a mischievous chronicler. They made sense and could be verified.

Through the professor's good offices we gained admittance to the former monastery buildings behind the cathedral. Here we stood, as it were, on the other side of Boniface's grave. Again excavations had revealed a little more of the past. Clustered in a semicircle around his tomb on the monastery side had been found the stone sarcophagi of various early medieval abbots. And beyond them the bones of monks whose lowly station meant they merited only perishable wooden coffins.

Most of the monks, however, had been buried outside the monastery, around the little chapel that is today Saint Michael's Church, the only remaining fragment of ninth-century Fulda. It has two towers, one squat and square, the second, at the centre of the church, tall, round, with a high, pointed roof. This one, the professor said, was the ninth-century heart of the chapel that once stood among the graves. The rest of the church is made up of later additions.

Even though it was a warm summer's day outside, the thick stone walls, with only tiny slits for windows, made this ancient chapel cool enough to raise goosebumps. Eight thick stone pillars held up the central tower. The simplicity of it all was breath-taking next to the ornament and cluttered detail of the baroque cathedral. It even boasted – like Wimborne Minister – a small Saxon turret, containing a staircase which led up to a higher gallery. I shouldn't have been surprised that the Anglo-Saxons had a shared architectural style, whatever the problems of communications and travel in the Dark Ages, but I was. And down below there was a small crypt where a thick central pillar, growing broader as it reached up to the ceiling, had for 1100 years held up the entire tower structure above it. White-walled, musty and damp, the crypt contained just one tombstone of an unnamed deacon.

Here, once more, was a building where the young Pope Joan might have knelt and prayed. And this time it was still in its original form, with a simplicity that focused your attention not with the gaudy signposts of details and images but via atmosphere, as intangible and alluring as is the God it was erected to honour. In a step I was transported back to an earlier age when the prayer and the sacraments, not the buildings that played host to them, were the focus of the Church. In any other town, certainly in Britain, Saint Michael's could have done a roaring trade in the current vogue for retreats geared towards ancient (usually Celtic) and more spiritual forms of prayer, reflection and meditation. Here, however, it stood witness to Fulda and its illustrious but not immediately obvious past.

Professor Schrimpf had another engagement, so had to leave. He wished me luck in finding the female pontiff. I must come back and share my findings with the seminarians, he added without a trace of irony. Again, as with the likeable Father Boyle, there was no embarrassment on the Church's behalf, more a slightly mischievous curiosity.

In the 1983 film *Yentl*, Barbra Streisand plays the eponymous heroine, a teenage Jewish girl in eastern Europe who disguises herself as a man in order to learn the Talmud or code of law. Such opportunities were widely denied to women in mainstream Judaism right up to the dawn of this century, the period when *Yentl* is set. For daughters, there was a separate and inferior school system, with a few crumbs of scholarship often offered by blind teachers who would not therefore pose a threat to the young maidens' virtue.

Based on a short story by the Nobel-prize-winning author Isaac Bashevis Singer, *Yentl* has Streisand's character told that 'a woman who studies Talmud is a demon'. Undeterred and disbelieving, she cuts her hair, dons male attire, adopts the name Anshel and tricks her way into a Yeshiva or rabbinical school. There she initially thrives, but her gender proves her undoing. She falls for a fellow student, Avidor, and is forced to reveal her true self and jeopardise all she has achieved.

The story, as recounted by Singer in 'Yentl: The Yeshiva Boy'[2] reflects not one particular case, but one of the most enduring stories in Jewish folklore. Like all such tales, it is essentially a parable, a narrative created to illustrate the particular point concerning women being denied an education.

Its point, then, is parallel to the 'message' in accounts of the young Joan. She, too, according to the chroniclers, saw her chances of further education after the age of twelve evaporate because of her sex. It was the way of the world in the ninth century. Even high-born women only managed a shot at scholarship after that age by entering a nunnery and taking vows. The time of convents offering education to young women without requiring them to sign up for life-long chastity, poverty and obedience was still far off. The trail-blazing pioneer Mary Ward only founded the Institute of the Blessed Virgin Mary with such a lofty educative mission in mind at the start of the seventeenth century.[3] Unless Joan was willing to join a religious order, then, her fate as a woman was to remain untutored in Latin, Greek, the scriptures.

Sister Lavinia Byrne is one who has chosen to follow the example of Mary Ward. A member of the Institute of the Blessed Virgin Mary, she is one of Britain's best-known nuns, a vocal feminist in her radio broadcasts on the BBC and a supporter of women's ordination. Like her fellow IBVMs, Lavinia Byrne remains passionate about the effect education can have on her sex – and therefore clear-sighted as to how it might have affected the young Joan. 'Education is the key to visibility and social mobility. Your aspirations change. You no longer collude with the traditional division of roles.'[4]

She quotes examples from the medieval period of women who were thus inspired by learning, like the twelfth-century nun and mystic,

Hildegard of Bingen. Her fine mind – she wrote two books on medicine – and talents as a musician and artist won her the respect of archbishops and kings. But – and here was the danger faced by educated women in the Church, Sister Lavinia points out – they also marked Hildegard out in the minds of some clerics as a trouble-maker, one with ideas above her station and sex. When she ignored a warning from her abbot to act in a more womanly and therefore subservient fashion and instead went on using her brain and her tongue, she was denied the sacraments for six months and her music was banned. In 1148 she stood trial and was only exonerated by a special synod.

Another example of that same deep-rooted fear of clever, resourceful women is the Beguines in the Low Countries, Germany, Italy and Greece in the thirteenth century.[5] Here were groups of independent-minded women who lived chaste lives in communities where scholarship and looking after the needy were twin concerns. It was a cross between the women's colleges at Oxbridge and a convent, a place of learning cleansed of the presence and the influence of men. The Beguines were free of the clerical control that shackled convents at the time.

For a period the Beguinage flourished. Cologne boasted some ninety-nine Beguine communities, some with just two members, others with as many as fifty. But the ecclesiastical authorities were hostile, fearful no doubt that such free spirits might infect other women, and the movement was persecuted and ultimately driven out of existence. The Beguines are typical not only of their period, but of the entire Christian period, save perhaps our own century. Women were denied learning and advancement and whenever they created an environment where at least the first could be achieved, they incurred the wrath of the ecclesiastical authorities.

Four hundred years before the Beguines, Pope Joan could have predicted their fate. Only by disguising her sex could she remove the certainty of restraint. Perhaps it is just a coincidence that the first chronicle references to Joan came at a time when the Beguinage was thriving. Many of the chronicle accounts of Joan lead back to Germany where the Beguine communities were strong. But perhaps the tale of the She-Pope had been revived after centuries of suppression as a way of countering this new tide of women's emancipation. You may think you're freeing yourself of Church strictures to pursue scholarship, Joan's biographers may have been warning their audience, but however fine your brains, your sex and your bodies will be your undoing.

Given the strength that subsequent generations of women derived from female solidarity in the convent, it is worth pondering for a moment why such a route did not appeal to Joan. She, too, might have gone down in history as a trail-blazer like Hildegard or the Beguines.

Joan's parents, as we have seen, were either co-workers of the ordained missionaries in Germany or possibly a priest and his wife. Celibacy for priests did not become the norm until the twelfth century and married clergy persisted until the Council of Trent in 1545. If her family worked alongside missionaries, a reluctance to consider the convent is odd, particularly given Joan's academic gifts. Among what today we would term lay workers, the missionaries would have been held in high esteem. For the clever young Joan to enter the convent would have been the equivalent in today's terms of the daughter of a school cleaner getting to be headmistress.

But if Joan's father was a priest, it could well have been that he felt a vocation to be a nun was potentially less fulfilling than one to the priesthood. Nuns have always been regarded by the Church as on a par with laity, rather than as a sub-section of the clergy.[6] For Joan's parents, proud of a young girl whom the chroniclers recall as prodigiously bright, the convent may have seemed second best, a repository of handmaidens to men; women who, whatever their talents, were destined to perpetual second-class status. Such was the practice of the Benedictine rule at the time.

Equally, the parental objections may have been earthy ones. In the lawless atmosphere of the Dark Ages, the protection once enjoyed by convents against the financial, practical and sexual threat posed by marauding bands of men had broken down. Joan would not be safe. In her history of nuns over two millennia, Jo Ann Kay McNamara writes of the ninth century: 'What is certain is that the civil wars of the mid-century left the most prosperous convent communities in jeopardy. Laymen, prelates and their erstwhile brothers in religion all cast hungry eyes on the remnants of what they possessed and let greed reinforce the competitive process of misogyny ... Lack of income discouraged vocations and shrank communities. Rapine and negligence both destroyed the communal economy.'[7]

Alternatively similar thought processes may have been initiated by Joan herself, based on her observations on the community at Fulda, the co-relation between male and female roles there with Lioba's followers relegated to a hillside above the town. Any decision about her future education would not have had to be made until she was eleven or twelve – the age at which bright young males were sent off to abbey or cathedral schools. A precocious twelve-year-old, an age then deemed adult enough to marry and bear children, may well have made her own choices. Fired by the story of the cross-dressing saints, she dreamt of more. Watching her female contemporaries and their elder sisters embark on a life of repeated childbirth and, very often, death by the age of twenty could also have helped her come to a decision.

Seen from different angle entirely, there was another practical and emotional drawback to the female religious life. Nuns had to remain celibate, while priests could marry. As her later life may be held to demonstrate, Joan was not naturally made for celibacy. She may have realised this early and cut her cloth appropriately.

While we are now too far distant in time to reach any conclusions on such musings, what cannot be denied is that seeking an education would be – and has been for other women down the ages – a first step to liberation from the subservient role. History shows that once women acquire learning they can move outside the world of the home and challenge men in the public arena.

The parallel between the 'message' concerning women's education in both Yentl and Pope Joan is clear, but did it go further than that? 'Yentl' is folklore, the original for the tale, if there was one, lost in the mists of time. Might Joan just be folklore and, moreover, might a Jewish story have seeped into the Catholic tradition and been given a Catholic name – Pope Joan?

The interchange of ideas between the two traditions is well established, especially in the medieval era, as I learnt when I visited the Warburg Institute. The Warburg is a funny old place. Just off Gower Street in the heart of London University, I must have walked or driven past it thousands of times without ever realising it was there. In an age when academic institutions advertise on television, wedged between life insurance and family hatchbacks, and when they have constantly to dream up headline-catching research in order to attract funding and students, the Warburg keeps an unfashionably low profile. Behind its front doors is another world of 1950s' municipal propriety – highly polished lino, old but not antique fittings maintained in apple-pie order, a deferential porter behind a utilitarian sliding glass screen, and neatly arranged notice-boards with worthy, self-improving gatherings to advertise. All that was missing was a faint waft of cabbage to complement the order, plain good sense and rationality.

Yet appearances can be deceptive, for the Warburg is anything but quintessentially English. Its origins are less in an Agatha Christie thriller than in 1930s Germany. The collection of books and manuscripts gathered by Aby Warburg were, after his death in 1929, shipped out of Nazi Germany in 1933 to London, where the Institute has resided ever since – though Hamburg has now invited it to return. As a source of enlightenment on the German folklore and oral history tradition in which both Yentl and Pope Joan thrived, it could not be bettered.

Archivist Dorothea McEwan's official work at the Institute is to translate and catalogue the letters of its founder. His interest in the history of thought is mirrored in McEwan's own academic speciality – the fables and folklores of her home country, Austria, and its neighbour Germany.

She saw the links between Pope Joan and Yentl, but found notions of historical truth or myth too rigidly defined.

Rather than truth, we should talk of itineraries or routes of stories, where a basic story that explains something is put in the form of a fable and then goes on a journey. When we do sometimes look at a story like a photographic exposure, a one-off, we are not able to trace its origin or itinerary. Rather, we have to examine it as if in slow motion to understand its real story, why it is retold, what are its different contexts, why it was important then, and why it is important now. We can see how ideas have changed and metamorphosed on their specific journeys.

Certainly the Joan story as a lesson to women should not, McEwan said, be seen in isolation. Yentl was part of that wider context but all societies have their tales to communicate collective expectations to women.

In some sub-Saharan African societies women's lives are understood in five stages of which three are highly desirable. While the birth of a girl is not a reason for celebration, the girl who has reached puberty, the virgin, has high value. A young mother of a male child is at the peak of her importance, whilst subsequent births just prove that she can give birth until finally, after menopause, she has lost this power. Yet, paradoxically, whilst losing the biological power of giving birth, she gains another power – that of grandmother, mother-in-law and in fact becomes highly important as a sort of honorary male.

Pope Joan, seen in this light, is simply the Catholic church's own chosen method for reminding women of their biology.

But where was its origin and was there a more direct link with Yentl via an interchange of ideas in medieval Germany? 'It is impossible to know,' McEwan said.

It is the same with most tales. Their starting point gets lost in the process of adapting a whole story from one society to another. Take Grimm's fairy-tales. People have tried to translate this collection as precisely as they can, but they still have their local details – wooden clogs in Holland, leather trousers in Italy. Such details are not literal translations – but the nearest approximation. As the story is passed down through the generations, the details become more and more important and the source and meaning of the story obscured.

Sometimes things can go dramatically awry in the translation. McEwan quoted 'the story of the glass slipper' that we call *Cinderella*. 'It was originally a French story and was about a fur slipper but the word for glass in French – *verre* – is very like that for fur and the translator made a mistake. By careless copying the story was corrupted. A fur slipper makes sense. A glass one not. No one could walk in a glass shoe.'

In the maze of myths, the importance of Germany as a breeding ground for the tale of Pope Joan was getting lost. Does the geography have any significance? 'When I was doing research on the ecclesiastical fines you had to pay in medieval times for having married priests,' McEwan said, 'I found that they were at their highest the further you were from Rome – in England, in Germany and in Spain. And these are the very places where this story of Pope Joan is sourced. It is therefore more credible as a story in the telling because it placed Joan in what were rebel provinces. Perhaps that is even part of the real story behind it.'

So one purpose in talking or writing about Pope Joan may have been to identify troublesome outposts of the papal empire and slander or libel them by association. Furthermore, in post-Reformation Germany, when Joan's story was at its most accepted, there was a popular oral and written tradition among Protestants and other dissidents called *Papstfabeln*. These all made the Catholic church look foolish and diminished its authority and standing among hearers. 'The best-known one,' said McEwan, 'was that of the donkey around at the end of fifteenth century who was pulled out of the Tiber and wore the papal crown. It was telling people the papacy was asinine.'

Another issue with the *Papstfabeln* is that their core message sometimes was not clear. In the hands of different interpreters, they could support any one of a number of different prejudices, not all of them anti-Catholic. Take the multi-purpose figure of Frau Jutta – literally Mrs Joan – a staple of the *Papstfabeln*. Dietrich Schernberg's *Ein schön Spiel von Frau Jutta – A Beautiful Play of Mrs Joan – was written in 1565 and was very widely performed for many years. Its central character mixes Faust with Joan. She makes a pact with the devil and thus armed dons male disguise to trick her way to the papacy. When uncovered, she is killed and goes to hell, where she suffers agony and torment, only to be saved by a timely intervention by the Virgin Mary. In one short tale a number of officially cherished but otherwise despised Catholic notions are gathered.

McEwan was, however, reluctant to concede the She-Pope any life outside the magic circle of the fictional *Papstfabeln*.

> Pope Joan belongs with these stories. All the elements of her are elements of other stories. It is just one way of mixing them together. The idea of Catholic rules being broken was always central. Like the many stories of abbesses giving birth which also overlap with Pope Joan. The abbesses mostly lived in southern Italy in old Benedictine houses and always fell for their confessors. It is a whole genre in German literature. Just like Joan they would hide their pregnancy under their robes, but unlike her they would bring up the 'orphan' child in the convent.

Yet McEwan's verdict seemed to me to underplay the very fact that Pope Joan had survived down the centuries at a popular level and in the face of clerical opposition, while the *Papstfabeln* quickly became, by and large, the preserve of historians. The difference is perhaps that Pope Joan has been translated into a timelessly appealing format, where the *Papstfabeln* are rooted in one time and place.

In such a situation the raw material, however distorted by the Chinese-whispers effect of being passed from generation to generation with the attendant struggle to survive, was less important. It was the itinerary that mattered – an itinerary that would have had to give the tale a structure that relates to readily recognisable stereotypes. Taking on a life of its own – whether it be from the starting point of a real historical event, Martin Polonus's chronicle, or even a Germanic folktale – the Pope Joan story had transformed itself with great tenacity into the form most likely to help it endure.

The most enduring story form in western culture is, of course, the classical model. We remember classical stories, plots, themes and characters. We return to them time and again in each generation and culture. One of the joys of classical stories is that while we may not be familiar with individual texts, we know what is going to happen because of the format. Events and personalities fit into a classic structure.

To take this deconstructing process inspired by Dorothea McEwan to its logical conclusion, the Pope Joan story could only be cast as a classic tragedy. It couldn't be comedy – that way she would have had to get away with being Pope and only be discovered when dead. The tragedy rests in her being hoist with her own petard. Hence her gruesome death in the Vicus Papissa. To complete the story as a tragedy, she has to be struck down by her fundamental flaw. It's no good her getting murdered or poisoned.

Had the tragic ending then be added to give a myth everlasting life? It made an interesting counterpoint to the argument that her pregnancy and death were simply a dire warning to women.

Yet this recasting was too simple for the Pope Joan story in the chronicles. Its details fit only with their period and not, in the classial sense, with every era and every situation. They are particular to a time and place. The recent memory of women saints and women heads of double monasteries, for example, suggests that Pope Joan slotted neatly into its own time. So, too, do the history of Fulda and of the English missionaries in Germany. It was time to examine the other elements to confirm the verdict.

Clothes maketh the man, the old saying goes, and in Joan's case this was literally true when, according to the chronicles, she set off at the age of twelve from Fulda for Athens to get an education in the company of a young monk who was, depending on your source, oblivious to her deception, a fellow scholar, her teacher or her lover – or a combination of any of them.

Joan's deception was based on disguising her sex by changing her dress. She would accept no constraints on her intellect or what is described as a challenging and lively manner. In hitting on cross-dressing, the religious life was something of a gift. 'As the French say,' wrote Sydney Smith to Lady Holland in the nineteenth century, 'there are three sexes – men, women and clergymen.'[8] With men of the cloth, few look beyond the uniform and gender is taken for granted. Where better for Joan to hide her sex without fear of close scrutiny?

Clerical outfits are androgynous. On an official visit to Rome, while still married to Prince Charles, the late Diana, Princess of Wales is reported to have entered a reception room at the British Embassy to the Holy See and greeted a gaggle of cardinals in their full regalia of black cassocks set off by red skull-caps and red cummerbunds with the words 'love the colour, chaps'. The world's best-dressed woman then smoothed the cloth of her own designer outfit and quipped, 'just as well we don't clash.'[9]

Princess Diana was not the first glamorous woman to tease a clerical audience. The actress Tallulah Bankhead is reported to have encountered a robed thurifer in an Anglican church, swinging his incense. 'Love the drag, darling,' she burst out, 'but your purse is on fire.'[10] The deliberate cultural misreading of priests' garments as women's clothing has, after all, gone on for many centuries. Even senior clerics have remarked upon it. Bishop Baumgartner, a retired prelate in the American Episcopalian (Anglican) church, once told an interviewer that he had sent four of his vestments to the dry cleaners. He called them an alb, a stole, a cincture and an amice. The dry cleaner listed them as 'one dress, long; one rope; one scarf; and one apron'.[11]

Like heraldry or cricket, ecclesiastical dress has its own strange codes and connotations. Red for a cardinal, purple for a bishop, white for a pope are just the most obvious catch-phrases of a sartorial language that few can interpret beyond a general symbolism of being apart from and indeed in contradiction of the secular world. And the gender ambiguities of churchmen's dress are considered by the chosen few who are *au courant* to be scarcely worth discussing – since priests have always been men.

Yet for the rest of society the issue is not so clear-cut. As Marjorie Garber pointed out in her history of transvesticism,

> . . . ecclesiastical or religious dress is particularly fascinating because of the ways in which particular items of clothing have tended to cross over gender lines, not through uniformity per se – although, as we will see, there have been attempts to make women's and men's costumes the same within specific orders or denominations – but rather by the migration of styles over time from one gender to another. In eighteenth-century England, for example, parasols were popular for ladies, but umbrellas became items of daily use for

clergymen who officiated at burial services – at least fifty years before fashionable gentlemen began to carry them.[12]

Even the terminology surrounding ecclesiastical dress is misleading – frocking and defrocking priests.

The notion that Joan could have disguised herself successfully as a man in religious garb is, then, not at all incredible. Indeed, the very sexlessness of clerical attire gives her story another ring of truth.

The particular style adopted by clerics down to our own times dates back to Roman and pre-Christian times and would therefore have been the norm in Joan's age. As with many of the forms and dogmas of the contemporary Church, there is a pagan root here, carefully hidden away and largely unacknowledged. The Romans regarded trousers as the sign of a barbarian. Early Christians had no desire to compound their offence to the rest of society in the first centuries by their dress. They followed the Roman style and blended in.[13]

The gown was then as much a universal item as jeans are today. But as the rest of the world moved on and developed a new wardrobe, the Church's dress-code clock stood still. In the catacombs under Rome are illustrations of the early Christian leaders wearing costumes that have changed little in the intervening two millennia, namely a gown-like chasuble, draping its wearer with ample, long and full proportions, a centre opening and a seam back and front. But for the surroundings, they could be standing at a contemporary high altar saying mass.

The early Christians' unwillingness to bother too much about formalising dress codes – or for that matter rituals and beliefs – sprang from their conviction that the second coming of Christ was imminent. Then came persecution, so there was a disincentive to develop any kind of uniform that would make Christians stand out from the rest of society.

Thereafter, the clerical style of dress became increasingly anachronistic, something that set priests apart from the rest of society. For the Church this was symbolism of a moral variety, but for others the strange religious dress of priests had other overtones. In eighteenth-century masquerades men often dressed as nuns and women as priests. There was an anti-Church, anti-Catholic edge here in Enlightenment times, questioning the bona fide of the cleric, ridiculing it even. In our own day the Sisters of Perpetual Indulgence, cross-dressers in full wimple and robe often seen at gay pride demonstrations, continue the tradition.

How might Joan's disguise have developed? It could all have started with a bit of harmless dressing-up, done with parental connivance, which then got out of hand. Circumstances also conspired to assist and even encourage her.

Until the ninth century, men of the cloth usually wore beards. The cross-dressing saints, we are told, either grew beards to resist men or were known as the 'beardless one'. In such circumstances, Joan would have stood out and invited closer scrutiny in a monk's gown with her hairless chin and upper lip. The Athenian writer Chalcocondylas pointed the way round this dilemma in his sixteenth-century *De origine et rubus turcorum*. At just the time Joan took up her disguise, priests stopped having beards on papal orders. 'It is well-known that a certain woman was made pope by reason that they knew not her sex; for all (almost) in the western parts of Italy shave their beards.'[14]

As her body developed, other aspects of Joan's femininity could easily have been hidden. Historian, psychologist and sociologist Dr Rosalind Miles has written about Joan in her *Women's History of the World*.[15] She has few doubts that Joan could have got away with her physical disguise. She says:

> If you think of the conditions in the ninth century, of often extreme physical deprivation, shortage of food, shortage of medical care, with many people living on the verge of inanition through the absence of basic supplies, that then reduces the difference between the sexes. It is only in a very ample culture that men can become tall, manly and well-defined and women are voluptuous. Most of the female curves are fat. The gender distinctions would be much less clear. Women, for example, would not have beautiful moisturised skin. And if both sexes did manual labour in childhood, they would both be brawny.

Contemporary feminism could be a help here, Dr Miles insists. 'It has long tried to insist that, although the tallest, hairiest person on the planet is likely to be male and the shortest, softest, sweetest person is likely to be female, there is so much physical overlap in between, that we are so obsessed by sex that we allow the gender and genital differences to blind us to the fact that males and females share hearts, lungs, livers, eyes, ears, brains.'

That overlap could be all the greater, Dr Miles goes on, in the case of someone disguising her gender and denying her sexuality. 'Female bodies, starved of full nourishment as under a regime of denial or the self-starvation we now call anorexia will grow a pelt. It's nature's way of protecting itself. But it "reads" like facial hair or a beard.'

Moreover, the monkish disguise Joan wore before she became pope was, for Dr Miles, the perfect cover. 'What better disguise for a woman to wear than something that is essentially a frock. The sleeves come down over your hands so you don't have to show you've got little female wrists and hands. The hood comes right over your head. Look at medieval paintings. It's not that the hood is round your head like that' – she traces a semicircle from ear to ear with her finger – 'it's like that so only the chin would be seen' – her hand now stretches under her eyes.

There were other aspects of Joan's disguise that she finds intriguing and entirely plausible. Like the covering up of her female curves:

> They would have been bound. Look at Elizabeth I. She was constantly totally flat for the same reason. Okay by then they were wearing stomachers – that was the convention of the time – but a lot of women if you really look at them don't have very much breast. Most of the tissue is fat and if Joan had been childless and never lactated, then the glands would have been small and unactivated. Even when she was pregnant at the end of her life and her breasts would be swollen, by that stage she was surrounded by very corpulent senior churchmen. By that stage, she would have been accepted as John.

Months or even years into her papacy, her physical appearance would have been beyond scrutiny, says Dr Miles.

> We don't have the capacity to keep paying attention to each other. And by then too she may have become quite sexless. If you look at people who live without sex, they become quite sexless themselves. Some of these dear old Irish bishops look like little old ladies with their rosy cheeks. Men become somewhat eunuchised and women could become masculinised. Freud teaches that personality is situational and flexible. If she had spent her formative years among monks, she would have behaved like a monk. We all would.

On the question of menstruation and how Joan might have disguised that, Dr Miles turns from the purely physical to the the psychological. 'Women don't all menstruate copiously every three weeks. Some women have light and irregular periods and they might be the ones who are attracted to a more masculine life.' She is convinced that

81

women can think themselves and their hormones into the part of a man. 'For women the hormones and the psyche are very closely related and we are slowly beginning to understand that. It's frequently been suggested that women in power have higher levels of testosterone and androgens.'

So, just as it has been suggested that contemporary women leaders like Margaret Thatcher produced unusually high levels of male hormones to match their masculine role in a masculine world, so, too, Pope Joan's body might have responded to the situation in which she found herself.

Rosalind Miles had touched on the psychological, but the mental strength that Joan would have needed to sustain her disguise over such a long period continued to fascinate me. Crucial to my accepting Joan as real in the historical sense was to be sure that she could have broken out of the mind-set that in her era relegated women to minor positions. From where did she obtain what might be termed a male sense of entitlement – that she had the 'power' or was authorised to accept the papacy, that she was entitled to stand up in front of crowds and teach, run the Church, give orders to her deacons?

The cross-dressing saints were one potential source, the women who headed double monasteries another. If she had read the tales of women priests in the library at Fulda, then she would have gained confidence from them. These sources, plus what the chroniclers speak of as a lively intelligence, could have given Joan the courage and determination to pursue an unconventional vision of a woman's role. Indeed, such a background would have made her stand out when she gave her sermons in Rome and explains why she caught the eye of Pope Leo IV. Her life experiences would have been so very different from anyone around her.

In George Eliot's *Daniel Deronda* one of the women characters talks about how terrible it is to be a woman with scholarly or mental attributes or aspirations, intellectual desires and 'to have your mind bound small like Chinese feet'. Joan liberated herself from that and therefore put herself into another mind-set.

Quite how she would have felt, hovering between male and female, is almost impossible to imagine. A clue, however, is provided by contemporary transsexuals. The writer and historian Jan – once James – Morris has spoken candidly of her sex change. While, unlike Morris, Joan underwent no surgery and was crossing the gender divide in the opposite direction, such revelations do give an oblique insight into the She-Pope's mental agonies.

'The more I was treated as a woman,' Morris wrote,[16] 'the more woman I became. I adapted willy-nilly. If I was assumed to be incompetent at reversing cars or opening bottles, oddly incompetent I found myself becoming.' Acting a part, then, can cease to be acting and become natural, almost instinctive. And Morris rapidly forged bonds with others of her new sex. 'I began to find women's conversation in general more congenial. Women treated me with a frankness which, while it was one of the happiest discoveries of my metamorphosis, did imply membership of a camp, a faction, or at least a school of thought: and so I found myself gravitating always towards the female, whether in sharing a railway compartment or supporting a political cause.' In the all-male atmosphere of the upper echelons of the Roman Church such a capacity to adapt would have been essential for Joan.

Morris also wrote of forgetting what it was to be a man. 'It is hard for me now to remember what everyday life was like as a man. Sometimes, by a conscious effort I try to recapture the sensation, and realise the contrast in my condition now. It amuses me to consider, for instance, when I am taken out to lunch by one of my more urbane men friends that not so many years ago that fulsome waiter would have treated me as he is now treating him.' By contrast, Joan's body was still that of a woman's and her change of gender was never until the end of her lifetime made public like Morris's, but this account does provide a glimpse of how she could have embraced emotionally and psychologically her affected masculinity. 'Soon it all came to feel only natural, so powerful are the effects of custom and environment.'

If, then, Joan's physical disguise was certainly possible and the mental courage she would have needed can conceivably be traced to available sources, the psychological leap into what others took to be a man's body was also becoming credible. I was still seeking final proof, but another niggling doubt had been removed.

Chapter Seven

'Lust, relying on secular power and mad and stimulated with the rage of dominion, claimed everything for itself. Then, as it seems, Christ was evidently in a deep sleep in the ship when, these winds blowing so strongly, the ship itself was covered with waves.'

Cardinal Baronius, *Annales Ecclesiasticae (on Rome in the Dark Ages)*[1]

Why Athens? This is a question that has bothered many who later came to examine Joan's story as told by medieval chroniclers. Emmanuel Royidis, a native of the Greek capital, wrote two books on the She-Pope in the 1880s, one a slushy romantic novel with a cynical anti-clerical undertow and the second a short volume setting out the evidence for talk of a female pontiff. In the latter, though he boasts that 'few ecclesiastical authors have had access to the University Library at Athens' and that he has therefore gained a new perspective on this 'hermaphrodite heroine', he uncovers no new sources. Indeed, he admits that 'we know nothing positive about the Athens of the period', save that it 'still retained its early splendour. The ancient monuments still existed and the language of the people was Greek.'

Athens was a pale shadow of its former glories in the ninth century. It had flourished as an intellectual centre, if not politically and economically, until the start of the sixth century. But in 529 the Emperor Justinian closed down the philosophical schools and transferred his patronage of learning to his capital Constantinople.

Yet in Constantinople the academic world in Joan's time was split between the warring factions of iconodules and iconoclasts, those who promoted the worship of images and those who opposed it. Athens, by then an outpost of Byzantine culture, may at least have been free from the conflict, a place where Joan could learn the Greek that was said by the chroniclers to have so distinguished her when she arrived in Rome, where many prominent clerics struggled even to master Latin.

Joan's fluency in both classical tongues was one of the accomplishments that helped her sparkle in an age of illiteracy and ignorance even in the highest church circles. As Gregorovius, the nineteenth-century German historian of Rome, pointed out when recalling her tale, a period of study in Athens, however diminished it had become as a seat of learning, would have given her a head start over most of Rome.[2] The

Greek city's position at the meeting point of western and eastern Christianity would also have given her a breadth of theological view rare among her contemporaries in Rome.

Short of evidence, others have tried to cut out the Athenian period of Joan's life, redirecting her as a wandering pilgrim in disguise who went to England – an alternative explanation for the title 'Joan the English'. This was the favourite theory of the seventeenth-century writer, Louis Contarini, in his *Vago e dilette e Vole Giardino* of 1602, a source quoted by Spanheim.[3] Others suggest that she went to study in Paris.[4]

There is not a shred of evidence for either of these alternatives. If we take the year 830 as a possible date for the teenage Joan fleeing Fulda, then she might have found some centres of learning in England, in the great monasteries like Ely or Wimborne, before their destruction by the invading Danes. In Paris, there was as yet no university. It was only in 829 that the Council of Paris had requested the Church to expand the public schools that were found in the precincts of cathedrals.

The final though by no means definitive word on Athens has to rest with its native son, Emmanuel Royidis. In his romantic novel on Pope Joan, rather than his slim history tome on the same subject, he conjures up this account of the She-Pope's Athenian exile with her lover, whom he named Frumentius:

> Joanna had seen no temples beyond a few druidic obelisks and a few battered Roman ruins. The churches in her native country were rough-hewn and blockish – as were the Germans who had built them. Now she gazed with wonder and surprise at the columns of the Parthenon and the Caryatids of the Erechteum, while the good Frumentius embraced the ankles of the latter and asked if they were not petrified angels.
>
> Early the following morning they awoke and, shaking the dew out of their habits and the sleep out of their eyes, they set off down the hill to visit Athens. Joanna's heart throbbed with curiosity and fear as she realised that she was soon to stand before the many idols of that famous city; idols which Gregory had considered to be a danger to Christian souls – just as the sight of a gay and lovely former sweetheart is a danger to the man who has married an ugly and frowning wife. But these hopes and fears were groundless. Some time before the pious Byzantine emperors had demolished the works of Myron, Alkamenes and Polykletos although they had enjoyed the esteem of St Luke and even of Alaric. These outrages had begun

during the tenure of Constantine and continued throughout the period of Theodosius the Little . . .

Not only the priests and learned men took to visiting Joanna; patricians and visitors of the New Rome also began to know the road to her cell. Many a time when she was surrounded by such a crowd she sighed as she thought how many more admirers she could win, and how much more fervent they would be if, instead of hiding her beauty away in a habit, like them a golden sword in a lead sheath, she could suddenly appear among them in a silken dress, her hair flowing about her shoulders. In the beginning Frumentius was glad of the fame that she won. But after a time he began to notice some small changes in the conduct of Joanna which alarmed him considerably. He became as worried as a coquette who notices that wrinkles are beginning to appear on her face.[5]

The novel does not make a compelling source. Fiction's place in an investigation based on fact is questionable, but with Athens such a closed book in this period it becomes a matter of imagining Joan in scene and then looking for obvious anachronisms or faults. In that restricted context fiction can play a role and Royidis, who had the advantage of knowing the city, its history and its people, constructed a perfect and seamless fit.

More importantly, however, what cannot be ignored is that the link with Athens and with Greek scholarship is central to understanding how Joan came to make such an impact on Rome and the Church there that she was elected Pope.

Martin Polonus gives no reason in his sparse account as to why Joan abandoned Athens for Rome. Royidis's suggestion of an emotional crisis, a break with the lover whom she had now outgrown intellectually, should be taken as lightly as the rest of his soufflé of a novel. The facts point to the pull that the centre of western Christianity would have exerted on a woman whose whole life had been spent either in Church circles or studying theological and spiritual matters. However far the city may have fallen since the days of the Roman Empire, Rome still claimed a theological hegemony in the Christian world. It was therefore the natural stage to display and enhance the much-praised talents Joan had developed while in Athens.

The links between Athens and Rome were unusually close in Joan's time. There is an abundance of historical and topographical evidence from the seventh century onwards for the growth of a Greek colony in

Rome, centred on land between the River Tiber and the Circus Maximus, once the emperors' great sports stadium.[6] This period coincided with dislocation around the Mediterranean, prompted by the rapid expansion of Islam as the banner of the Prophet was carried through Syria, Palestine, Egypt and Persia into eastern Europe and via North Africa into Spain. It was also a time of dispute within the eastern church, with Greeks often in the minority and therefore forced into exile.

Greek refugees built their own church in Rome, Santa Maria in Cosmedin, home to the 'Bocca della verità' (or 'mouth of truth').[7] To this day the church is used by Greek Catholics, mainly of the Melkite rite, who are in communion with the Pope. In Joan's time, however, it was known as Santa Maria de Schola Graeca – Saint Mary of the Greek colony – and was the base of a thriving Greek community which integrated fully with the Romans and even provided several popes from John VI (701–5) through John VII (705–7), the son of a Byzantine official, Constantine (708–15) from Syria to Zacharias (741–52), a Calabrian of Greek parents.[8] In all there have been thirteen Greeks on the throne of Peter and the word Pope itself comes from the Greek, *papas* being the popular diminutive of *pater* (father).

The Greeks in this period had a profound impact on western Christianity. They founded monasteries, bringing with them ideas from the east pioneered by Saint Basil.[9] By 680, there were said to be twenty-four. And the Greeks also imported to Rome a passion for sacred relics that the west took to its heart. The manger of the baby Jesus arrived in the great church of Santa Maria Maggiore thanks to the Greek Palestinian pope, Theodore (642–9). Moreover, the Greeks ensured that icons became commonplace in western churches, while trends in liturgical decoration, furnishings and layout were all affected.

Learning continued to be valued in Rome, however low its political stock had fallen. From 536 when Pope Agapetus (535–6) had urged a university in the city, the Lateran Palace and various churches had played their part in encouraging learning, developing libraries, hosting writers and supporting what today would be clumsily termed 'cultural events'. Again, such devotion to scholarship was an area where in the seventh and eighth centuries Greeks flourished. 'The intellectual life of this period', writes Peter Llewellyn in his landmark study *Rome in the Dark Ages*, 'was dominated by Easterners – Greeks and Syrians from the East or Sicily – who made their mark through the increased Hellenism of the Church; rising swiftly over the less educated native

Roman clergy, they formed a preponderance of influence and learning.'[10]

The Greek colony took the lead in the production of books. Thanks to their handiwork, Pope Paul I (757–67) was able to flatter Charlemagne's father Pepin into a political alliance by presenting him with a library of works on grammar, geometry and orthography – spelling – as well as the writings of Aristotle and Dionysius the Areopagite.

Evidence of the enduring influence of Greeks and Greek scholarship on Rome and the Catholic Church comes in the early decades of the fifteenth century with Theodore of Niem, secretary to several popes, a learned doctor of the Church and a scholar. In 1413, Theodore published *de Iuris Dictione Autoritatis*, a history of Rome and of the rights and privileges of the emperors.[11] He records that the Greek School in Rome continued to thrive in his day, offering Greek, Hebrew, Arabic and Pagan Studies on its curriculum. Drawing on ancient and now lost documents, he asserted that the school had a long, distinguished but sometimes controversial past. Among its former star teachers were, he wrote, in the fifth century Saint Augustine of Hippo, *éminence grise* of Christianity and the fount of its sexual hang-ups.

The Greek community in Rome enjoyed a special significance because their mother tongue was also the language of imperial bureaucracy, government, culture and commerce. However tenuous the ties had become, Rome remained part of the empire based on Constantinople. So in 664, for example, Pope Vitalian, his priests and the Roman nobles all had to bow and scrape when the Byzantine Emperor Constans II visited the city. They were, however, on their guard. Ten years earlier Pope Martin I (649–55), had been seized from his sick-bed by the Emperor's men and dragged off to face charges of treason in Constantinople. Constans appeared quite happy to see the Pope publicly flogged, then put to death, but was persuaded to change his mind by the Eastern Patriarch. Martin, however, never recovered from the ordeal and died before he could see Rome again.[12]

Constans treated Rome much as he had treated its spiritual leader. He behaved as if the city were his personal property and accordingly looted it of statues, gilded bronze tiles from the roof of the Pantheon and even insisted on writing his name on the inside of the Column of Trajan. But he was the last emperor from Constantinople to make such a pilgrimage of plunder. By the time of Joan's arrival, Byzantine

88

influence had declined into indifference and been replaced by more sympathetic if no more reliable alliances.

After the Emperor Constantine decamped and moved his capital to Byzantium in 330, Rome's status as the glittering hub of the world had waned. It had become an anachronism, a province of a declining and overstretched empire, but still had all the pretensions of an imperial capital. Pushed to the periphery of the emperors' minds, it languished without the political weight or the troops to defend itself as it fell prey to successive invasions. First in 410 came the Visigoths under Alaric, intent on destruction, pillage and a quick departure. Their plunder caused Augustine so to despair for the future of civilisation that he wrote his deeply pessimistic *City of God*, a book that has had a profound influence on Christian thinking ever since.

Later the Vandals, then Attila the Hun pillaged the city, with the Emperor in the east unable or unwilling to prevent them. Rome was a derelict second-class backwater of a weak Asian empire. Even when the Vandals were not baying at the doors, they were active in the Mediterranean and Italian peninsula, cutting off the city's food supplies. So precarious did Rome become that the emperor's exarch – or representative – in Italy moved his base to the east coast and the port city of Ravenna from 539 until the hegemony of Constantinople finally ended in 750. Rome was left to its fate.

The sole native institution to survive these tumultuous centuries was the Roman Church and its leader, the pope, the Bishop of Rome. So into the vacuum left by Constantinople's slow and uneven withdrawal stepped the papacy. When the Goths arrived menacingly at the gates of the city in 410 it was Pope Innocent I (402–17) who went out to meet Alaric, their leader, and persuaded him to spare Rome's churches. Leo I (440–61), one of only two 'Greats' among the popes down the ages, took the process one step further and made a distinction between the dignity and importance of the office of pope and the personality and actions of any individual holder of that office. It was the papacy itself that mattered and endured. It could be enhanced by good popes and reduced by bad, but it was bigger than any one individual.

Leo sought to invest the throne of Peter with a new and universal authority. 'As his 150 surviving letters show,' writes the papal historian Nicolas Cheetham, 'he [Leo] insistently reminded them [his correspondents] of their dependence on the see of Saint Peter as the fount of all authority, of their duty of obedience to it, and of its own duty of caring for them all.'[13]

Increasingly the emperor in Constantinople and the papacy vied for the right to run Rome and its hinterland. Every time there was a strong man in either office there were tensions. The Emperor Justinian, seeking to reassert Constantinople's hegemony, had Pope Vigilius (537–55) kidnapped, brought to the imperial capital and imprisoned for eight years. When he was finally released Vigilius was so broken by his experiences that he died on his journey back to Italy.

The tactic succeeded in reasserting the emperor's right to be consulted on the appointment of the pope, a veto that was maintained, albeit in name only, until 741. By that time Constantinople had too many problems of its own to worry overly about a far-flung city in the west, while the papacy had found new allies in its continual struggle to protect Rome from invaders. In the eighth century, King Pepin of the Franks worked closely with the great English missionary Boniface and was so impressed by his spiritual mentor that he gave vast tracts of land to the papacy. With the crowning of Pepin's son, Charlemagne, as Emperor in 800, Rome came firmly under the protection of the Frankish kings.

Yet their empire was too stretched and Charlemagne's successors too fractious to give Rome real security. The Romans for their part resented their new protectors and despaired at swopping subjugation to one failing empire for subjugation to another, seemingly in the ascendant. Exploiting such chaos and ill-feeling, the Saracens sailed up the Tiber and pillaged the city without meeting any opposition.

Europe was dominated in the ninth century by three great powers – the Church, the marauding pagan tribes of northern and eastern Europe and the remnants of Charlemagne's Holy Roman Empire, at its peak in 800 but in a slow decline thereafter. The vacuum this created was steadily and stealthily filled by the Church. The office of pope – in the early Christian centuries simply a title claimed by the Bishop of Rome with no enforceable wider authority – grew in importance and scope as a consequence.

The Rome that greeted Joan in the late 840s was still recovering from a brush with Islam. In 846 the Saracens had attacked Rome from the sea and looted the city at their leisure. Churches were stripped of their riches. The interlopers carried off the offerings of eastern and western rulers over a period of five centuries – statues, altar pieces, candelabra, gold and silver, paintings. The Saracens had targeted the suburb on the slopes of the Vatican Hill. Its focal point, the Basilica of Saint Peter, was ransacked for its lavish ornaments and the saint's tomb attacked with its macabre contents scattered.

The Emperor Aurelian had dismissed this side of the Tiber as too marshy for important buildings – the land was said to be plagued with malaria – and therefore left it outside the walls he constructed to defend Rome. It contained, however, Nero's pleasure garden where Christians had once been forced into leather jerkins, liberally daubed with pitch and set alight, and where, in AD 64, Saint Peter, the fisherman pope, was crucified upside down. Early Christians established a shrine there to mark the site of Peter's martyrdom and his grave. By the fourth century it had grown into a basilica, thanks to the efforts of the faithful and – according to Christian legend – support from Constantine himself.

The building was, however, something of a jigsaw, pieced together with marble and stone from nearby tombs and from temples destroyed in the many attacks on Rome. The basilica's isolation from the centre of Rome and its jumble-sale character emphasised Christianity's position as a late arrival at the table of the deities. As the papacy and the Church grew in power, efforts were made to upgrade the basilica. By the seventh century, its great doors were plated with silver and the cult of Saint Peter was developing apace, with pilgrims travelling from across Europe to see his grave and offer gifts in the hope of his intercession with God in heaven on their behalf. So generous were these visitors that by the eighth century the silver on the doors had been replaced with gold.

It was therefore an obvious target for the Saracens in 846. It had only survived up to then because most invaders were either Christian or had a healthy respect for offending the Christian God. When the Saracens, the forces of militant Islam, began to advance up the Italian peninsula they had no such scruples.

With Saint Peter's in ruins, Joan would have found much of the rest of Rome likewise run down, a hotchpotch of *ad hoc* styles, akin to a ninth-century shanty town. The aqueducts had long since fallen into disrepair and the lack of water gave the whole place a smell to rival modern-day Venice on a hot summer's afternoon. Several times in recent memory the Tiber had burst its banks and contributed to the destruction of the fabric of the city. Yet most of the damage that had befallen the city had been done by Romans themselves, dismantling the classical heritage for the most humdrum of reasons – burning marble to get lime to make plaster. When Constans visited in 664 on his mission of self-aggrandisement and looting, it was reported that the old imperial palaces on the Palatine Hill were in ruins, overrun with weeds, while the catacombs had been ransacked and remains and relics scattered willy-nilly.

It was not a universally bleak picture. The Saracens' raid had been a shock, but it had not obliterated all the fruits of a minor renaissance that had been inspired and funded by Charlemagne. Churches had been restored, the Aurelian Walls reinforced and fortified and at the Lateran a grand dining-hall erected to rival the Hall of Nineteen Divans in the great palace of the emperors in Constantinople. Charlemagne's money had even begun the task of improving agricultural land outside Rome, now a part of the increasingly large dowry that accompanied the see of Peter, property and potential revenue that made the papacy an ever more attractive option for ambitious and greedy Roman families.

One major project dominated Rome at the time of Joan's arrival from Athens. Pope Leo IV, elected in the year of the Saracen raid, had determined to rebuild Saint Peter's and enclose it within a new city wall. In 848 work began on what are known to this day as the Leonine Walls, huge fortress-like structures that surround the Vatican enclave, running from what had been the Mausoleum of Hadrian (now the Castel Sant'Angelo, so named because legend had it that the Archangel Michael had once appeared on its summit) on the Tiber, up the Vatican Hill, round and back down to the river again. Saracen prisoners taken in the raid were used as slave labour and Christians throughout Europe gave money to finance the project. By 852 the work was finished and the basilica safe. The walls were consecrated by Leo in 852, attended by barefoot clergy with ashes strewn in their hair, chanting prayers of praise.

Joan would have attended the ceremony, perhaps even sat on the papal podium. For from the time of her arrival in Rome, the chroniclers tell, she had caused a stir by her learning, her fluency in Greek and her erudition. People realised that she was different. She worked as a teacher at the Greek School on the Aventine Hill, near Santa Maria in Cosmedin, but her work would not have been restricted to a classroom or children. The school would have included adult pupils, while it would have prided itself on the public lectures and debates it staged for a wider audience. Joan, in such gatherings, made a mark and soon her reputation had reached the ears of Leo IV, a pope who valued learning and loyalty as much as he did civil engineering.

Theodore of Niem, in his testimony to the enduring influence of the Greek School on Rome and the Church, mentioned earlier, places Pope Joan, along with Saint Augustine, among its ex-alumni. Writing of the school in the ninth century, he records:

John, called English, who was a woman born at Metz, and studied at Athens, going in man's apparel, where she profited so well in the arts, that coming to Rome, she read there the liberal sciences, and was held so sufficient a reader that many of the better sort became her ordinary hearers. Afterwards with one consent she was chosen pope, and lived in it two years and upward. But betaking herself, more than before, to her idleness and pleasure, she could not live continently as she did in her poor estate, when she plied her book diligently; whereupon one day, as she went with the clergy and people of Rome, according to the custom of the time, in solemn procession, being attired in papal manner, she was delivered of her first-begotten son, begotten by one of her chamber, near the Temple of Peace, which stands in the city; as is evident by an old marble image, which stands there to this day, to denote so much in a figure. And hereupon it is, that when the popes go from the Vatican to St John Lateran's, and back again, they go not the direct way thither, but by other streets further about and so make their journey longer.[14]

So another element in Joan's story – as told by Martin of Poland in 1265 – can be verified by an outside and weighty source. Theodore of Niem testifies that the Greek School existed in 1413 and had existed for many centuries. This papal secretary, perhaps consulting records there or as a result of conversations, links Joan with the school. He mentions her not in any approving way, but as a source of shame who should be noted in the interests of historical accuracy.

Despite being a fixture of all medieval accounts of the papacy, even today Joan's name is missing from most chronicles of popes, or at best tacked on in an appendix. Perhaps it is because there is a deep-seated desire to make the papacy – the only institution within the European and western orbit that links the immediate post-apostolic period with the atomic age – seem somehow venerable. It has after all witnessed the birth, growth, prosperity, decay and even disappearance of powerful nations, empires and even whole civilisations. Popes have created emperors, deposed monarchs, inspired wars and in the process touched human society and culture at every point.

Yet at the same time as rejecting Joan, many questionable and historically tenuous figures from the Dark Ages are given official blessing as having held the Petrine office. Do they not equally besmirch the good name of the successors of Saint Peter? Those who illegally seized the office – now deemed 'anti-popes' – are welcome. So long as they are men. No matter how venial, corrupt or unsaintly.

But where is the incontrovertible proof of their existence in this ill-documented period? With many of the more significant popes – those who left their mark on the world – there is an abundance of proof in the form of accounts by respected church historians and mumismatic details – old coins and medals. With others, though, the case is far from proven. For most of the early popes, Eusebius's *History of the Church*, written in the fourth century, is the only source.[15]

While Eusebius (260–339) is known as the 'father of ecclesiastical history', it is not beyond the bounds of possibility that, writing in an age of poor communications, few written documents and a lively and often colourful oral tradition, he may have made mistakes. And though the situation improves in later centuries, there are still yawning gaps in the papal roll of honour. Of John VI (701–5), J. N. D. Kelly writes in his *Oxford Dictionary of Popes*: 'Nothing is known of his background except that he was Greek by birth.'[16] He continues that 'few glimpses of his reign survive'. On Pope Lando (913–14) the record is equally opaque: 'Nothing is known of his earlier career or the circumstances of his election, and nothing is recorded of his reign except a benefaction to the cathedral of Sabina.'

'The ninth century is so utterly confused that the odd pope may possibly have dropped out here and there,' says Britain's leading light on the history of the papacy, historian and ex-Jesuit Michael Walsh. 'The whole system was so corrupt.'[17]

A brief glance over the history of the papacy in the ninth century up to Joan's election confirms his assertion. Paschal I (817–24) built a successful working relationship with Charlemagne's son, Louis the Pious, guaranteeing him freedom of action within his lands and the protection of the Frankish emperor, but he was a harsh and self-willed ruler of Rome. He made many enemies and when he died was so detested that a popular uprising blocked the plans he had left to have his body interred in Saint Peter's. It was left unburied and rotting – this was an age before refrigerators – for several weeks until his successor,

Eugene II (824–7) arranged a more discreet final resting place. A classic example of the constant rewriting of church history, Paschal was celebrated by Cardinal Baronius (one of the most vocal of anti-Joanites) in the late sixteenth century,[18] but in 1963 his feast day (14 May) had been deleted from the Church's calendar as an unsuitable and shadowy role model.

Of Eugene's successor, Valentine (August to September 827), all that is known comes from the *Liber Pontificalis*, a book of sometimes questionable accuracy concerning this period as we have already seen.[19] A patrician Roman, he was elected by priests and people, and died forty days later. Gregory IV (827–44) was of aristocratic background. His partisan position in a struggle between the various factions that arose among Charlemagne's sons and grandsons fatally weakened his authority and the Frankish commitment to defending Rome. But beyond this, little is known of his lengthy pontificate.

His death was marked by violent demonstrations. The people of Rome seized the Lateran Palace and installed as pope their own candidate, a deacon called John. The ransacking of the papal apartments on the death of a pope was carried out as if by right by the Romans. The leading aristocrats, however, had no time for John, summoned their retainers, ejected him from the Lateran and installed one of their own, an elderly, gout-ridden priest called Sergius, as pope. John's life was spared, but apart from that nothing is known of him, though even on this flimsy evidence he has gone down in the papal record as a pretender, but not of sufficient weight to be given a number.

Sergius may have had the backing of the Roman aristocracy, but the Frankish Emperor Lothair had not been consulted and sent his army south to take his revenge on the papacy. A beleaguered Sergius capitulated but kept his throne. Once the immediate danger had passed, he handed over the day-to-day administration to his corrupt brother Benedict. The latter made himself a bishop, sold other dioceses off to the highest bidder, and turned the papacy into a trinket shop for the well-to-do.

The Saracen raid on Rome in 846 came as Sergius lay dying, a judgement, many felt, on his corrupt and inept rule. As we have seen, the scholarly Leo IV, a Roman of Lombard descent, injected new vigour and rigour.

If Joan's name is taken next in line, the account of her elevation sits easily with many of the precedents set in previous decades. First, it is said that she was elected by the people. This was the practice at the time and would have permitted an outsider – one who did not have powerful backers among the Roman families or curial officials – to succeed over more conventional candidates, especially if she had the blessing of Leo. Indeed, though the chronicles describe her as a monk, she would not even have had to be ordained to become pope. Certainly the current practice – that the pope is chosen from among the cardinals of the Church – only came much later. Cardinals first appear around the eleventh century. And bishops were barred from the papacy by the fifteenth chapter of the Council of Nicaea (325), the landmark Church council that settled the format of the *Credo*. There it was decided that to be first a bishop of another town or city and then be elected pope and Bishop of Rome was tantamount to bigamy.

We know this rule held in Joan's time because Pope Marinus I (882–4), himself once a bishop, moved formally to set it aside. His success allowed the election in 891 of Formosus, already Bishop of Porto. However, Formosus's successor but one, Stephen VI (896–7), took violent offence at this bigamy and had the body of his predecessor exhumed so that he could stand public trial. Stephen's real argument with Formosus had been a political one over alliances with different factions in the Frankish empire, but under the guise of a Church court, a corpse, dressed in papal vestments, was unsurprisingly found guilty. Its punishment was to have three fingers of its right hand hacked off, be undressed and thrown into the Tiber. The spectacle did little for Stephen's esteem in the eyes of the Romans. He was arrested and put in prison, where he died at the hands of assassins. Details of Formosus's trial, though placed in the Lateran archives, were subsequently destroyed by those who wished to expunge all mention of this unhappy chapter from the Church's history. Fortunately records existed elsewhere. There are undoubtedly precedents for removing all references to Joan's pontificate.

One tradition, dating back to the fourth century, that may have aided Joan's passage to the papacy was the habit of reigning popes to gather around them a group – often seven – of deacons, men who had taken a set of fairly undemanding vows that are the first step on the road to the priesthood. 'Indeed,' writes Cambridge historian Eamon Duffy in his history of the papacy, 'it was routine for the Pope to be elected by the senior clergy from among the seven deacons.'[20] When Joan caught Leo's eye, he may well have elevated her to his inner circle of deacons where she would have attended him, dressed like a pope in a distinctive wide-sleeved robe with two purple stripes, and, on his death, been in the front rank of potential successors.

Joan's age – given that within two years of assuming the papacy she was pregnant, she could not have been more than mid to late thirties when she was elected – would not have stood against her. Today we have grown used to popes in their late sixties, seventies and sometimes eighties, rivalled on the international stage only by the leaders of communist China. But in the ninth century, with considerably shorter life expectancies and wealthy Roman families keen to push their sons forward for high office, youthful pontiffs were commonplace. The ages of Joan's predecessors are unknown, but of her successors Nicholas I (858–67) took office at thirty-eight, while in the next century, John XII (955–64) was elected at eighteen.

It is true that around Joan's time there was a trend towards Roman or Italian popes, but as we have seen, the run of Greek or Greek-speaking popes had only recently ended. The tradition of an exclusively Italian papacy – broken in 1978 by Karol Wojtyla after 455 years – was not established until much later. By the standards of the time, a Greek-speaking German with English roots would not have been excluded on any racial grounds.

The general picture that an account of Joan's predecessors and successors conjures up is that of a Church in crisis, caught up in political events mostly outside its control, neglecting the spiritual and in some cases auctioning off the sacred. Just as Sergius II handed over control to his brother, others employed artifice and simony to get elected. Formosus is said to have purchased the papacy from the Duke of Spoleto. Boniface VI – who reigned briefly between Formosus and Stephen – was according to Cardinal Baronius, in his sixteenth-century *Annales Ecclesiasticae*, 'a disgusting monster', deposed for adultery and homicide.[21]

This epoch of the church was 'the obscene century', said Baronius. The conduct and learning of the priesthood had become a scandal. 'In 846 priests had become so ignorant', writes John Potter in his *History of Christianity*, 'that they baptised infants *in nomine Patria et Filia et Spirita Sancta* instead *in nomine Patris et Filii et Spiritus Sancti*.'[22]

It was such circumstances that made Leo seem an attractive candidate – a man of learning untouched by corruption and with his mind firmly set on the needs of Rome rather than the sectional interests of one or other of the Roman oligarchies and their clerical minions.

Indeed one of Leo's concerns – given form at a synod of 853 – was to force clergy to withdraw from secular business.

This same context may even have helped the anti-pope, John the Deacon, in 844. And it would certainly have made Joan a strong candidate.

Popes, Cardinal Baronius wrote, 'ascended the holy chair by trampling over the dead bodies of their predecessors or opponents'.[23] In such muddled, treacherous and confused circumstances, when the most unsuitable of men aspired to or had the papal throne thrust upon them, the notion that a clever, articulate and astute woman, disguised in male clothing, could rise to the top of a rotten pile becomes increasingly credible.

Chapter Eight

Whoso doth the breeches wear
Lives a life as free as air.
Old French proverb

It was time to return to Rome. It was only four months since I had ambled out there in the spring sunshine, a bag full of crumpled clothes, novels and good intentions to do very little. And now here I was, complete with best suit, smart shoes that had never fitted since my wedding day, tape recorder, batteries, pencil, pad, camera and even a neater haircut, ready to try to be an insider in the city of the popes so as to pin down the truth about the She-Pope.

And there was no comfortably scruffy flat for my base this time round. It was booked out by holiday-makers revelling in the autumn sunshine. Instead I stayed just behind the Trevi Fountain in a brisk, business-like hotel whose starched mood matched my own and whose bedside tables were strong enough to support a pile of weighty reference books. Only Georgina Masson survived from first time around.

Top of my list of citadels to breach was the Vatican. One potential lead to be followed up there came with a 1970s' version of Joan's history. Written when feminist writers and historians were taking up the woman pope with gusto, Frenchman Henri Perrodo-Le Moyne's 1972 account *Un Pape Nomme Jeanne* is a rather shrill polemic.[1] In the final section, '*Femmes, Levez-vous!*' – 'Women arise' – he concludes: 'The day when woman frees herself, that day she will no longer be the "spare rib" . . . the papacy and the Church in its entirety will no longer blush concerning John VIII, the Papessa.' Working himself up to this climax, Perrodo-Le Moyne recounts a meeting with an unnamed but senior Vatican prelate who 'reveals' that 'some very important documents concerning this woman are secretly concealed in chests and under the papal seal'.

Though unimpressed by the book itself and its attempt to overlook historical detail in the rush to recruit Joan to a contemporary cause, this reference had made me pull up short. The Vatican's Secret Archives – misnamed since its existence was never publicly denied, though access was barred to all but a chosen clerical few – might just have been behind this allusion. And, thanks to a new if tepid Vatican spirit of *glasnost* in dealing with journalists, it might just be possible to follow it up.

Until recently, the Vatican was one of the most secretive of societies. Probing writers made few inroads into the citadel, and even the most mundane of details – like what the Pope ate for breakfast – were treated with the same reverence as the third and terrible secret of Fatima, imparted by the Virgin Mary in a vision to a young Portuguese girl in 1917 and now known only to the Pope.

However, the bizarre events following the death of Pope John Paul I, when the Vatican's inept attempts at news-management, covering up medical details and embellishing the pontiff's last hours with pious details, merely inflamed curiosity and led to the publication of an international best-seller which speculated that he had been murdered.[2] The truth was both more banal and more poignant – that an elderly man who had never wanted the job couldn't cope with the strain and his health had failed.[3] But because of the veil that descends over everything to do with the apostolic palace, rumour and wild theories multiplied.

In an attempt to learn from the experience, the Vatican – now under a new Pope, John Paul II, who initially at least showed himself adept at courting and manipulating public opinion and the cameras – revamped its press office and the grandly entitled Pontifical Council for Social Communications, bringing in a charismatic American, Archbishop John Foley, to charm the media rather than block them at every turn.

It has been only partially successful. Most figures in the curia still regard the press as about as savoury as estate agents or the Reverend Ian Paisley. But one of the fruits of reform has been to make admission to the secret archives possible in theory. And through Father Boyle's good offices and some frantic phoning and faxing, I was indeed granted access to this inner sanctum. My clerical guide, though, made it plain that any indulgences he granted me on our tour were strictly on a non-quotable basis. He might answer my questions or not, but it was all unattributable – the Vatican equivalent of 'lobby terms', that quaint Westminster practice where British politicians tell reporters intimate details of policy and personality for print but refuse to be named as anything other than 'a source close to the government'.

The smooth 'Monsignor Sottovoce' showed me the edited highlights of the archive, officially founded in 1880 and today comprising over 100 kilometers of shelving. I had imagined caskets of medieval manuscripts, decaying relics and a procession of locks and keys. Instead, the public rooms – if somewhere that is not open to the public can have such facilities – were calm and very discreet. Huge, heavy cupboards lined each chamber and crossed them at regular intervals, the reddish, mottled but enormously dignified wood of their great solid doors carved with the papal crest and accompanying designs. The smell of wax and old paper filled the air. The lived-in, slightly irregular but highly polished floorboards could have graced any Islington drawing-room. And tucked away in various cubby-holes, dwarfed by the cupboards, were a handful of clerics and nuns, working away on ancient typewriters, whispering into bakelite telephones, glancing up briefly and suspiciously at me as my feet squeaked across the floors.

Monsignor Sottovoce's workstation was an oasis of paper and bustle in a desert of beautiful but blank fittings and fixtures. As we settled in for a chat, I tried to work round his hostility by making a few general enquiries to encourage him to let down his guard, before I got on to the potentially vexatious subject of Pope Joan.

Relics seemed like a good ice-breaker. Did the archive contain the skulls, hands or other body parts of saints, or – and this leapt straight into my mind after almost three decades from my primary school where they were much talked of – any fragments of the cross on which Christ died?

The provenance or not of such items did touch on the work of the archive, I was told, since much of the documentation detailing their past travels lies in its files and documents. But reaching judgements on them can be nigh on impossible. How can you be objective, I was asked, when confronted with something like the stole worn by Thomas à Becket and kept in the reliquary at Santa Maria Maggiore? Yes, the blood-stains are in the right place and it is the right sort and age of cloth, but Becket's blood group is unknown and the documentation is at best sketchy.

Sometimes the archive can conclusively show that something is fake – like the cult of Saint Philomena. In the nineteenth century in Naples a cult grew up around the bones of an adolescent girl found in the catacombs. She was said to have been an early martyr and her skeleton to possess healing powers. A great shrine was built at Mugnano and a feast day established in the Church's calendar, but when science in the early 1960s raised a question mark about the dating of the body and the nature of its death, the Church drew on its own records in the archive to explode the cult of Philomena, closing down the shrine.

Lulled into a sense of intimacy, I ventured to mention the name Pope Joan and got a dusty answer. Did, I asked, the archive contain anything that might cast light on the legend of Joan that could now be released under the Vatican's equivalent of the thirty-year-rule?

No. Files in the archive dated back to the eleventh century and letters from Pope Gregory VII to William the Conqueror. What, then, about evidence of official attitudes once Martin Polonus's account had ruffled feathers in the fourteenth century? Again a blanket denial, but this time accompanied by a warning. I should be careful of such chroniclers and their recourse to poetic licence. But, I interceded, he was a bishop. Another writer on Joan was secretary to the pope. Oh, came back the reply, they're the worst. No wonder he wished to remain anonymous.

It was his last word. I was ushered out, sure that I had just been brushed off, but in the nicest possible way. Whether this was simply a tactic taught to all officials by the new regime at the Pontifical Council for Social Communications – and therefore no more sinister than a bad stab at PR – or whether it was a screen for something else, I had no way of knowing but it redoubled my determination to get to the bottom of this riddle.

My investigation had strayed many miles from its birthplace, the Vicus Papissa, but my return to this Roman byway on a dismal September afternoon was not merely nostalgia for the adjoining square, its shopkeepers or even the anonymous provider of floral tributes at the one-time shrine to Pope Joan. Now thoroughly briefed on the history of the place, I was anxious to pit the facts against the geography.

What had become increasingly apparent in the intervening months since my last visit was that many of the details of the She-Pope, as bequeathed by the medieval chroniclers, are credible. They fit snugly with their period, with other better documented tales from that time and can be woven into a convincing whole. The backdrop around the shadowy character of Joan is thereby enlivened with colour and congruent detail. The challenge for me now was to move the spotlight from the stage to the star.

That day there were no flowers attached to the grille over the shrine. All in all it was looking rather forlorn, almost obscured by triple-parked cars and the ubiquitous fly-posters. I clambered over assorted plastic bumpers and bull-bars, and peered into the gloom of the strange little unattended sentry box. Even in this downbeat light the Madonna and Child fresco, though faded, was too garish to be ancient. Perhaps fifty years old or even, to stretch credibility, two hundred and fifty, it certainly did not date back to the early medieval period. My initial theory that this mother and child might be an ambiguous image – Christ's mother and the holy infant in the eyes of the righteous, the She-Pope with her bastard boy for the *cognoscenti* with a glimpse of the skeletons in the Church's cupboard – was not going to hold.

Moreover, most of the medieval writers – chroniclers, residents of Rome and pilgrims visiting the seat of Christianity – speak not of a fresco but of a statue. Potentially the earliest references to it come in various editions of one of the later medieval period's 'best-sellers', *Mirabilia Urbis Romae*, a pilgrim's guide to the city, the forerunner of Georgina Masson. *Mirabilia Urbis Romae* speaks of a statue of the female pope 'nigh unto the Colosseum'.[4]

While in a general sense correct in terms of the legend, this description raises more problems than it solves. Principally it depends on which version of the text you consult. Though some hold that editions existed in the twelfth century, our knowledge today rests on fourteenth- fifteenth- and sixteenth-century copies, several of which refer to the statue near the Colosseum. Others are silent on the subject, but one edition, from 1375, tells an entirely different tale – that the woman pontiff's body was buried 'among the virtuous' in Saint Peter's itself.[5] Such an honour would, of course, have been accorded to most ninth-century popes, but did not come as a right, as the tale of Paschal I, mentioned earlier, demonstrates. If he was excluded because he was unpopular, then Joan's deception would surely have made her *persona non grata*.

Wherever her grave was, it is now lost. I did consider taking the train out to Ostia Antica, where archaeologists have begun the task of piecing together the ruins of what was between 300 BC and AD 300 the flourishing port of Rome. We know that there was once a large Christian cemetery at Ostia since it is recorded that the formidable mother of Saint Augustine, Saint Monica, was buried there in 387. And we know from Martin Polonus that Joan's son, born in such inauspicious circumstances, went on to be Bishop of Ostia. Perhaps he had her remains transferred there and buried in the cemetery. Or perhaps he erected a shrine to her. My memory of a previous visit to Ostia Antica was of a few well-documented sites and then mile after mile of rubble, awaiting the attention of archaeologists and historians. My dream was that now I would wander around these neglected areas and chance upon an inscription to confirm my theory, but cursory enquiries dissuaded me. There had been extensive, brick-by-brick searches for Saint Monica's grave in the past and they had taken teams of workers months to complete. It would be like searching for a single word in the Domesday Book without even knowing that it had been there in the first place.

Yet, unreliable as it was, this reference in the *Mirabilia* to Joan being buried stayed with me, stored alongside other questions and queries thrown up by documents about the She-Pope that I hoped either to prove or disprove during my time in Rome.

If the *Mirabilia* cannot be counted an infallible guide, the *Diarium Italicum* of the French Benedictine monk, Bernard Montfaucon (subsequently published in English in 1712 as *The Travels of the Learned Father Montfaucon from Paris through Italy*) also falls somewhat short of being incontrovertible.[6] Montfaucon claims to have consulted a thirteenth-century manuscript in Rome's celebrated Barberini Library that mentions a statue of Pope Joan which had disappeared by the time of the monk's visit to the city. Yet his reference is not specific and cannot be followed up.

The first certain description comes in *Graphica Aurea Urbis Romae*, a late-thirteenth-century manuscript in the Laurentian Library in Florence.[7] It refers to an open space near the Colosseum where there was a statue of the woman pope and a boy. The timing of this reference coincides with the wide dissemination of Martin Polonus's chronicle, suggesting that it may have prompted interest in the She-Pope among visitors to Rome. With the spread of the Dominican scholar's text, her statue may have become as much a fixture on the itinerary of visitors to Rome as the Colosseum itself. Just as today's tourists in Amsterdam combine the Van Gogh Museum and the bulb fields with a darker side of the Dutch city when they take a harmless but mildly titillating evening saunter round the Red Light district and druggy cafés, so pilgrims to Rome, after a long day of churches, basilicas and ancient ruins, might have sought out a counterpoint in Joan's memorial.

On a visit in 1510 to a city he later came to regard as hell on earth, Martin Luther mentioned seeing the memorial to Joan – in his description a woman in a heavy papal-style cloak, holding a child and sceptre – but expressed surprise that the popes allowed it to remain. Later writers echo his description.[8] None is more distinguished than John Burchard, Bishop of Strasbourg and Master of Ceremonies of the

Pope's Chapel under Innocent VIII (1484–92), Alexander VI (1492–1503) and Julius II (1503–13). In 1486 Bishop Burchard organised a procession for Innocent VIII which took the party down the Vicus Papissa. The papal official records reactions in his *Liber Notarum*, an original copy of which is held in the King's Library in Paris:[9]

> The Pope Innocent VIII returning in state on horseback, passed through the street in which the figure of Pope Joan is placed in memory of her lying-in. Now it is pretended that the popes, in their cavalcades, ought never to pass through the street; the Pope was therefore blamed by the Archbishop of Florence and some other prelates for having gone that way.

So the statue existed and popes by tradition shunned the street. Yet neither fact in itself proves Joan's existence. It could have been that a cult grew up around her after Martin Polonus's chronicle, that a statue then was erected to embarrass the Church authorities by rebellious Romans, or then folklore overtook fact in dictating that pontiffs did not take the most direct route from the Lateran to the Vatican for fear of giving credence to rumours. Yet – and perhaps this thought was in Bishop Burchard's mind, though he has left us no clue – surely the best way to scotch the rumours was to process down the street. Avoidance only gave credence to the story. Alternatively, of course, the good bishop may have been ignorant of the truth of the tale and was only later enlightened by the Archbishop of Florence – possibly with the aid of some now lost documentation from the august Laurentian Library.

In centuries to come those who dismissed Joan had all sorts of reasons to offer for the papal detour to avoid her would-be shrine. The growing popularity of the statue, it is said, coincided not only with Martin Polonus's account but also with the exile of the papacy to Avignon between 1308 and 1367. In this interval, the legend was able to take hold without fear of official contradiction and once returned to the Vatican, popes no longer felt able to use the Vicus Papissa. More popular was the explanation that the road, though straight and direct, was too narrow for all the pomp and finery of a papal progress.

It certainly is narrow, especially as you climb from the little square, past the sentry box and up towards the Church of Santi Quattro Coronati, but no narrower than any of the alternatives around about or, for that matter, many of the most popular *vias* of the historic centre of the city. And, as I was able to observe, a funeral procession could fit through without an unseemly crush despite the lining of parked cars. Hearses were becoming something of a motif for my investigation.

Eyes down in the leaf-filled gutter as if expecting the remnant of a 1000-year-old blood-stain suddenly to reveal itself, I could only find one clue in the geography here. That was the sharpness of the climb and descent, sharp enough to bring on a birth in my expert opinion, having recently read my way through every pregnancy and childbirth manual in anticipation of the arrival of our first-born.

What, though, if it wasn't anti-clerical hands that had erected the statue of Joan? Could the Church itself have played a part? Theodore of Niem, the scholarly secretary to several popes, adds weight to this view in his *de Iuris Dictione Autoritatis* of 1413: 'There existed at Rome a marble statue representing the fact as it took place; that is to say, that of a woman who was delivered of a child. That statue was erected by Pope Benedict in order to inspire a horror of the scandal which took place on the spot.'[10]

He did not make clear which Benedict he meant. It is tempting to think it could have been Benedict III (855–8), Joan's immediate successor, but with the weight of manuscript evidence pointing to Martin Polonus at the middle of the thirteenth century as the great promoter of the She-Pope, Benedict XI (1303–4) or Benedict XII (1334–42) seem more likely. The latter, though one of the Avignon popes, did invest heavily in building works in Rome, restoring and re-roofing Saint Peter's and refurbishing the Lateran. And the former, though short-lived, was Dominican Master-General, head of Martin Polonus's order and hence also of that of many of the proponents of Joan's authenticity.

The scandal the unnumbered Benedict intended the statue to generate was no doubt geared towards bringing the faithful back into line with the ecclesiastical authorities. Yet it generally had the opposite effect, as Martin Luther bears witness.

Even if it was a miscalculation on the part of Pope Benedict, he remains the only figure associated in any of the chronicles or accounts of the statue with commissioning it. This has given rise to another suggestion – that the figure of a woman with her child was an existing but unspecific sculpture that was simply reassigned to Joan, perhaps because it happened to stand in the right place, the very street I was now pacing trying to work a way through this mental maze.

The inscription – *Petre, Pater Patrum, Papisse Prodito Partum* – originally quoted in 1225 by de Mailly as being on Joan's tombstone, and subsequently taken up in amended form by later chroniclers, has led some iconoclastic writers to suggest that the statue of the She-Pope predated rather than postdated her papacy. And by some five centuries. J. C. von Orelli in his 1828 study of Roman antiquities, *Inscriptionum Latinarum*, went to great lengths to show that the abbreviated form of the inscription – PPPPPP, shared by the accounts of all the chroniclers – was not uncommon in Rome.[11] The phrase *Pater Patrum* – Father of Fathers – which is again quoted in all accounts, was not originally a Christian form of words, von Orelli argued, but belonged to the Mithras cult which thrived in Rome in the early Christian centuries.

This once-fashionable Near Eastern mystical credo had seven levels of enlightenment, ending with that of high priest, or *pater patrum*. Von Orelli suggested that the statue in the Vicus Papissa, which senior churchmen in the medieval period took to be Joan, was in fact one of a number of monuments to Mithraic priests from the second and third centuries. It had been neglected in this comparative backwater and survived the demise of the cult it celebrated, but was brought back into service 1000 years later as Martin Polonus's account gained in popularity and attracted pilgrims to the spot.

It was rather like the annexing of William Blake's 'Jerusalem' to the cause of British patriotism. How many of those who wrap themselves in a Union Jack to sing of 'England's green and pleasant land' remember that the lyrics about 'dark satanic mills' were written with irony and a mildly revolutionary intent?

The Mithras idea was another plausible and ingenious theory, but again with little scope for definitive proof. I had spent the morning before my *passeggiata* checking out a more hopeful lead concerning the fate of the statue. At the dawn of the twentieth century, the Italian archaeologist Giovanni Tomassetti had raised the question of whether the fabled statue of Pope Joan had ended up relabelled in the labyrinthine Vatican Museum.[12]

I had worried irrationally that my earlier act of sacrilege in sitting in the *sedia stercoraria* might have been recorded on the museum's secret camera and that 'Wanted' posters with my face had been blazoned over every entrance point to its hallowed corridors. So this time I made sure that I had absolutely no contact with the officials and kept my gaze modestly averted as I wandered through to the Chiaramonti Gallery, home to the sculpture collection. The statue of a robed and crowned woman suckling her child is labelled as Juno – to the Romans, the buxom guardian of marriage and protector of women – and

Heracles. It is said to have come from the gardens of the Palazzo Quirinale, now official residence of the Italian president but once a papal palace.

These gardens were created by Pope Sixtus V (1585–90) and filled with ancient statues brought from other Roman sites. Though the landscaping is well recorded, there are no details of from whence individual items were brought. Another problem with the woman and child in the Vatican Museum is that they bear little resemblance to Luther's description. The sceptre is missing, though Tomassetti contended that the right arm and shoulder had been restored – you can still see the marks – and therefore it might have been modified.

The most often repeated account of the statue has it thrown into the Tiber by Sixtus V as part of his wholesale rebuilding programme in Rome. Yet even this assertion is open to question. Saint Robert Bellarmine (1542–1621), the celebrated Jesuit who taught theology at Rome's Gregorian University, refers to the statue in the past tense in his *De Summo Pontifice*.[13] Since this was published in 1577, the memorial to Pope Joan would have disappeared before Sixtus ascended Peter's throne. Moreover, Bellarmine, a staunch defender of the papacy, insists that the statue was of a man, a pagan priest, he claimed, preparing for a sacrifice.

Bellarmine's description is so at odds with other accounts that they cannot be reconciled. Either he hadn't seen the statue – unlikely since he worked in Rome – or he had seen a different one. Or, perhaps, his passion as a propagandist for Catholicism got the better of him. His fellow Jesuit Elias Hasenmuller, writing in *Historia Iesuitici Ordinis* in 1593, may simply have been copying and enlarging on his illustrious colleague's account. According to Hasenmuller, Pope Pius V (1566–72) had the statue thrown into the Tiber 'that he might extinguish the memory of that shameful act'.[14]

Certainly the statue was there in 1565 when the English pilgrim, Thomas Harding, reports in *A Confutation of a Booke Intituled An Apologie of the Church of England* seeing a memorial to an androgynous She-Pope 'graven in stone, after the manner of a tombstone, pitched upright not far from the Colosseo'.[15]

My walk in the Vicus Papissa was getting me no closer to sorting out these conflicting references. After a last despairing look at the *edicola* – I was almost tempted to address a novena to its statue of Our Lady for guidance in sorting out the historical muddle – I walked back down towards the Tiber, stopping off on the Aventine Hill to look over Saint Peter's from a park at its summit.

Gazing over the roofs and towers of the Vatican City, wondering where to go next on this Roman leg of my investigation, I remembered from previous, less frenetic visits, a favourite view just along the street. Next to the park is the Basilica of Santa Sabina, ancient but timeless with its simple grey marble interior. And then comes one of those wonderful Roman curiosities. Pressing my eye against the keyhole of the locked and bolted gate that leads on to the garden of the residence of the Knights of Malta, I could see down through an avenue of trees to the silhouette of the dome of Saint Peter's, stripped of its surrounding pomp and paraphernalia.

Take away the distractions and focus on one point, I told myself walking back to my hotel. There was a statue and it celebrated Pope Joan. The cult surrounding her could no longer be in doubt. Nor could the fact that many high-born and high-minded people, clerical and not, believed in the historical truth of the story it celebrated.

Chapter Nine

'As the weeks slipped by, I began to experience a sense of exhilaration at the knowledge I was getting away with it . . . As time went on I became more and more daring.'

Valerie Arkell-Smith aka Colonel Victor Barker, speaking after her disguise was exposed in the press[1]

Rome was enjoying an Indian summer and the heat was only adding to the frustrations of sorting out fact from fiction. Rome's charms as a holiday destination, I was discovering, did not transfer to the workplace. Endless phone calls and faxes to the Vatican produced repeated brush-offs. Libraries were closed at irregular and irrational times. Books and documents I sought were impossible to trace and shut off to all but those with at least four doctorates' and a letter of recommendation from the late Mother Teresa.

Without a deep, pink armchair to sink into beside an open window, I decided on the next best thing – escape. Outside Rome, there were two more reported sightings of Joan that post-dated her disappearance from the Vicus Papissa. The first, filed by Bishop Burnet of Salisbury in 1686, came from Bologna where he says local people believed a bust in front of the Church of Saint Petrino to be that of Joan.[2] The authorities, the good bishop wrote, denied the rumours and insisted it was Pope Nicholas IV (1288–92) – another example of the ambiguous messages a single image can give out. A telephone call to Bologna, however, failed to locate the church and dissuaded me from driving hundreds of miles to amble round the several hundred houses of God in search of a clue that no subsequent writer had mentioned.

The second sighting in Siena, however, was much easier to trace. While the statue of Joan in Rome recalled only her fall from grace, in Siena she once took her rightful place in a gallery of popes in the cathedral.

The journey was quick, refreshing and hearse-free. Siena stands in the heart of Tuscany on what used to be known as the Francigena Way, linking Rome via Florence to northern Italy and hence the rest of Europe. Old and new come together charmingly as a modern motorway follows its course, not in sunken six-laner British style, all high embankments and no view, but rather a picture-postcard drive, where the main problem was too much visual stimulation beside the road. The route from Rome to Siena was guarded by endless hill towns, glimpsed in the intervals between the road tunnels that plough through all natural obstacles.

Once in Siena, however, I found that a car was useless. The medieval heart is a pedestrian zone. A maze of narrow alleys and streets, up and down steep hills, lead one on to the main shell-shaped square, the Campo, a suitably impressive centre-piece to what was once a thriving and important republic.

It's not just the absence of cars that gives Siena, within its ancient walls, the air of a place where time has stood still. Any new buildings – homes, factories and offices – were way back near the *autostrada*. The shop-fronts were deliciously and individually old-fashioned to my eyes, accustomed to anonymous high streets full of colour-co-ordinated chain stores.

Yet, behind this set-in-stone air, there was one change that had taken place that was crucial to the riddle of the She-Pope. In a letter dating back to the mid-fifteenth century the Parisian theologian Jean Launoy describes how Archbishop Enea Silvio Piccolomini of Siena, later Pope Pius II (1458–64), discussed with Cardinal John Carusial a statue of Pope Joan that stood in his cathedral.[3] Even the virulent nineteenth-century anti-Joanite, Dollinger, saw the significance of this: 'In the fifteenth century hardly any doubt about her [Joan] shows itself. At the beginning of the century the bust of Pope Joan was placed in the cathedral of Siena . . . and no one took offence at it. The church of Siena, in the time that followed, gave three popes to the Roman see – Pius II, Pius III [1503] and Marcellus II [1555]. Not one of them ever thought of having the scandal removed.'[4]

By the early years of the seventeenth century, however, Antoine Pagi, provincial of the Franciscan order from Arles, recorded in his diary of a stay at the Franciscan house in Siena various conversations with his brethren, priests of the cathedral and finally an anonymous gentleman of the city about the fate of the bust of Pope Joan.[5] It had recently been removed, Pagi was told, on the orders of Clement VIII, with the backing of the Duke of Tuscany and inspired, he claims, by the priest-historian Cardinal Caesar Baronius, one of those who worked hardest in post-Reformation times to downgrade the history of the She-Pope to legend.[6] Pagi suggested intriguingly that, rather than remove the bust and make a replacement, masons had simply chiselled its features into a more manly profile and renamed it Pope Zachary.

Pagi's is not an isolated account. Alexander Cooke, a Protestant writer who seized on Joan in a tract first published in London in 1625 to make the Catholic church look foolish, refers to a memorial of the female pope in Siena cathedral 'which the bishop of that place would not suffer to be defaced, at the last repairing of that church, though your Jesuits did earnestly request him to deface it'.[7]

The Benedictine Jean Mabillon, a monk of Rheims and a prolific writer around the middle of the seventeenth century on archaeological subjects, is another who rehearses the story in his *Itineria Italia*, published in Paris in 1687.[8] It is an account of a journey he undertook around Italy in 1685 and 1686. In Siena, memories of the bust of Pope Joan were still fresh, he recounted, while he quoted an Abbot Jacobus Mignanellus as an eyewitness to the existence of a now lost likeness of the She-Pope.

I came in the wake of Mabillon and millions of other pilgrims to Siena's Cathedral or Duomo. It is an extraordinary building, towering above the town from its highest spot, its steeple and side walls made entirely out of black and white marble like a huge liquorice allsort. From the road into Siena it had looked as if it half filled the town. In the flesh it was only slightly more modest.

Indeed, had the Sienese had their way, it would have dwarfed even Saint Peter's. Begun in 1260 when the Sienese forces won a famous battle over their long-time rivals from Florence at Monteaperti, the cathedral was planned on a massive scale as a celebration of victory, independence and prosperity. Work was still going on in 1348 when a terrible plague killed half the population of the city and in its aftermath the dream had to be scaled down. The cathedral I could see was but the transept of what was planned. Only a few pillars and a fragment of façade to the rear of the cathedral piazza were left of that scheme.

Inside the Duomo, the array of marble and graphite, frescoes and statues, blues, golds and whites was as dazzling as the strong autumn sun outside. So dazzling, indeed, that the gallery of some 170 busts of popes, starting with Peter, on the right-hand side of the crucifix in the middle of the apse, and continuing in more or less chronological order right round the main body of the church back to the cross with Pope Lucius III (who died in 1185), seemed like a minor detail.

This gallery was why I had come to Siena. Made of terracotta and at one stage – as I later discovered by consulting various weighty and labyrinthine published extracts from the archives of Siena – painted blue and gold, the now pale-grey and dusty statuettes have been a feature of the Duomo since the late fifteenth century and may be at least another hundred years older. The triple tiara that each pope wears, for example, may date back to the early fourteenth century. Among the archives, too, was a note of 7 August 1600, from Marquess Tommaso Malaspina, governor of Siena, to Giugurio Tommasi, craftsman of the cathedral, ordering him to take down the bust signed John VII but said to be of Pope Joan.[9]

The bust of Zachary, mentioned by Pagi, cowered in a corner above the main entrance. A brief reconnoitre confirmed that there was no spiral staircase, organ loft or viewing gallery. It was going to be impossible to get close to the display of heads. The best view I could get was neck bent, peering up into the gloom.

Yet even at this distance, Pagi's theory seemed unlikely. There was little evidence that Zachary had been any more knocked around than his neighbours. A spot of erosion here by the wastes of time. A crack on the cheekbone there. And he did have what looked like a bad case of acne on his left cheek, but he was undoubtedly manly, strong-chinned, fleshy with deep-set eyes, thin lips and a big nose.

Zachary was in more or less the right place for the eight-century Pope Zacharias, one of the last of the Greek pontiffs. However, the Duomo's chronology was not exact. To his left – i.e. in theory his predecessor – was Gregory II. History tells us that it should have been Gregory III, who in Siena's roll of honour came later. Some pontiffs are repeated, others missed or replaced by anti-popes.

Moving on to the time when Joan was said by chroniclers to have sat on the papal throne, Leo IV, Benedict III and Nicholas I stare out impassively, the first with a look of gentleness and wisdom, the second the spitting image of Jeffrey Archer and the third, decidedly feminine, a plain but regal face in the Queen Victoria mould, jowlly, with heavy-lidded big eyes. Might this once have been the profile of Pope Joan?

If just getting a good look at the busts was difficult, then I couldn't begin to imagine the upheaval of removing or exchanging various heads – ladders, scaffolds, masons etc. Popes may have ordered Joan's removal, but for the men charged with the hard labour of completing the task and filling the resulting gap, it would have been quicker and easier simply to change the name painted in big black letters under the offending bust.

Reinforcing my suspicion was the fact that every recorded attempt to match up the physiognomies on show in Siena with other portraits of the popes has failed. Once I had accepted that the busts were not in any

113

real sense likenesses but simply a range of human faces, all with the same tiara, alb crossed over their chests in gold and tied with a toggle, it was easy to take on board that the relevant name in the papal chronology had simply been attached. Some of the faces on show were very masculine, others softer, some androgynous and others – admittedly just a few – camp or feminine. Leo VI, for example, with his square jaw and boxer's face was undeniably male. But Sergius III a few spaces further along could have passed for a memorial to the late Dame Edith Evans.

The busts, then, were a pack of cards, capable of being shuffled at will and reassigned like trumps in any new hand by the simple device of giving them a new name. If the bust that was once Joan was here in the Duomo, it was now undetectable. It could have been any or all of the heads and shoulders on display.

Despite this realisation, I was still surprised that this last official sighting of the She-Pope should be so little remarked upon in Siena. The cathedral guides were vague, the piety stall not much more helpful. Perhaps, I reflected over a cappuccino in the Campo, it was her claim to be one of the few women to merit a place in the firmament of the Catholic Church that had left Siena unmoved. The town, after all, has plenty of other female role models.

In the Palazzo Pubblico, the Gothic town hall facing me, there were numerous representations of the Virgin Mary and a handful of another female patron of Siena, the She-Wolf. A fifteenth-century gilt-and-bronze statue used to stand outside the Palazzo on a column but it had now been replaced by a replica and brought indoors for protection against the elements. The Sienese had borrowed the image of the She-Wolf from their Roman overlords, and later adapted it as the rallying point for their republic. 'Lupa, lupa' ('wolf, wolf') was the battle-cry of the Sienese soldiers.

The third of this female trinity to captivate the Sienese and eclipse Pope Joan was Saint Catherine, the fourteenth-century mystic, celebrated for her political interventions with popes, spiritual raptures, stigmata and closeness to Saint Francis of Assisi, and a native of the town. All around Siena in the narrow lanes were statues to her. She has her own church, and in the Palazzo Pubblico was a portrait completed in her lifetime by Lorenzo di Pietro (called the Vecchietta).

Catherine offered only an indirect link to Pope Joan. She had, as we have seen, named Euphrosyne, one of the cross-dressing saints, as her role model. But perhaps it was enough. With such a complex and saintly figure interwoven in their collective folklore, the people of Siena had little time for the She-Pope.

Back in Rome, the Vatican was still resisting my every effort to persuade a senior cleric to talk about Pope Joan. Professor Cesare D'Onofrio was the next best thing to an official spokesman prepared to hear me out. A self-styled 'historian of Rome', with over thirty publications to his name, D'Onofrio has access to officials and records at the Vatican that are denied to others. He had turned this raw material into a series of well-received books, which he sells through his own bookshop – run by his wife in the shadow of the Pantheon and stocked with just his own titles in a variety of bindings and editions, plus a few photographs he has taken.

A sprightly, dapper man in his seventies, prone to the addiction of older Italian men to wear clothes more suited to those half their age, Professor D'Onofrio was certainly treated with great deference at the Foundazione Besso, a charitably funded library and study centre in the heart of Rome where we had arranged to meet. His name was whispered in almost hallowed tones by first the doorman then the receptionist as I was ushered into an odd book-lined antechamber, taller than it was broad and therefore seeming as if it had been turned on its side. In the middle of this peculiar room sat the *professore*. Italians love a title and I was introduced, flatteringly, as Dottore Stanford.

As if sensing that his unusual publishing and distribution methods made me doubt his academic bona fide, Professor D'Onofrio began our interview by listing some of his plaudits and admirers. Among those who had liked his book on Pope Joan, published in 1979, D'Onofrio quoted her successor, Pope John Paul II. The Polish pontiff had written to say so, he told me, and that wouldn't have happened unless 'the Jesuits had first checked my facts'.

Despite the disparity in our titles and ages, we quickly established common ground. Professor D'Onofrio too had sat in *sedia stercoraria*, though with his impeccable credentials at the Vatican he had done so with the full approval of the authorities. It wasn't a commode, was it? This English technical term tripped him up slightly. After much vaguely scatological gesturing, he understood.

Can you imagine lying down like that to do your toilet? No. It is a birthing chair, where women lay down for birth. There are still others – in Constantinople. They were used at the coronation of the pope in San Giovanni in Laterano for symbolism. When the Pope sat in the chair at his coronation, the Laterano was claiming to be mother church of the world and the pope was claiming for his church the role of mother – *ecclesia mater*.

There were originally, the professor explained – slightly wearily – two chairs, the one in the Vatican Museum and another that Napoleon looted, took off to Paris, left in the Louvre which had now been 'lost'. The thought of a cover-up flashed briefly in and out of my mind, but the professor was away on what sounded a bit like his standard lecture on the subject. Both chairs were used in the papal coronation in the Chapel of Saint Sylvester in San Giovanni. The new pope sat in first one, then the second.

To be the mother church of Catholicism is certainly a claim the Lateran makes. *Mater et Caput Omnium Ecclesiarum* – 'Mother and Head of All Churches' – reads the inscription on its façade. But where was the supporting evidence for this elaborate theory, I asked the professor, and what exactly was the symbolism of two rather than just one chair?

> The symbolism of a mother caring for her children was common in rulers at that time. That is what gave me the clue. When the Roman emperors were crowned, their empresses would sit in what would otherwise be a birthing chair. That was their role. As mother of their people. So the popes borrowed this, men borrowing female symbolism just as they took over the emperors' authority in Rome. It established historical continuity and the continuity of the papacy – one pope giving birth to the next.

But why two chairs? 'Look at Bishop Burchard,' the professor ordered. In addition to his account of the Vicus Papissa quoted earlier, Burchard, papal master of ceremonies, recalls the coronation of Innocent VIII in September 1484:

> The Pope was led to the door of Saint Sylvester's Chapel, near which were placed two plain porphyry seats, in the first of which, from the right of the door, the pope sat, as though lying down: and when he was thus seated, the prior of the Lateran gave into the pope's hand a rod in token of ruling and correction and the keys of the Basilica and the Lateran Palace, in token of the power of closing and opening, of binding and loosing.

Pope Joan giving birth in the street (above) and being executed, along with her lover and child (below): from an illustrated account of her life, published in 1600, by the Protestant writer Johannes Wolf as part of his popular history of the shortcomings of the papacy, *Lectiones memorabiles et reconditae*.

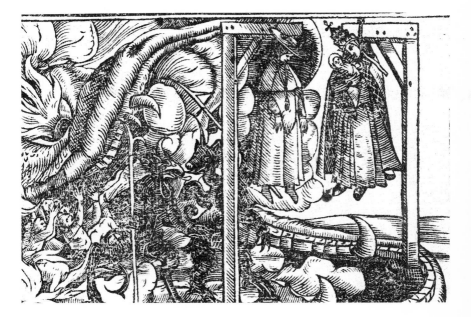

Pope Joan with her child: from the chronicle of the German writer, Hartmann Schedel, published in Nuremberg in 1493.

The cover of a collection of texts by Catholic authors rejecting the story of Pope Joan, published in 1616.

A fifteenth-century portrait of Joan from one of the frescoes in the Piccolomini Library in the Duomo in Siena.

An illustration that accompanied an account by the Swedish traveller, Lawrence Banck, of the coronation in 1644 of Pope Innocent X. Innocent is seated in the *sedia stercoraria* and having his testicles felt by a young cardinal as a way of ensuring that he is a man.

The little *edicola*, or shrine, on the Vicus Papissa, that is believed to mark the spot where once a statue of Pope Joan stood before it was removed on the orders of the Papacy.

The Vicus Papissa - or "street of the woman pope" - leading from the Colosseum to the Lateran Church in Rome. Because Joan gave birth and died here, papal servants reported that successive pontiffs refused to travel along the street thereafter.

The bust of Pope Zachary in the Cathedral of Siena. Writers and travellers report that in the sixteenth century this bust replaced one of Pope Joan that had stood among the gallery of pontiffs peering down on the nave of the cathedral.

The *sedia stercoraria* in the Vatican Museum. It is kept in a small room with no mention of its infamous past role.

The crypt of the Church of Saint Michael in Fulda (below) which, along with its Saxon tower (right), is one of the few remaining ninth century parts of The German Town that is as it was when Joan began her education there.

The eleventh-century pontifical, *Parisinus Lat. 5140*, in the Bibliotheque Nationale in Paris: Pope Joan is not mentioned in the text but between Leo IV and Nicholas I there is a puzzling gap where, historian Joan Morris believed, an account of Pope Joan had been hastily edited out.

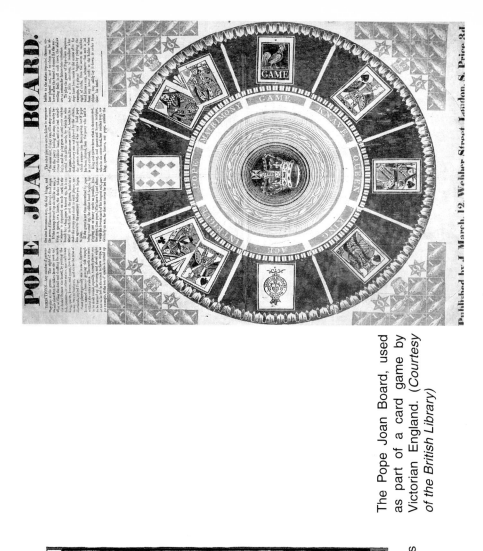

The Pope Joan Board, used as part of a card game by Victorian England. (*Courtesy of the British Library*)

The "papesse" or female pope has long been a feature of tarot cards.

Bernini's *baldacchino*, over the main altar in Saint Peter's, is decorated at the foot of its four columns by eight apparently identical versions of the Barberini crest (above left). But, under the papal crown that is part of the design, a woman's face contorts through seven of the versions (above right and below left) and in the last one is replaced by a baby (below right). Various other details - gargoyles and transmuting folds at the foot of the crest - combine to indicate that the story being told is of a woman pope giving birth.

Innocent then got up and sat in the second chair from whence he handed back the keys, ready for his successor.[10]

Closing and opening, binding and loosing. It certainly could be applied to labour. And the notion that the rod and keys belonged to the office, not to the individual, had been common since the time of Leo I (440–61), the first pope to realise that the authority of the papacy had to be greater and more enduring than any individual who might be pope.

Burchard is an impressive witness, but the idea of mother church – either for the Lateran or for Catholicism as a whole – is nowhere explicit in his account. And set against him has to be the account of other witnesses who spoke of the pope's testicles being felt.[11] 'Symbolism can become confused later,' the professor said, 'and I would want to be sure the writers were eyewitnesses. At such an intimate moment, would there have been a crowd of onlookers?'

We both shuffled nervously at the idea of being involved in such a public spectacle. I couldn't help thinking of that scene in *Crocodile Dundee* when Australian bush-ranger Paul Hogan descends on a fashionable New York bar, chats up a male-to-female transvestite, is shocked to discover his mistake and then insists on grabbing the crotch of the next woman he meets to verify her gender.

Yet the professor was doing a disservice to the eyewitnesses of this strange ceremony to check the pope's masculinity. By consulting records, I had now discovered that Hadrian VI (1522–3) abolished the use of the *sedia stercoraria*. Hence the account of the Swedish traveller, Lawrence Banck, whose 1644 report I had uncovered on my first investigation in Rome, would now seem dubious. But the Milanese historian, Bernardino Coreo, and Adam of Usk, writing contemporary and intimate accounts of papal coronations in 1492 and 1401, cannot be so lightly dismissed. Was it being suggested that they simply made up this extraordinary ritual or took it on trust that it had happened on the other side of a crowded basilica?

Professor D'Onofrio was anxiously flicking through a copy of his own book in front of him. He was changing the subject. He began showing me endless diagrams of birthing chairs. In ancient times high-born women would have used one of these to deliver their child, he insisted. 'In your own British Museum, there is such a chair. In blue stone.'

He must have seen my doubts but tried to convince me. 'Later the Vatican tried to take the two chairs – as a symbol of its authority over the Laterano. This was the time of Martin Polonus, when the popes came back from Avignon and the Vatican and the Laterano struggled for supremacy. Part of that was a struggle as to who had the chairs. You have to remember that in those days, to have sacred relics was to have authority and to have income.'

The Lateran held on to them, though the Vatican usurped its powers. It wasn't until the time of Pius VI (1775–99) that the chairs were finally transferred across the Tiber (by way of the Vicus Papissa? I wondered). In the interim the Vatican – and here the good professor was speculating – tried to play down the real significance of the chairs. It invented the legend of Joan to deny them and hence the Lateran any importance. But their creation, he claimed, took on a life of its own and ultimately turned against the Church.

In this scenario the Vatican was Martin Polonus's unknown source, the official mouthpiece in a battle with the Lateran. Only the strategy backfired spectacularly.

The professor's use of the word 'legend' had caught my attention earlier. And here he was using it again. He seemed to be offering confirmation of his own scepticism. Was he saying that Pope Joan was simply that – a story? 'Not a story, but a *storiella*.' I looked puzzled. 'In English a myth, a legend.' Are the two same, I asked, conscious of my own belief that a myth expressed a truth, while a legend could be a story? 'Myths', Professor D'Onofrio announced, as if handing down a papal pronouncement, 'are where the gods are involved. Legends are when it is something to do with the people, a popular story.' And Pope Joan? 'A legend – no gods.'

The professor seemed to sense my exasperation at his failure to give chapter and verse to buttress his speculations. He changed tack. 'But even if this is a false story,' he said, switching to the gentle tone of a doctor at a child's hospital bedside, 'all the elements are true.'

I had already worked that out, I replied, and began recounting my inconclusive ramble around the Vicus Papissa of the previous afternoon. 'Ah, yes,' he interrupted, 'the topography of Rome explains this. It is called "Vicus Papissa" because it ran alongside the home of a family called Pape. They are in the records as living there.'

He reached again for the copy of his book and showed me the relevant pages and the references.[12] Ancient street-plans of Rome, some dating back to the tenth century, identified the Papes. 'At that time it was the custom for wealthy families to take responsibility, as an honour, for lining and decorating part of the street that the pope would pass along. The Papes were a rich medieval family. We know that Giovanni Pape and his family lived up to his death in 973 opposite the Santi Quattro Coronati and had their own chapel. It would not have been unusual for such a pious family to have a street named after them, or even a female relative.'

The Vicus Papissa was then not 'the street of the woman pope', but 'the street of Mrs Pape'.

Just as Professor D'Onofrio was about to declare judgement against Pope Joan, he suddenly and playfully threw in a twist. Had I been to Saint Peter's, he asked. And had I examined Bernini's *baldacchino* – or canopy – over the main altar? Then I should. 'Pope Urban VIII (1623–44) understood the old symbolism of the Church. He was a very intelligent, cultivated pope. So he asked Bernini to incorporate in the *baldacchino* the idea of the papacy representing mother church, of one pope giving birth to another.'

Was this well-recorded, I asked the professor? He was vague. Like many of his theories it was a hunch, part of what appeared a personal folklore that he had fashioned around his city. 'Go and see for yourself. It was a secret. Only Bernini and Urban knew what it meant. They did not even tell the craftsmen.'

I've never been a fan of the principal shrine of world Catholicism. Swamped every day by legions of tourists, Saint Peter's has little of the feel of a house of God. It is a museum, a victory monument to Rome's medieval success in imposing its will on Europe. It offers no more invitation or inspiration to pray than the Empire State Building. It's all a question of size.

Designed by Carlo Maderno at the start of the seventeenth century, the façade illustrates the point. It strains so to be imposing that it ends up out of proportion. It is too long for its height – as if an extension has been tacked on to either side of a hitherto balanced frontage. The details match, but the overall impression jars on the eye.

It was not Maderno's fault. He wanted to keep it shorter. The two bays at either end were added on the orders of a later pope, swayed by Bernini's ambitious plans for two towers. But the master of the baroque had miscalculated. When building began the towers were too heavy for Maderno's foundations and had to be dismantled, leaving only their bases as unwanted and ugly additions to the front. Later the damage was made good, but by over-extending in the style of what was already there.

Some great churches have the name of just one architect attached to them – Christopher Wren and Saint Paul's in London for instance. But Saint Peter's is associated with many. Michelangelo is credited with the great dome but it was dreamt up by Bramante and completed by Domenico Fontana, Maderno's uncle. Michelangelo wanted the nave to be a simple Greek cross, with four equal branches, but Maderno changed this into a more standard Latin-cross shape. And dominating my approach to the basilica were the outstretched arms of Bernini's colonnade.

Entering the great empty cavern of the interior of Saint Peter's, Bernini's *baldacchino*, crowning the main altar from whence only popes can say mass, dominates all the other visual treasures on display. Because the tomb of the first pope lies beneath the altar, Bernini based his design on an original canopy that had stood over the martyr's remains in the first Saint Peter's.

The closer I got the more outsized the *baldacchino* became, rising up out of the great swathes of marble like some monumental and incongruous Victorian folly on a tranquil green hillside. Everything in Saint Peter's has to be the biggest, the best, but even under the biggest dome and above the best altar, this canopy is in a superlative league of its own, the height of any other cathedral.

Some say it is accursed. To support such a structure, deep foundations had to be dug – Bernini had learnt his lesson after the débâcle of the towers – but that meant disturbing old graves and relics. This caused protests from local people who, despite living in the shadow of the headquarters of Catholicism, maintained age-old pagan superstitions about incurring the wrath of the dead. Behind the blanket control Rome once imposed on Europe with its Inquisition and burnings at the stake, older traditions still survived. When several of the workmen died, the *baldacchino* was declared by some sacrilegious.

Though he himself was struck down by a mystery illness many blamed on Bernini's desecration, Pope Urban VIII did not lose faith in his architect. To hurry the project – and hence reduce the duration of the protests – he allowed Bernini to strip some of the bronze he needed from the portico of the Pantheon. This concession by Urban, one of the Barberini popes, outraged the Romans. 'What the barbarians did not do, the Barberini did,' according to a popular rhyme of the day.[13]

The millions who cast admiring glances at this canopy each year know little of its checkered and sinister history. Once the most unpopular feature in Saint Peter's, today it is one of its most readily recognisable and least controversial.

If Professor D'Onofrio's theory about the *baldacchino* had any mileage, it lay in the close relationship between pope and architect. It was a major commission for Bernini, then a young (thirty-four when it was completed), untried and – among his peers – unpopular architect. They pointed to his miscalculation on the towers and suggested he was a man promoted above his ability. He responded with sardonic ill-humour and a calculated disdain for his rivals and their work.

Urban made his own life more difficult by sticking with Bernini. Yet the Pope saw in him a genius that later ages came to appreciate. A literary connoisseur, owner of a fine library, a poet and a composer of hymns in his spare time, Urban was a gifted and unusual man. He had the breadth of vision to befriend such original and challenging thinkers as the father of modern science, Galileo (though he also later allowed him to fall into the hands of the Inquisition).

There was obviously something in Professor D'Onofrio's paeon of praise for this pope and a basis to suppose a meeting of minds with Bernini. Did this, though, extend to architect and patron incorporating a secret code in the design of the *baldacchino*, in effect their own private joke?

I waited my moment for a gap in the throng and walked carefully around the *baldacchino*. On the two outside sides of each of the four posts holding up the canopy, the Barberini crest is emblazoned at the centre of an elaborate, almost heart-shaped, off-white marble design by Borromini. Walking round the altar, the common features of these eight embellishments immediately became obvious. At the centre of each were the three bees of the Barberini emblem. At the top they all had the papal crown, and under it the rod and key of Peter, symbols of the highest office in the Catholic church.

These were constants. On my second or third circuit, I started to spot the differences. Tucked in underneath where the key crossed the rod was a woman's face. Her expression altered from one plinth to the next. And on one, she was replaced by a cherub. And right at the bottom, where the crest ended in a profusion of flourishes and frills, the contours of the triangular point were undergoing some sort of transmutation.

These were, admittedly, minor details. The second in particular was invisible unless you were of a particular frame of mind. My fellow scrutineers were unmoved, concentrating on the bigger picture – necks cricked to see the dome, eyes agog at the ostentation of the *baldacchino*. One elderly American, though, was amused and intrigued by the sight of my nit-picking examination and followed in my footsteps, copying my gestures. I smiled. A theory was coming to me and I wanted to share it. I felt I had discovered something that had lain unremarked upon for centuries – save, of course, by Professor D'Onofrio. That last sobering thought drew me up short. My co-conspirator had by this time lost interest and moved off to join her group as they descended the narrow stairs to Peter's tomb.

The faces did indeed tell a story. The starting point appeared to be the emblem to the left of the main altar, as approached from the great doors, and facing back to the entrance. There the woman's face was peaceful, even happy, though up on the papal crown, at the top of the design, a gargoyle appeared menacingly among otherwise innocuous decorations. By the third crest this demon had gone, but the woman was by now in considerable pain, her mouth open, her eyes screwed up. From four to seven, she contorted her face this way and that, her hair falling across it. Then in the eighth she was replaced by what at first glance seemed a cherub, but on closer examination was a chubby-cheeked, smiling baby. Down below, meanwhile, the flourishes at the bottom of the crest began by appearing as the jaws of a fierce creature but gradually contracted as if something large was about to pass out between the folds. In the final crest, with the baby's head above, the folds returned to their earlier shape.

This was the story of a pregnancy. The woman was in labour and in the eighth crest she was replaced by the baby. The folds at the bottom all the way round represented her vagina contracting to give birth to the baby and then returning to its original shape. The gargoyle on the first design, plus the jaws at the bottom, made clear that this was a wicked story and an evil woman using her sexuality. Seen in this context even the shape and positioning of the Barberini crest – round, swollen and central – represented the stomach of a pregnant woman.

For Professor D'Onofrio, the private code was that of *mater ecclesia*, the Church as mother earth. With no evidence to back up his theory, he was again speculating. And in such uncertain circumstances, for me it suggested something else – Pope Joan and her child. The image of a mother, wrapped up in the symbols of the papacy and given a sinister turn by the gargoyle, was not a wholesome or approved one. Mother earth would not have been demonised and given a wild creature's jaws – even in the private joke of Bernini and Urban.

That left just two options – a damning indictment of all women, their genitals as plundering animals and their sexuality inspired by the devil, or the story of a particular woman. The first was possible. The medieval Church, as I had already discovered, had little respect and much loathing for women. What this series of images most immediately brought to mind in that respect was the once common notion of incubi – women having sex with copulating male demons, often disguised as animals, and then giving birth to the devil's disciples.

Yet Urban was a cultured man and by the mid seventeenth century, with the craze for burning witches on the wane, the Church had begun to tire of such imagery. And, even if it hadn't, why hide the warning against women in a secret code in the *baldacchino*? The story of incubi had been broadcast from every pulpit in its time. There was no cause of shame that made it something to be hidden away in the crests on the plinths beside the altar.

Without any hard-and-fast evidence of Bernini's intention, these images had to be left in the realm of speculation and it seemed to me more likely that it was the story of a woman who was close to the papacy. But given the position of the trappings of papal office, the message appeared clear. This wasn't a pope's mistress, but a woman who was pope. Pope Joan, still in the 1640s well known though frowned upon, might have been what Bernini had in mind. He was, after all, a man with an odd sense of humour which could unsettle and even disturb his colleagues. He maintained, for example, with all apparent seriousness, that the dilapidated Hellenistic 'Mastro Pasquino' was the finest of all antique statues. He was also a man of contradictions – attending the Church of the Gesu for vespers every day, exact in seeking out the confessional, yet promiscuous, with an insatiable and often health-threatening appetite for women.

What better way to excite his sardonic humour, to express both sides of his personality, than to play with an image alongside the papal altar in the principal church of the world-wide Church? On the surface he was representing in images one of the most ancient boasts of the Church, that it was *mater ecclesia*, but at the same time he was dropping a dark hint about a tale his employers had done their best to sweep under the carpet. Urban may have been in on the first part of the equation, but not the second.

Moreover, that disputed *Mirabilia Urbis Romae* of 1375 suddenly came to mind,[14] referring to Joan as buried in Saint Peter's. Was

Bernini picking up on a popular misconception and alluding to it in his design?

As I flew back to London, gazing out on the tips of the Alps peeping through the clouds, I could almost imagine Bernini sitting out there with his harp, looking down on Rome and Saint Peter's, and smiling to himself at the irony as pope after pope stood at this altar saying mass, oblivious of the twist in the convoluted frame of his *baldacchino*.

Part Two

THE PAINTER AND THE PORTRAIT

Chapter Ten

'Every portrait that is painted with feeling is a portrait of the artist, not of the sitter.'
Oscar Wilde[1]

My investigation was now moving into a new phase. Placing Joan in history, checking the details of events and sightings, searching out the clues she may have left behind was the first part. Understanding why the memory of her lived on, in the face of such hostility from the Catholic church and historians, was the next stage.

Pope John Paul II received a hostile reception when he visited Germany in June 1996. Almost two decades into his pontificate the travelling pope had grown accustomed to muted receptions and local criticism of his conservative message on morality. The heady days of the late 1970s and early 1980s, when the sight of a pope making use of the jet engine to move beyond the confines of the Vatican City generated mass hysteria wherever he touched down, had been replaced by a feeling that his trips had the air of a bygone era of spectacles, of world fairs and centenary exhibitions, of the British fleet sailing majestically into the great harbours of the globe to show the flag and rally the troops.

In Germany that summer there was a new twist. In Berlin, thousands of participants in an annual gay street festival gathered on the Friedrichstrasse to send an uncompromising message to their visitor – that he was unwelcome and that his teaching on homosexuality, 'a strong tendency towards an intrinsic moral evil' as the Vatican has deemed it,[2] was offensive. To give expression to their hostility, they staged a mock papal coronation with a Hamburg prostitute crowned as Pope Joan. Berlin's Cardinal Archbishop, Georg Sterinsky, was outraged at the insult to the Pope. It had put him in mind, he fumed, 'of the very worst period of the French Revolution'. His memory was obviously selective.[3]

That Pope Joan should be so publicly remembered in Germany, that she should act as a rallying point for opponents of Rome, and that celebrating her memory should invoke memories of the anti-clerical French revolution are all significant. The riddle of Pope Joan has refused to die and continues to beguile dissenters.

Germany was the principal battleground of the Reformation and it was there in this period that the memory of the She-Pope, for the two centuries since Martin Polonus's chronicle taken as read by most papal historians and church-goers, first became a matter of dispute between the reformers and the forces of the Counter-Reformation.

Martin Luther – who had seen the statue of Joan in the Vicus Papissa in 1510^4 – focused much of his wrath with Rome on the question of the nature and role of the papacy. He and fellow Protestant critics sought to discredit the Pope's claims to universal jurisdiction and a direct line back to Saint Peter (and hence God) by pointing out that a woman – one, in the thinking of the time, of the weaker sex – had once held the pontifical office.

Both sides then cried foul. After centuries of grudging acceptance, Rome denounced Joan as a Protestant put-up job, ignoring the army of distinguished Dominican chroniclers who had first promoted her tale. The female pope was the work of an army of anti-Catholic forgers who had, the papal line went, broken into libraries and amended key works of history.

The reformers, as we have seen, could quickly shoot down this argument. They countered that the real lie, exposed in all its hollowness by the tale of Joan, was the papacy's claim to unrivalled power by act of God. It was a lie, the Protestants pointed out, that the current incumbent of Saint Peter's throne had anything in common with Christ's first apostle. It was a lie that the papacy had been anything other than one bishop among many for the first centuries of the Church. And it was a lie, they concluded, that there was any divine succession stretching from the current pope back to Peter.

Joan was caught in the cross-fire. A series of Catholic historians queued up to kill her off, a sacrifice for the greater good of Rome. The more sophisticated and ultimately the more persuasive papal propagandists – conscious of the fact that the Protestant forgery hypothesis did not hold water – looked for more complex explanations for the growth of what they deemed a fabrication. They came up with a bewildering variety of solutions to the conundrum, none of which on its own was enough to convince, but which collectively managed to crush existing belief in Joan by sheer weight of numbers.

However dishonest and unjust, it proved one of the few notable successes of the Counter-Reformation. Just as later generations were to edit out the contribution of other women to the growth of Christianity, or of blacks to the development of the United States, Joan was covered up in a widespread conspiracy of silence and historical lies.

Key to this act of vandalism was the damning of Joan's sex. The focus was placed on her ultimate downfall – the con-woman caught out for what she was by giving birth to a bastard child in the street. It was her sex that was her weakness. Through Joan, womankind as a whole was labelled lustful, deceitful and unfit for any authority. Oh how typical of a woman, cried Joan's attackers, leading men astray, having her wicked way and then falling pregnant. If any one belief had the power to unite the warring factions of Christianity – Lutheran, Protestant and Catholic – it was this one. All ultimately found a common interest, whatever their initial differences, in the suppression of the story of Pope Joan. It reinforced their fundamental misogyny and may indeed have perpetuated it.

Though the story of Joan was widely accepted between the writing of Martin Polonus's chronicle and the Reformation, it would be a mistake to imagine it was told with much relish. The celebrated historian Bartolomeo Platina, keeper of the Vatican Library under Pope Sixtus IV (1471–84) and another of Father Boyle's predecessors, epitomises the mood of the times. In his *Lives of the Popes* (1479), he gives an outline of the tale of the She-Pope and then adds: 'These things that I have mentioned are popularly told, though by obscure and untrustworthy authors, and therefore I have related them briefly and plainly, so that I should not be thought obstinate and pertinacious in omitting what all men then believed true.'[5]

Another figure from this pre-Reformation period whose interest in Joan should not be overlooked is Bernard Guy, a senior member of the Inquisition under Pope John XXII (1316–34) and Bishop of Galicia. Father Boyle, at the very outset of my investigation, had mentioned the enigma of this arch-inquisitor, a man who prided himself on seeking out the truth, leaving the story of Joan 'up in the air'. Guy is credited by history with discovering and correcting many errors in the chronicles of earlier writers, but he retains the integrity of the tale of the She-Pope. The historian Frederick Spanheim in his later exhaustive survey of every medieval document to mention Joan lists a source in the library at Leyden, apparently in the hand of Guy but now lost.[6] It states: 'I read and compared a number of chronicles in order to discover clearly and with certainty the truth of each circumstance' concerning Pope Joan. It reluctantly concludes that she should be included between Leo IV and Benedict III.

Some, though, exploited Rome's discomfiture. The Renaissance pre-dated – and was one of the inspirations for – the Reformation. The Renaissance cast to one side the gloom and despondency of the medieval period and promoted a new faith in the potency of the individual, in learning and in free thought. Its relationship with the ecclesiastical authorities was understandably a difficult and often unhappy one. The prospect of greater education and mental emancipation was not one that clerics welcomed, especially among their flocks. It was not for humankind to try to understand God's will, they stressed, merely to await and endure the fickle turns of divine whim.

A great fascination of the Renaissance, according to the historian Marina Warner, was the lore of Amazons – larger-than-life women who turned convention and gender roles on their head and achieved greatness despite their sex. They became, she writes, 'a motif of dazzling and compulsive popularity in Renaissance Europe'.[7] Warner had in mind the later Renaissance period and its use of the lore of Amazons to provide a context in which Joan of Arc 'appeared natural, explicable, though still unusual'.

The same judgement might be made, though, of Pope Joan and the fascination she held for the poets Petrarch and Boccaccio, two of the greatest of Renaissance men. Petrarch (1304–74) had once been a deacon, but neither he nor Giovanni Boccaccio (1331–75) had much respect for the late-medieval church. Petrarch, thwarted in love but seeing some enduring value in organised religion, retired to Venice where he wrote a chronicle of popes and Roman emperors. It passes quickly over the conventional details of Joan's pontificate. After charting her election, he writes simply, 'she was revealed' (as a woman).[8] However, he then gives his imagination full rein with a description of God's anger at the profanation of the Holy See, let loose on the day Joan died: '. . . in Brescia, it rained blood for three days and nights. In France there appeared marvellous locusts which had six wings and very powerful teeth. They flew miraculously through the air, and all drowned in the British Sea. The golden bodies were rejected by the waves of the sea and corrupted the air, so that a great many people died.'

Joan Morris regarded these apocalyptic lines as the poet's attempt to express his distaste for Joan's deception, 'a deviation of natural phenomena which Petrarch somehow connects with the horror of the unnatural act of Pope Joan.'[9]

The echoes of Old Testament plagues and the aftermath of Christ's death on the cross are missing from Boccaccio's more playful account of Joan in the 101st chapter of his celebration of women in history, *De claris mulieribus*,[10] a fourteenth-century precursor of Rosalind Miles's *Women's History of the World*.[11] The author of the *Decameron* ignores any link between Joan and Germany, and has her coming straight to Rome from England. His emphasis, as the French historian Alain Boureau pointed out in a learned paper published on Joan in Paris in 1984,[12] was that 'this was the story of a woman who became pope and not that of a pope who was discovered to be a woman'. He stresses the shame brought on the papacy by being duped, but leaves Joan – whose Greek learning appealed to him – to die in the relative dignity of a dungeon rather than in the street.

Boureau saw this transformation in the usual pattern of Joan's story in the hands of Boccaccio as a device to give her the classical grandeur and tragedy that obsessed Renaissance writers. It also enabled Boccaccio to draw parallels between the She-Pope and one of the poet's heroines from antiquity, Semiramis, who dressed herself as a man to hold on to her dead husband's power until their young son came of age. She succeeded all too well but was discovered when she committed incest with her child.

Perhaps Boccaccio's greatest legacy to future generations searching for the truth about Pope Joan, however, is the many illustrations and wood-carvings of her story which in years to come brightened successive editions of his always popular works.

An enlightening – from the point of view of Joan's credibility in this pre-Reformation period – and well-documented event was the Council of Constance, called in 1413 in northern Italy to try John Huss, self-styled and popular 'Apostle of Bohemia', who had rejected papal authority. Huss was brought in chains before twenty cardinals, forty-nine bishops and 272 theologians to answer for his dissent. The trial record shows him mentioning Joan in his examination. 'Was not the church without a head and without a ruler during the two years and five months Joan occupied the See of Rome?' Huss asked.[13] He went on to use Joan as an example of sin and error, and argued that mere election was not sufficient to make a pope. You had to be worthy of the office. It won him few converts and he was condemned to death.

Yet not once in debating his views did the august gathering contradict him on Joan or tell him to stop bringing up fairy-tales.

John of Huss was one of the precursors of the Reformation. The chain of events set off by Martin Luther's act of defiance at Wittenberg in October 1517 proved a crucial moment for the standing of Pope Joan. Just as John of Huss had sought to exploit her story as Rome's Achilles heel, so other reformers queued up to ridicule an office that claimed quasi-divine authority but had been seized by a woman.

The Jesuit historian Bower, professor of rhetoric, history and philosophy in the universities of Rome, Fermo and Macerata, candidly assessed the role of the Reformation in altering perceptions about the She-Pope in his *History of the Popes* (1759). 'She owes her existence and promotion to the Roman See, to the Roman Catholics themselves. By them, the fable was invented; it was published by their priests and monks before the Reformation, and was credited with their authority, even by those who were most attached to the Holy See, Saint Antonius, Archbishop of Florence, being among them. Nor did they begin to confute it till the Protestants reproached them with it.'[14]

The Reformation concentrated minds. In England, the war of words between John Jewel, Bishop of Salisbury (1560–71) under Elizabeth I and the exiled Catholic polemicist, Dr Thomas Harding, shows how Pope Joan became a standard debating point. Harding's *Confutation* of 1565 denied her existence on the by now usual Catholic grounds.[15] Jewel, two years later in his *Defence of the Apology of the Church of England*, took issue:

> And why might not Pope Joan, being a woman, have as good right and interest unto the see of Rome, as afterward had Pope John XIII, who, being pope, had wicked company with two of his own sisters; or others, whom for their horrible vices and wickedness Platina called *monstra et portenta*, 'monsters against kind, and ill-shapen creatures'? . . . Yet neither would so many chronicles have recorded, nor would the whole world so universally have believed these things of the pope more than any other bishop, had there not been wonderful corruption of manners, and dissolution of life, and open horror, and filthiness in that only see above all others.[16]

Such circumstantial evidence would be thrown out by a court of law, but in its time it found a ready popular echo. Alexander Cooke's 1625 pamphlet, *Pope Joan: A Dialogue between a Protestant and a Papist*, rehearsed all the old arguments, giving the Protestant all the best lines.

It achieved great popularity. 'My purpose', Cooke wrote, 'is to lay open the Catholic authorities shame in denying known truths . . . most apparently their impudency appears in denying the report of Pope Joan, which is proved by a cloud of witnesses, in this discourse, for they are driven to feign, to forge, to cog, to play the fools, and, in plain English, to lye all manner of lyes for the covering of their shame in this.'[17] Cooke's aim was that 'the simpler sort (for I write not for the learned) may have a taste, by this, of the honesty, or rather dishonesty, of Papists in handling of points of controversy . . . Papist or Catholick, choose whether name thou hast a mind to . . . I offer unto thee here a discourse touching Pope Joan (if thou darest read it, for fear of falling into thy Pope's curse) whose popedom I will make good unto thee.'

His 140-page pamphlet was the latest in a long line of attacks that exploited the popular conception in England that Catholics were against the Crown and agents of a foreign power. A succession of plots to restore a Catholic to the throne simply served to prolong the appeal of such an approach. From the Gunpowder Plot of 1605, through the defeat of James II at the Boyne in 1690, to Jacobite risings in 1715 and 1745, Catholics were vilified. Even when a measure of toleration was introduced with the first Relief Act of 1778, mobs flooded out on to the streets in the Gordon Riots with cries of 'No Popery'.[18]

By that time in continental Europe, the dividing line between the two denominational camps over Joan had become rather more clouded. In 1647 a French Protestant minister, David Blondel, broke ranks and argued against Joan on the basis of the historical evidence.[19] He was later rebuked by his fellow countryman, Pierre Bayle: 'The Protestant interest requires the story of Joan to be true.'[20]

In the next century Catholics, too, began standing back from their partisan positions. Abbé Lenglet-Dufresnois in his *Methode pour étudier l'histoire* (1729) wrote: 'I am astonished at the obstinacy of Catholics of the present day in denying the existence of Joan. One ought, on the contrary, to seek at all costs to establish the truth of this history because she contributed a great honour to the Holy See; for, according to the testimony of all the historians, Joan reigned as Pope with piety and wisdom.'[21]

If Lenglet-Dufresnois was running up the white flag, other Catholic writers played into the hands of their opponents with poor tactics. Exiled English Catholics joined in Antwerp in 1566 to produce *Dialogi Sex Contra Summi Pontificatos*, claiming that Joan had existed but that she was hermaphrodite.[22] This generated a small publishing industry in itself, with Protestant propagandists queuing up to knock down the theory. Few were more withering than *The History of Pope Joan and the Whores of Rome*, printed in London in 1687, by an anonymous author fearful that the Catholic Stuart king, James II, then on the throne, was intent on restoring papal influence at court:[23] 'Can any ingenious person ever believe that such a wise nation as the Romans are, and always have been, could be so greatly imposed upon, or that they should be so sottish or stupid, as not one of them to know a woman from a man, neither by her voice, countenance nor costume?'

A measure of how confused the various positions became as the centuries rolled on, yet how interest remained as lively as ever, comes with the example of a member of a reformed church going so far as to endorse the obvious falsehood that the story of Joan had been created by Protestants breaking into libraries. This was the favoured theory of Anglican minister, the Revd Sabine Baring-Gould, writing in the late nineteenth century in his *Myths of the Middle Ages*. 'It need hardly be stated that the whole story of Pope Joan is fabulous and rests on not a single historical foundation . . . A paper war was waged on the subject, and finally the whole story was proved conclusively to be utterly destitute of historical fact. The great champions of the myth were the Protestants of the sixteenth century.'[24] Baring-Gould was of the Petrarch school in seeing Joan's story as an addition to the Book of Revelation: 'I have little doubt myself that Pope Joan is the personification of the great whore of Revelation, seated on the seven hills, and is the popular expression of the idea prevalent from the twelfth to the sixteenth centuries, that the mystery of iniquity was somehow working in the papal court.'

Another peculiar feature of the ongoing debate about the riddle of the She-Pope has been the tendency of historians to return to the subject in packs. One writer taking a favourable look has always prompted another to rush out a condemnation. In 1843, for example, the Dutch Professor Kist produced *A Woman in the Chair of Saint Peter* with his theory that Joan was the widow of Pope Leo IV who took over her dead husband's office.[25] The following year Professor J. H. Wensing, also Dutch, responded with a condemnatory volume addressed directly to his rival.[26] Not to be left out, the Italian Antonio Bianchi-Giovani brought out in the same year his *Critical Examination into the Documents about Pope Joan*.[27]

Three names, however, stand out above all others in the post-

Reformation's gladiatorial battles over Pope Joan – Frederick Spanheim, Cardinal Baronius and Ignatius von Dollinger, one a Protestant academic with encyclopaedic knowledge, another a papal propagandist with impeccable credentials in the inner circles of the Vatican and the third a doughty German, loyal to the papacy but at odds with various incumbents, who was determined to end debate on Pope Joan for ever.

The first, Frederick Spanheim, a Calvinist, born in Switzerland and a professor at the University of Leyden, concentrated on collecting every reference to Pope Joan he could find. He let the facts – running to two volumes and covering 500 sources – do the talking. His research was first published in 1691 and went on to sell in many popular editions, especially in France, throughout the eighteenth century. Unfortunately for contemporary historians, some of his sources are now lost, while his references to others contain too little detail to follow them up with any hope of success.[28]

The second, Cardinal Caesar Baronius (1538–1607), was credited with persuading the Pope and the authorities in Siena to remove the bust of Joan from their cathedral. He studied her story as part of his research for *Annales ecclesiastici* and in a short section of his book damned most of the evidence on the grounds of its historical unreliability. Yet though Baronius was quoted as gospel by those who denied Joan, his scholarship was not without its drawbacks. For instance, elsewhere in his carefully researched text he recounted with the utmost seriousness the destruction of the Temple of Peace at Rome to coincide with Jesus's birth, the martyring of 11,000 virgins at Cologne in 237 and the sleep of the seven Epimenides of Ephesus for nigh on two centuries.[29]

The third in this trinity, Ignatius von Dollinger, was Professor of Theology at the University of Munich. According to his admirers, Dollinger produced in the nineteenth century the last word on Joan.[30] The Jesuit, Father Herbert Thurston, distilling Dollinger's weighty tome on Joan into one of the penny Catholic Truth Society booklets that used to grace the porches of every church, freely acknowledged his plagiarism: 'Since his [Dollinger's] time no scholar with a reputation to lose has ventured to defend the historical existence of Pope Joan.'[31] (Thurston, incidentally, was writing in 1929, on the crest of another wave of interest in Joan – made up of Richard Ince's *When Joan Was Pope*[32] and Clement Wood's *The Woman Who Was Pope*.[33] Such sustained interest at least throws into question his assertion that

Dollinger had finally put any lingering doubt about Joan's existence to one side.)

Dollinger's *Fables Concerning Popes of the Middle Ages* came out in 1863 and is a familiar run through the historical sources, reiterating their drawbacks. His assertion that Jean de Mailly's *Chronica Universalis*, potentially the source for Martin Polonus, was lost is an odd one, since it is still available to this day. Though he trumpets that to believe in Joan 'one must do violence to every principle of historical criticism', Dollinger's thorough sifting of the evidence is such that he never quite manages to explain away why so many chroniclers got it so wrong. He suggests a whole list of reasons, but gives the impression of not entirely convincing himself. And he falls back mainly on the accusation that it was Protestant forgers who promoted the legend, even if Martin Polonus first wrote about it.

You get the sense that Dollinger had another agenda and that his measured but strangely open-ended explanations are all geared to that. Joan Morris, in a note in her archive, ventures a solution: 'The opinion of Dollinger is of no great importance. He separated himself from the [Catholic] church because he was unable to believe in infallibility as decreed at Vatican I (in 1870). He wrote his book to show how fallible popes and Church theologians and authorities could be.'[34] For all his efforts to uphold the integrity of the papacy Dollinger was excommunicated in 1871 and, on his deathbed, refused the offer of the last rites from a Catholic priest. As a spokesman for Catholic orthodoxy Dollinger was an unlikely candidate and can hardly be counted as a dispassionate searcher after truth in the case of Joan.

Baronius was more imaginative than Dollinger in suggesting other explanations for the rise and enduring popularity of Joan's story. He advanced two theories. The first was that Pope Joan was a name given to the 'real' Pope John VIII, who in the official list of pontiffs reigned from 872–82. He might have been called a woman, Baronius wrote, because of his 'easy and pliable nature', particularly in regard to a dispute with the Patriarch of the eastern half of Christianity, based in Constantinople.[35] Besides providing an insight into Baronius's view of women, this explanation is at odds with the little that is known about John VIII – that he was above all an aggressive statesman and politician who worked to fight off the Saracen threat to Rome.

In his second attempt to explain away Joan, Baronius gave credence to reports that another reputedly effeminate character, a ninth-century

Patriarch of Constantinople, may have been the source for the riddle. In their haste to cover up their own shame at a less than macho patriarch, Baronius wrote, the eastern half of Christianity, separated from Rome since the eighth century, invented the story of Pope Joan as a slur on the throne of Saint Peter and a smoke-screen – 'a tissue of fables without proofs, in every part lying, mad, absurd, vain, frivolous, loose, contradictory and devoid of any appearance of truth' – to distract attention from the alleged skeleton in its own cupboard.

Baronius was not the only source for this story-line. The tenth-century *Chronicle of Salerno*, of which today a fifteenth-century manuscript remains (i.e. one that is two hundred years older than Baronius himself and which therefore cannot be accused of following his lead), told of an otherwise just and good patriarch some time in the ninth century who developed a liking for his niece.[36] In order to have her live with him, he ordered her to dress in male attire, pass herself off as his nephew and work as his secretary in Constantinople. On his deathbed, the Patriarch commended his niece as a suitable candidate to be his successor without revealing her gender. The young woman was duly elected, but was discovered when the Neapolitan Prince Arichis of Benevento was alerted to the deception in a dream. The prince sailed east to Constantinople to investigate further and uncovered the scandal. The duplicitious patriarch was expelled from the palace she had usurped.

This tale from the *Chronicle of Salerno* gains credibility when other sources speak of Pope Leo IX in 1054 writing a long letter to his opposite number, Patriarch Michael Cerularius. It was a competitive, point-scoring communication under the veneer of diplomacy and Leo mentioned the elevation of a woman to the patriarchate, though he then tried to soften the implied insult by adding that he could not believe such a terrible thing could be true.

The earliest reliable mention of this letter comes in an eighteenth-century collection, and it was dismissed as a fake by Dositheus, Patriarch of Jerusalem in *Histoire des Patriarches de Jerusalem*. Moreover, there is no chronicler of the Eastern Patriarchate who even hints at such occurences and in this epoch no patriarch is recorded as having been expelled from his post.

In the war of words between the estranged Christian siblings it is hard to know who might have been calling the others' bluff. Certainly there is a much greater weight of evidence for a female pope in the Vatican than there is for a female patriarch in Constantinople.

The eighteenth-century historian, Edward Gibbon, briefly took the Pope's shilling while a student at Oxford, but after fourteen months in the Roman fold recanted, 'cured', it was said, by a Calvinist minister. He spent the rest of his life an unrepentant agnostic. If he were then to be suspected of displaying a bias in his interpretation of the story of Joan, it should be anti-Catholic, yet in his six-volume *Decline and Fall of the Roman Empire*, published between 1776 and 1778, still a set text on many a history degree course, he dismissed contemptuously talk of a woman pope. He offered an alternative explanation as to why the story ever arose:

> The influence of two sister prostitutes, Marozia and Theodora, was founded on their wealth and beauty, their political and amorous intrigues. The most strenuous of their lovers were rewarded with the Roman mitre, and their reign may have suggested to darker ages the fable of a female pope. The bastard son, the grandson, and the great-grandson of Marozia – a rare genealogy – were seated in the Chair of Saint Peter.[37]

For Gibbon, Pope Joan was a coded reference to the power that two women and their descendants exerted over the papacy from the end of the ninth century to half-way through the eleventh. Gibbon's confidence that he had answered the riddle of Joan is weakened, perhaps fatally, by the fact that he got the most basic detail wrong. Marozia and Theodora were mother and daughter, not sisters.

Their story, however, is a remarkable one and shows just how low the papacy had fallen only thirty-five years after Joan died. Theodora first appeared in Rome with her husband Theophylact around 890. He amassed great power and influence before his death in 920 – as a senator, a judge and a duke in charge of the papacy's finances and the Roman militia. His wife was also appointed to the senate, but her ambitions ran much higher. She was determined to found a dynasty, for the House of Theophylact to become the new emperors of Rome. The papacy, with its *de facto* status as protector and administrator of Rome, stood in her way. So Theodora first connived with her husband to have their candidate elected as Sergius III in 904. Sergius was given the couple's fifteen-year-old daughter, Marozia, as part of his reward and duly got her pregnant. She gave birth to a son, John.

Theodora's control over the papal court was soon complete. On Sergius's death in 911, she ensured two of her nominees took over the papacy – Anastasius III (911–13) and Lando (913–14). She followed them with her lover, John X (914–28). Whatever the impropriety of his accession, he showed that he was made of sterner stuff. He worked alongside Theophylact, Theodora's husband, and the new husband of Marozia, Alberic, Marquis of Camerino, a German soldier of fortune, to shape a coalition of Italian rulers under the papacy. This grouping vowed to defend Rome and, when the Saracens attempted a raid on the city in 924, proved remarkably effective, decisively repulsing the menace of the infidels for two generations.

By this time both Marozia's parents had died and, despite Pope John's aspirations, she was the effective ruler of Rome. She had borne Alberic a son, but was notoriously free with her favours. Beautiful, cold and intelligent, her fellow citizens were loyal to her because she fed their ambitions of recapturing past greatness. The victory over the Saracens was presented as the latest of a long line of great Roman victories stretching back to ancient times. Part of her plan was to create an hereditary papacy. Blind to its spiritual and universal side, she saw the throne of Peter simply as the badge of success for her family. She began scheming to be rid of Pope John, her mother's ex-lover. She wanted to replace him with John, her own bastard son by Pope Sergius.

When the Pope sought military and moral support from Hugh of Provence, Marozia outmanoeuvred him and married Hugh's brother, Guy, a feudal lord in Tuscany. He proved the more effective of the two brothers and with his private army Marozia took the Castel Sant' Angelo, the gateway to the Vatican, and in effect laid siege to Saint Peter's. Pope John held out for two years but finally, with the crowd behind Marozia, capitulated. He was imprisoned and later murdered.

Marozia contented herself initially with two placemen – Leo VI (928) and Stephen VII (928–31) – but they were only keeping the throne warm for her son John. In 931, aged twenty, he became John XI. However, Marozia's machinations became too much even for the Romans. When she discarded her husband Guy and married his brother, her erstwhile enemy Hugh of Provence, the crowds rose under the leadership of another of her sons by Alberic – also called Alberic – and deposed her.

The young Alberic took charge of all temporal matters and left his hopeless and dissolute half-brother with only ceremonial functions. After John's death in 936, he was succeeded by a series of four nominees who did Alberic's bidding. On his deathbed in 954, Alberic extracted a promise from the Roman nobles and clergy that they would elect his teenage son, Octavian, to the papacy when next it fell vacant.

The following year eighteen-year-old Octavian was duly elected as John XII.

His sternest critics said that he turned the Lateran into a brothel and was the Christian Caligula. Threatened by the Huns, John formed an alliance with Emperor Otto of Saxony in 961, but once the danger had passed reneged on the deal. In fury, Otto called a synod in 963 to investigate John's dissolute ways. When the Pope refused to co-operate, he was deposed and replaced by Otto's candidate as Leo VIII. The Romans, though, rose up against the Emperor's presumption and helped John cling on until 964 when he was murdered by an outraged cuckold who found him *in flagrante* with his wife.

A final group of candidates from the House of Theophylact held the papacy in the next century. Benedict VIII (1012–24) and John XIX (1024–32) were both great-grandsons of Marozia. Benedict IX (1032–48), little more than a teenager at his accession, was Marozia's great-great-grandson.

The era of the House of Theophylact remains one of the most unhappy in the history of the papacy.[38] Commentators down the ages have outdone each other to find portentous enough words of condemnation. For Cardinal Baronius it was a time of 'pornocracy' when Marozia and Theodora as 'vainglorious Messalinas filled with fleshly lust and cunning in all forms of wickedness governed Rome and prostituted the chair of Saint Peter for their minions and paramours'.[39]

Yet Baronius in no way predicted Gibbon's theory linking Joan to the Theodora/Marozia period. Indeed, no subsequent chronicler of the papacy was shy about mentioning their history, the more sanguine reflecting that in a time of corruption they were simply the most corrupt. Though the *Encyclopaedia Britannica* slavishly followed the great historian on this subject, Gibbon and his theory fall on the grounds that no respectable writer on the papacy needed Pope Joan as a code with which to talk of the Theophylacts. Their history was well attested and witnessed by countless official and semi-official writers. Furthermore, Luitprand of Cremona, who deemed them 'shameless strumpets', was a contemporary chronicler of all their misdeeds, so there can be no question of the truth of what was alleged.[40]

A weak variation on Gibbon's theme was the suggestion by Onuphreus – one of the Counter-Reformation's most industrious anti-Joanites – that Pope John XII, grandson of Marozia, was so effeminate that later writers confused him for a woman. History records, however, that when John was indicted at the synod of 963, the list of charges read as follows:

> . . . committing incest with two sisters, of playing dice and invoking the devil to assist him to win, of creating boy bishops for money, of ravishing divers virgins, of converting the sacred palace into a seraglio, of lying with his father's harlot, with a certain Queen Dowager and with a widow called Anna and his own niece, of putting out the eyes of his father confessor, of going hunting publicly, of going always armed, of setting houses on fire, of breaking windows in the night . . .[41]

So far, none of the alternative solutions had amounted to much. All they had done was show the papacy in the worst possible light and make the story of Joan's deception seem less shocking and more credible by comparison. The final suggestion, however, that her emergence in the writings of Martin Polonus and her repeated championing in the writings of his fellow Dominicans owed something to a row between that religious order and the papacy had been on my agenda since my first crucial meeting with Father Boyle.

Ignatius von Dollinger was adamant that the solution to the riddle of Pope Joan lay with the order founded by the charismatic Spaniard Dominic Guzman in 1217.[42] The Dominicans started the story, Dollinger stated, because of their rivalry with the papacy and their desire to do down the office. It then survived because of the 'wanton frivolity of Italian literati and the stupid indifference of ecclesiastical dignitaries'.

Dollinger was correct in highlighting an unhappy period in relations between the papacy and the Dominicans. Guzman's followers came initially largely from the educated merchant or aristocratic classes and were therefore more willing than some of their confrères in other orders to stand up to the presumptions of a papacy which was nearing the apex of its earthly powers and pretensions.

In the period when Dominican writers are credited with the first tried and tested mentions of Joan – Jean de Mailly in 1225, Martin Polonus in 1265 and 1277 and Stephen de Bourbon in 1261 – the order was, as Dollinger alleged, engaged in a series of disputes with Rome. They clashed most spectacularly with Pope Innocent IV (1243–54) over their stranglehold on professorial chairs at the University of Paris. Other orders were jealous of the influence of the clever and ambitious Dominicans. Innocent (with ultimate temporal authority over this Church institution) decided to put them in their place. He backed a decision to permit only one chair per religious order and rejected out of hand an appeal by the Dominicans for special treatment. He added insult to injury with his 1254 bull *Etsi animarum*, in which he removed other jealously guarded Dominican privileges.

Innocent died soon afterwards – the result, it was said at the time, of Dominican prayers of intercession – and was replaced by Alexander IV (1254–61) who had a greater respect for the Dominicans. The tension, however, remained, and later in the century the order joined forces with the less intellectual but more practical Franciscans to resist the efforts of Pope Boniface VIII (1294–1303) to control their properties and reserves. The two orders then lined up alongside the French King, Philip IV (the Fair), a ruthless and amoral autocrat who had persecuted the Jews and disbanded the Knights Templar, when he tried to arrest and prosecute Boniface.

Over central issues of policy and the enforcement of Christian teaching, the Dominicans were often to be found in this period out of step with the papacy. However, there was, I suspected, a temptation to over-exaggerate the idea of Dominicans and the papacy in conflict. For example, even when horns were locked over university appointments, Innocent IV appointed thirty-five bishops, nine archbishops, a patriarch and a cardinal from the ranks of the order in just over a decade. More crucially, the notion that the Dominicans would have reacted to a set-back in their relations with the papacy by magicking a story out of the air about a woman pope is simply not credible. If they wanted to make either individual popes or the office they held look foolish, the Dominicans had plenty of live ammunition without resorting to fakes. Playing on the excesses of the House of Theophylact would have done the job admirably, encompassing excess, immorality, political manipulation and the danger of the female sex. If it was the question of the papacy's unbroken line back to Saint Peter, there were many examples to quote for the prosecution from the Dark Ages of shady and unpleasant characters without having to fabricate the story of a woman. If the story were true, however, it would be another matter. Indeed, the Dominicans' repeated use of it, in preference to other lurid tales, is a powerful argument in favour of the historical reality of Joan.

Dollinger's certainty that Pope Joan was born in the Dominicans' wicked imaginations stretched the credulity of even his most devoted admirers. The Jesuit Father Herbert Thurston, whose 1929 pamphlet largely reproduced Dollinger's arguments, here parted company with his mentor and suggested that the Dominicans fabricated the story simply because they wanted a gossipy and sensational story to pull the crowds, a medieval version of tabloid journalism.

However, the link between Joan's emergence in the thirteenth century and the Church battles of that period has continued to intrigue historians. The French writer Alain Boureau, in his 1984 paper on Pope Joan, focused the spotlight afresh on the dispute between Philip the Fair of France and Pope Boniface VIII. Boniface's predecessor as pope was Celestine V, an eighty-five-year-old hermit monk when he was elected in 1294 as the compromise candidate to unite warring factions among the cardinal electors after a twenty-seven-month stalemate.[43] (Choosing a pope had now moved to the system that exists to this day, the product of a two-thirds majority among the most senior clerics gathered in secret conclave.) Celestine soon realised that he was totally ill-equipped to be Pope and abdicated after a few months with the cardinals' full consent, making him the last pope officially to give up the office before he died.

Philip, in his subsequent battle with Boniface, sought to cast a shadow over his legitimacy and suggested that he had connived to remove Celestine and then murdered him. Therefore the question of whether a pope could abdicate and whether the cardinals could accept such a decision became an issue. In Boureau's prognosis, the Dominicans, as allies of Philip against Boniface, got caught up in the mêlée.

Cardinal electors, it was argued from Rome, were guided by the Holy Spirit and could not then be mistaken either in choosing a pope or in accepting a pope's abdication. In response, Philip, aided by his Dominican allies, made up the story of a woman pope to show just how fallible the electors had been in the past. There is an obvious flaw here. Joan was not chosen by the cardinals and her deception of a popular electorate would have had little bearing on Celestine's case. Clever Dominicans would surely have realised this weakness.

Yet, as well as coinciding with the publication in 1294 of another version of Martin Polonus's chronicle, the fight over Celestine's abdication was also reflected, Boureau argued, in the writings of a Dominican mystic, Robert of Uzes. His *Liber Visionum* of 1296 was a collection of visions of the future of the Church and contained a passage where the author found himself before a chair 'where it is said the Pope is proved to be a man'. On the story of Joan, however, Robert of Uzes was silent.[44]

The difficulty with Boureau's theory is the same as with Dollinger's idea that Dominicans created Pope Joan to spite the Vatican. If Philip the Fair had wanted to make the claims of the papacy look foolish and the whole election process comical, he need only have turned to the well-documented and scandalous period of Marozia and Theodora. All talk of Joan being a veiled reference to these women, or other shortcomings in the Vatican, relies on opponents of the papacy being too inhibited to mention them but seemingly unabashed in alleging that a woman dressed up as a man to rise to the highest office. It does not add up. Indeed, a careful examination of the evidence points in the opposite direction. If enemies of the papacy quoted Joan against it rather than the well-documented case of Marozia and Theodora, then they must have been absolutely convinced that they were backing a winner.

Chapter Eleven

'Orlando had become a woman. There is no denying it. But in every other respect, Orlando remained precisely as he had been. The change of sex, though it altered their future, did nothing whatsoever to alter their identity. Their faces remained, as their portraits prove, practically the same. His memory – but in future we must for convention's sake, say "her" for "his" and "she for "he" – her memory, then, went back through all the events of her past life without encountering any obstacle.'

Virginia Woolf, *Orlando*[1]

I chanced upon novelist and feminist theologian Sara Maitland's interest in Pope Joan quite by accident. We were both sitting in one of those soulless and misnamed hospitality rooms at a television studio in Liverpool, waiting to appear on a regional religious chat show to be broadcast in the early hours of the morning for insomniacs of a spiritual bent and church-going shift workers. Awaiting the summons to ordeal by sofa, I was reading Donna Woolfolk Cross's novel *Pope Joan*,[2] recently arrived from the States.

'Not that old chestnut,' Sara cried out as she peered over my shoulder. 'It's a nuttogramme.' There was a peculiarly savage edge to her voice.

'A what?' I queried with a thin smile and a measured tone.

'A nuttogramme,' she repeated, if anything more abrasively. 'You know, one of those religious subjects that flushes out the nuts, with some point or other to prove.' Quite an accolade. It didn't sound the sort of club that any self-respecting individual flaunted his or her membership of. Fortunately I was saved that particular disgrace as we were dragged off to hold forth in a debate before camera with an evangelical vicar on the future of sexual morality.

Later, perhaps out of our common cause in the face of an intolerant opponent, Sara took on a more pacific tone. 'When I said Pope Joan was for nuts, I meant me as well. I've written a short story about her. I'll send you a copy if you'd like.'

'The Dreams of the Papess Joan', first published in the early 1970s in the feminist magazine *Spare Rib*, was later collected in *Telling Tales*, a volume of Sara's stories.[3] It re-creates some of the details of Joan's life in a series of increasingly disturbed dreams. In the first, tossing and turning, she recalls her childhood in England and the determination she voiced to her sister to 'do anything she wanted' that led to her rise to the papacy, and her fall in her seduction 'by a fat-fingered cardinal, mummering and slobbering, making the words "your Holiness" into the obscenest joke in Christendom'.

In the second, Joan struggles to decide what to do with the baby that is coming. 'They are bound to guess soon . . . His Holiness is sick every morning, faints sometimes in the council, has started to put on weight, weeps when he blesses children, gives charity to poor mothers suddenly, although he never did until a few months ago; but they don't seem to guess.' There is almost a note of desperation, willing others to uncover her secret.

Falling back to sleep, she senses herself slithering back to where she started – as a young girl who wanted to be a man. 'Why, I ask myself, but I cannot ask Joan anymore because she does not exist; I have come too far and there is no way back.' In the fourth dream, she is back in a convent in England, having been excused her duties in Rome and bringing up her daughter. And in a brief final 'dream', Joan miscarries a son while heading the papal procession and is stoned to death.

So was it all a dream, and where, if anywhere, did the female cross-dressing saints fit in? 'Who's to know,' replied Sara Maitland. She gave a laugh that lit up the otherwise stuffy café where we were having lunch. As a novelist, she explained, it was not her task to find the answer. But questions of gender and blurring of distinctions fascinate Sara Maitland. One of her best-known books is her life of Vesta Tilley, a big star in the music-halls and popular theatre at the turn of the century with her drag act. Dressing up as a man brought her the largest earned income of any woman in Europe at the time, though now she's almost completely forgotten. 'Perhaps her problem was that, unlike Pope Joan who has gone on for centuries, Vesta Tilley didn't have a disastrous end. She retired from the stage, married a Conservative MP who was later knighted and become a lady. But', and she was visibly warming to her theme, 'there's another important distinction with Joan – Vesta never disguised her gender. Being a man was a performance, but at the end of the show she came out of the stage door as a woman. Even Joan of Arc didn't disguise her sex, though she never recanted men's clothes even as she burnt. But then she was a paradigm of the inverse – the wrong gender, the wrong class *et cetera*.'

Pope Joan's attempt to conceal her true identity may have been one of the reasons her story caused offence. 'People don't like being conned. Of course at a rational level it doesn't matter and shouldn't affect how we feel, but it's interesting, isn't it, how odd and unnerving we find androgyny in adults. We can't relate to it and find it threatening, but with children . . . I was sitting on the bus the other day and was smiling at a baby. I'd no idea if it was a boy or a girl, but it didn't matter. It didn't stop me relating to it. Gender was not absolute.'

Surely this was part of the attraction of Pope Joan for novelists? For once she paused before providing a comprehensive answer. 'The many angles of the story undoubtedly increase its appeal – and we love smut about the Church. Smut is not filth and this story was long enough ago that no one who matters was part of it. And then there is the element of cover-up. A cover-up with smut. Great. It all plays into the hands of conspiracy theorists.'

Yet she would presumably not put herself among the conspiracy theorists? A theologian, a defender of Christianity in her writings and journalism, and a recent convert to Rome, Sara Maitland is no anti-church rebel, although she can be a harsh critic of its more foolish and sexist excesses. 'What intrigues me is that with her story you have just enough information to whet your appetite. It's a bit like the death of Pope John Paul I in 1978. We knew just enough to make us suspicious that all was not right, but not enough to enable us to either confirm or rule out those suspicions. And so a small publishing industry was launched.'

Again Sara found the comparison with Joan of Arc enlightening. 'She is a good example of someone about whom we have all the information we want – in the trial documents. But still she is open to any reading you want. Hers is such a real voice. Pope Joan by contrast has no voice – and part of her attraction is precisely that – that like other women in history she has no voice but this time we know just enough to attempt to give her one.'

Sara Maitland was by no means the first novelist to be intrigued by Pope Joan. In the 1000 years since she is said to have run the Catholic church and the 600 since she became a feature of medieval chronicles, the She-Pope has continued to attract regular revivals of interest. Or rather, the dramatic events of her story have. Her deception of the Roman authorities and its brutal discovery have become celebrated in their own right, transcending in the process the medium, the environment and even the person who first generated them. The central character of Joan has been pushed to one side and, in the scramble to understand her motivations, has been kidnapped by a succession of fashionable causes and pressure groups. Few have been more attracted to her than writers who have turned to Joan to give dramatic expression to their own mainly anti-clerical or feminist viewpoint.

Seen through such a filter, the She-Pope has endured in a fashion denied to most of the women of history. Though she fits none of the obvious categories that have given women immortality – neither famous queen, courtesan, beauty, mother, artist nor saint – she has confounded all attempts to write her off and has maintained an allure for successive generations and centuries.

Such fame in the hands of creative and opinionated writers has, however, come at a price. When so little is known about Pope Joan, the polemicists permit themselves open season on the basis of the few facts that are passed on by the chroniclers. Lucy Hughes-Hallett, biographer of another stock and much manipulated female character of history, Cleopatra, has noted how this process distances the woman from the ensuing myth. 'A story is a protean thing, changing its nature as well as its shape when viewed from different angles. A single set of facts, arranged and rearranged, can point to a variety of contradictory conclusions – even the simplest piece of information can be made to serve a polemical purpose. The story-teller is – willy-nilly – something of a propagandist.'[4]

In the immediate post-Reformation period the principal arena for such propaganda was the pulpit, but as the Protestant and Catholic ecclesiastical authorities sought out new means of damning each other's claims, their battle spilt over into literature, art and theatre. And hence so did Pope Joan. Dorothea McEwan had mentioned Dietrich Schernberg's *Ein schön Spiel von Frau Jutta – A Beautiful Play of Mrs Joan* – written in 1565. Twenty-five years later came the first recorded English stage play on the theme of Joan – *Poope Jone*, performed by Lord Strange's Men at London's Rose Theatre. 'At poope Jone the 1 of marche 1591' Philip Henslowe recorded in his diary.[5] The cast would have been all male, as was the tradition in Elizabethan times, giving the central drama another twist – the male pope who was a woman was a man.

The script is, however, lost, and it is not until 1680 and Elkanah Settle's *The Female Prelate*, staged at the Theatre Royal, London, that there is a text which has survived.[6] Conforming with the anti-Catholic milieu of Protestant England, Settle portrays Joan as a scheming murderer and sex siren who nonetheless achieved the highest office in the Church of Rome. The stage is littered with the dead bodies of past and present lovers before Joan meets her customary end. As an epilogue, the cardinals gather and agree to instigate a test to check all future popes' masculinity:

> Thus when the Coronation Porphyry,
> On which Rome installed Bishop, Heavens
> Lieutenant takes his great Commission,
> Shall thro' it have that subtle concave form'd
> Thro' which a reverend Matrons hand . . .

The naked antipathy of the play to Joan and Catholicism remains its most striking feature. Unfulfilled plans in the 1920s by the occultist and writer on black magic, Montague Summers, to stage a revival only serve to emphasise the close link in the mind of subsequent generations between Pope Joan, the work of the devil and opposition to the Catholic church.

The English, however, cannot claim to have been the most ardent exploiters of the memory of Pope Joan. That honour has to be divided between the French and the Germans, with the latter's initial advantage slowly overtaken by the former. The French Revolution of 1789 was fuelled by anti-clericalism and inevitably Pope Joan's name came up among the heroes and heroines of the rebels. Voltaire, forerunner of the Revolution, makes a passing reference to her in his *Essay on Morals* (1756), but it was Charles Bordes's 1777 narrative poem on Pope Joan that made the greatest impact among the educated classes and *philosophes*. Bordes, a provincial rebel and writer whose main claim to fame was the blessing Jean-Jacques Rousseau had bestowed on his *Blanche de Bourbon* of 1736, brought together not only the anti-clerical tone of the times, but also the erotic and burlesque elements that were attached to the tale of the She-Pope in this period.[7]

Bordes's poem begins with a celestial council with assembled angels and saints worried about the disrepute of the papacy. The women saints in particular push for one of their own sex to be given a chance to restore the fortunes and reputation of the throne of Peter. They point to Joan, a woman of learning and spirituality who lives as a man at Tivoli, outside Rome, where she mourns the death of her lover, René. Through the intercession and trickery of the angels Joan is duly elected, though the cardinals are unaware of her true sex. Cardinal Marcel is sent out to convey to Joan the news, but Marcel is in fact

149

René who did not die but, forsaking any hope of ever seeing Joan again, had made a life for himself as a prelate.

The two recognise each other, are overjoyed and rekindle their passion before heading for Rome. Marcel/René knows that there some of the cardinals have prepared a gender test for the new pope, so he and Joan devise an ingenious way round the ordeal in the chair:

> In the best-known convents,
> For all their enclosure and chaste locks,
> There is an art of imitating jewels:
> Strawberries and cherry reds are always amongst us,
> As far as genitals are concerned, they're as good as an apple.

Just as Christian Davies in the seventeenth century had worn a silver dildo – 'a silver tube painted over, and fastened about her with leather straps' – to trick her way into the British army and fight at the Battle of the Boyne,[8] so Bordes's Pope Joan convinced those who checked her masculinity with a cunning use of fruit.

Bordes recounted this theatrical tale in the form of a poem because, in pre-Revolutionary France, it was forbidden to make fun of religious habits on stage. The events of 1789 removed such censorship and in the process unleashed a whole series of comedies and vaudeville performances based on Pope Joan. The year 1793 must be counted as that of the She-Pope for, in January alone, there were three versions of her life running on the Paris stage.[9]

After refusing initially to condemn the Revolution outright, by 1793 the papacy had become its sworn enemy. Pius VI in 1791 declared the Civil Constitution of the Clergy, which made French priests into civil servants, schismatic. Later he poured scorn on the Declaration of the Rights of Man and gave his blessing to the foreign armies who sought to overthrow the Revolution and restore the Bourbon monarchy. While the revolutionary army defended the new regime on the battlefield, authors and actors in Paris cocked a snook at their detractors in Rome by celebrating Joan.

Pierre Léger's 1793 account of Pope Joan had its heroine joining her long-lost childhood sweetheart, Florello, on the papal throne as equal partners, a moral tale in the politically correct, anti-marriage, equality-of-the-sexes atmosphere of Revolutionary France. Here was a model of how a reformed papacy might act, Léger was telling his audience. His play had its moments of humour and burlesque, but Defauconpret's version of the She-Pope went for laughs with a drop-your-trousers-style farce. The cardinals responsible for Joan's election – one the leader of the young faction, one the leader of the old and both her lovers – spent most of their time jumping out of beds and through windows. The attendant/narrator recalls the moment of revelation in the Vicus Papissa as comic:

> How the people will smirk and shout
> When this story at last is out,
> We approached Saint John's, we were nearly there,
> When a horrid event threw us into despair.
> The procession was halted, feet slid around;
> Thud! the Pope fell to the ground.
>
> The Holy Father groaned and shouted,
> The fear in the crowd was quite undoubted;
> Who could help him? Was there none?
> Suddenly the Pope . . . gave birth to a son.

The third of this remarkable trinity of plays was by Carbon Flins des Oliviers, but his text has been lost and confirmation of his homage to Joan comes only fleetingly in the journals of the author, soldier, diplomat and Christian apologist Chateaubriand when he records that the playwright has fallen in love with his sister.

When Napoleon Bonaparte seized control of revolutionary France in 1799 the violent anti-clericalism of the previous decade gave way to something more controlled, political and cynical. A last flourishing of that fading spirit of anarchy and rebellion was seen in 1801 in the work of playwright Theodore Desorgues. His *Le Pape et le Mufti ou la Reconciliation des cultes* gave a new twist to the outline of Joan's story. Taking a fashionably eastern theme – Napoleon had been battling with Nelson off the coast of Egypt for control of the Near East – the play had the Turks of Mufti Ali besieging ninth-century Rome. The Pope was a young Turkish woman, Azemis, who had disguised herself as a man and risen through the ranks of the clergy in order to be with her lover, Cardinal Azolan.

When Mufti Ali entered Rome, he settled down to a set-piece confrontation with Azemis, the claims of Islam set against Christianity. Mufti Ali was particularly scathing not just about the history of Catholicism and the papacy but about Christianity's claim to be based on divine revelation. 'In order to preach wisdom,' says Mufti Ali, 'this God of yours translates into bad Greek the thoughts of the wise men of ancient Greece, then pretends that what he says is new. Without their sermons, perhaps the clerics wouldn't exhaust their lungs making a thief who died on the gallows, the subject of proselytising. He died in public but was brought back to life in private. He became the son of god, this son of a carpenter. The world would have suffered less had he made that his trade instead.'

Aside from its missionary message, the play followed in the traditions of 1793 with a comic and farcical ending. Azemis turned out to be Mufti Ali's long-lost daughter. She had escaped from him to be with Azolan when their love had been forbidden. The couple then married with his blessing, but not with that of the populace of Rome who ran them out of town and the Church. Islam was presented as wise and far-seeing; Catholicism was steeped in intolerance and bigotry.

While Pope Joan has always had an appeal for polemicists, in the nineteenth century she was swept along by the vogue for slushy romanticism. The sharper edges of eroticism in the plays of the French Revolution were blunted, if not wholly neutralised, in this more prudish era.

Emmanuel Royidis, whose 1880s' novel remains one of the few well-researched sources on the Athens of Joan's time, exemplifies this genre. In Royidis's overblown romantic imagination Joan becomes the classic innocent abroad, a victim of fate, clinging to the strong arms of men who promise to save her, only then to be disappointed as they let her down. Royidis, though, makes good their failings and wraps Joan in an exaggerated tenderness. There are occasional hints of sexual impropriety, but they are, as befitted the period, restrained.

Royidis's work later attracted the English novelist Lawrence Durrell, who translated the novel in the 1950s. Durrell saw Joan as a latter-day incarnation of the god of love in an era that frowned upon such a figure. '*Pope Joan* is a sort of brief record of the history and misfortunes of Eros after his transformation by Christianity from a god to an underground resistance movement.'[10]

Behind the romance, however, Royidis was, like many promoters of Joan down the ages, virulently anti-clerical. Part of the appeal of his heroine was undoubtedly the opportunity she afforded him to give vent to his dislike of organised religion. Publication brought him excommunication from the Orthodox church in his native Greece. *Pope Joan* was banned there for many years but, in the heightened atmosphere of turn-of-the-century Europe, falling foul of clerical censors was a sure way of gaining an audience. To radicals and authors across the continent, Royidis became the equivalent of the writers who today suffer under totalitarian regimes. His was a *cause célèbre*. In France, with church and state locked in conflict over schools and an ongoing government drive to remove clerical influence from national life, *Pope Joan* clocked up 100,000 sales.

Royidis, though, was not the most famous name associated with Joan in nineteenth-century France. That honour goes to the novelist Stendhal. A lover of Italy, he spent many years there and recorded his observations in *Voyages en Italie*.[11] Joan merited a detailed discussion. Stendhal began by expressing surprise that Joan's legend lived on in Rome. 'Who would believe that today there are people in Rome who attach a great deal of importance to the story of Pope Joan?' But when he was forced to review the evidence, in conversation with a 'Joanaclast' in Rome's Barberini Library, he came to the conclusion that the shocking nature of the story should not blind readers to the facts. 'It would be pointless to argue against the existence of Pope Joan by saying that the thing was improbable. The exploits of the Maid of Orleans also go against all the rules of common sense, and yet we have a thousand proofs of them.'

Stendhal's willingness to believe may have been influenced by his own anti-clerical streak. His best-known novel, *Le Rouge et Le Noir*, presents an unholy and unattractive picture of clerical life in the upper echelons of the ecclesiastical world.

However, Stendhal was little read in his lifetime and only achieved popularity after his death. Royidis, for all the success of translations of his work in France after they had been banned in Greece, was an acquired taste. The She-Pope's biggest audience in the nineteenth century came in sixpenny illustrated paperbacks like G. W. M. Reynolds's *Pope Joan*, subtitled 'the People's Edition' and published in 1888 by Dick's English novels.[12] Other titles in the series included *Wagner the Wehr Wolf* and a sugary account of Grace Darling.

Reynolds – possibly a pen-name since nothing else is known of the author – started his book as a standard romance at Fulda, but *en route* from Germany to Rome, via Spain, the young, beautiful, waif-like Joan stays overnight in Calatrava Castle with her lover. There she gets wrapped up in a Gothic horror story, before emerging on the last few pages to hurry to Rome and be elected in disguise. 'Cardinal John Somanois [aka Joan] was remarkably handsome with a somewhat delicate expression of countenance. His features are, however, masculine, but the absence of beard gives them a feminine aspect.'

Reynolds's text was peppered with illustrations in the style of the Pre-Raphaelites, one of only a handful of occasions since the late medieval period when her life had inspired artists. Tall, oval-faced and somewhat distant throughout, Joan abandoned the curves, ruffles and plunging necklines of the early illustrations in favour of a final androgynous garb. But her shape, facial expressions and even ringleted hair were only thinly disguised, as if to emphasise the folly of the papal electors in believing her to be a man.

Reynolds and his illustrator understood the prejudices of Victorian England against the papacy. Though the first Catholic Relief Act had come in 1778 and Catholic Emancipation in 1829, the veneer of tolerance could not always disguise distrust and hostility at 'left-footers', as Catholics were dubbed. Occasionally this undercurrent broke out on the surface, as, for example, in 1850 when the Vatican named the first resident English Catholic Cardinal since the Reformation. The Prime Minister, Lord John Russell, led the way, denouncing the 'insolent and insidious' actions of the papacy. Queen Victoria took such offence that she is said to have remarked, 'Am I Queen of England, or am I not?' *The Times* added its voice: 'If this appointment be not intended as a clumsy joke, we confess that we can only regard it as one of the grossest acts of folly and impertinence which the court of Rome has ventured to commit since the crown and people of England threw off its yoke.'[13]

Such violent antipathy among the ruling classes was short-lived in the public domain, but in private it prospered in such banal activities as a simple round of cards. 'Pope Joan' was at the time a favourite game, played with cards on a tray-like, rotating circular board, divided into areas called 'Pope Joan', 'Matrimony', 'Intrigue', 'Ace', 'King', 'Queen', 'Knave' and 'Game'. Some boards were elaborately, if gaudily, embellished in lacquer and mother-of-pearl. For the lower classes there was a tuppenny variation, a flat printed sheet with the same divisions and categories as the three-dimensional version. A normal pack of cards was used, without jokers, and thirty counters or matchsticks. The nine of diamonds was Pope Joan and the aim was to play your cards in such a way as to win as many counters as possible.

Historians believe 'Pope Joan' was based on the German card and board game 'Poch', dating back to the sixteenth century. It may have been imported, it is said, with the Hanoverian kings. It was first seen in the salons of Georgian England, but reached its high point as a polite afternoon game for prosperous upper-class and bourgeois Victorians.

Like many other seemingly innocent games, 'Pope Joan' has an unsavoury purpose, according to Caroline Goodfellow, a historian at London's Museum of Childhood. 'To name a card game where you have to trick and deceive after Pope Joan was', she says, 'part of an unspoken anti-Catholic prejudice in Victorian times. It may have been dressed up as innocent fun – just a card game – but in fact expressed a dislike that ran deeper. You see the same thing with anti-Semitism, with money games called simply "Jew".'[14]

Pope Joan's attraction for romantic novelists has persisted throughout the twentieth century, though in keeping with the mores of the time, accounts have become laced with an eroticism that borders on the pornographic. And, as at other times in her long history, interest in Joan has come in unpredictable bursts. The 1930s was a particularly fruitful decade. So well known did she become that G. K. Chesterton – a devout Catholic convert who had none of the anti-clericalism or anti-Catholicism of her usual admirers – made her the key to unlocking a Father Brown mystery, *The Doom of the Darnaways*. However, his attitude was perhaps rather more dismissive, for the plot of this story hinged on the fact that a 'cultivated man' would know 'there was no such person as Pope Joan'.[15]

Richard Ince's *When Joan Was Pope* (1931) was the tamest of the decade's attempts to tackle the She-Pope, but claimed the most flamboyantly romantic source – a manuscript called *Disquisitio historica de Johanna, Papa Foemins docta Graecis Literis*, written by 'Nicephorus, monk, mystic of Monte Cassino' and discovered, Ince alleged, 'amongst mouldering piles of wallpaper and pots of hardened paint flung aside by the builders' in a remote Hebredian library.[16]

If he held back on the sex, Ince gave Pope Joan's life a new twist to appeal to the tastes of his audience. On her travels, she meets the god Pan who teaches her the joys of the 'old religion' which Ince then contrasted with the decadence of Rome that greets Joan on her arrival in the Eternal City. In the 1930s paganism was enjoying a revival, promoted by scholarly but much-discussed research into the origins and survival of witchcraft, and heralded by the sinister society figure, Aleister Crowley, who delighted in describing himself with the satanic epigram 'the beast 666.'[17] As if in homage to Crowley, though more correctly the Book of Revelation, Ince's account ended with Joan giving birth in the street to a baby boy who had the number 666 on both palms and was killed at once as a reincarnation of the anti-Christ.

Clement Wood's *The Woman Who Was Pope*, published in the same year at Ince's novel, also had devils and demons,[18] but it was Renée Dunan's *Pope Joan*, appearing first in France in 1930 and subsequently in English translation, that was the raciest.[19] It began with the young Joan turning up, in disguise, as a novice monk at Fulda Abbey. Her lustful gaze falls first on Brother Wolf, but when she is rejected, she seduces Brother Gontram:

> At the mere thought of Gontram her body would tingle as if bathed with liquid fire and in vain she besought God to deliver her from her sin. At length she subjugated her passionate, lustful body, and that body commanded her to yield to the demands of her womanhood. She wept and chastised herself severely for her sins. She passed whole nights in the chapel, lying outstretched in the form of a cross, repeating Latin prayers to the Creator. It was all in vain. When she arose, she resembled a Bacchante, and would fly to her cell all passionate impatience to fling herself into Gontram's arms.

While this may sound relatively tame by the standards of the 1990s, screen kisses were still being censored in Dunan's time. Dunan went on to have Joan caught locked in Gontram's embrace and sentenced to be burnt alive. She escapes and by a convoluted plot ends up on an Arab ship, where her use as a sexual plaything by the captain and his crew is candidly recorded. Disembarking in Africa, she joins a harem – again reported in detail – but works her way back to Rome, where she finds favour with Leo IV on account of her brains not her body. Cerebral matters cannot sustain her wayward soul, however, and she slips off by night to Naples where she works as a prostitute before and after her election as pope.

Dunan added a new soft-porn angle to the traditional anti-clerical-ism associated with telling Joan's story. Joan was part of the author's attack, from a liberated viewpoint, on Catholicism's strict code of behaviour on sexual morality. The ironic heart of the novel – heavily signposted – was in the hypocrisy of exposing a past pope not particularly as a cross-dresser but as a nymphomaniac.

Again the time of publication gives a clue. In the 1930s, the mainstream Protestant churches began the process of relaxing their anti-sex gospel in line with a slowly more emancipated society. The world-wide Anglican Communion, for example, decided at its 1930

Lambeth gathering to leave the question of artificial contraception up to each individual believer, having previously outlawed it as sinful. Catholicism's long, lonely and ongoing vigil against such practices was just beginning.

Most decades of the twentieth century have seen a new novel on Joan. In the 1940s it was surgeon George Borodin's *The Book of Joanna*,[20] set in 'the darkest corner of the ninety-ninth grotto of hell' and going into great anatomical contortions to rewrite the traditional ending. Joan collapses in the Vicus Papissa but her swelling is the result of a burst abdominal ulcer. In the 1980s, Claude Pasteur's *La Papesse*[21] returned to more traditional romantic territory with the tale of 'a mysterious pilgrim with a beautiful face who walks the roads of France' in the years between 840 and 855, rising ultimately to become Pope Benedict III. And in the 1990s, Donna Woolfolk Cross's *Pope Joan*[22] matched its literary pretensions – likening its central character to 'Dorothea in George Eliot's *Middlemarch*, Jane Austen's Emma and other heroines who struggle against restrictions their souls will not accept' – with a straight romantic plot, taken from the chronicles, that casts Joan as one of history's dreamers.

After the stage bonanza of 1793 in Paris, the She-Pope became largely the preserve of novelists. That trend is now changing. The late twentieth century's chief contribution to the Pope Joan industry has been the revival of her theatrical fortunes.

Precursor of the new wave was Bertolt Brecht. Just twenty-three and still some way off forging his reputation as one of the greatest dramatists of his age, Brecht toyed with the idea in 1921 of writing on the She-Pope. 'I've been to see the Matisses, I'm going to the Cezannes, I'm doing a play "Pope Joan" for Tilla, I'm working on three different film treatments,' he wrote to his friend and collaborator, the artist Rudolf Casper Neher.[23]

'Tilla' was the actress Tilla Durieux, one of the stars of her day, once a sitter for Renoir, though by 1921 her career had begun something of a slow decline as she entered middle age. Brecht was a great admirer and planned the play as a vehicle for her talents. Two months before his letter to Neher, however, he was already having problems with it. Joan, he records on 25 October, he saw as 'a strong, stocky, peasant girl who looks as if her face was made of earth and is good at facts, sums, power and cynicism'.[24] As an assessment of her character, based on Brecht's reading of the medieval chronicles, it is an interesting one, devoid of the romanticism of most of his contemporaries who examined her history.

The very next day, however, Brecht was frustrated by the lack of accompanying details as he revealed in an entry which suggests a common problem a Dark Ages character like Pope Joan presents to authors and dramatists:

> Now that I have established the plan of those incidents that took place in Rome in the year 860, as specified by my iron will, a certain childish curiosity, along with a desire to get my hooks on words, errors, matters of fact, led me to hunt up the available literature about Joan. There isn't any. Those country bumpkins and plagiarists who batten on the tolerance of grown-up elementary school-kids, those impotent source-mongers who are acquainted with everything and know nothing, who write political history five hundred times over from five different points of view without ever communicating a picture of the period that might let you see, for instance, what the Pope ate and drank, how he loved and was served, and how he felt about smoking ... And not one single account of the fashions, crafts, business transactions or the social situation of merchants, soldiers, priests. There were no novels to help out, and history with its umpteen fat volumes comes nowhere near supplying as much of the essence of public life as one gets from one solitary newspaper. Look where you will, you find nothing, nothing but ideological think-pieces and miserable attempts to insinuate a meaning into the whole external calendar of European public sensations ...[25]

The project was never completed. Only a handful of fragments remain. Romantic imaginings were perhaps the only way to make good the gap Brecht highlighted, but he made his reputation by developing a theatre that denied its audience the satisfaction of emotional involvement. His style was more brutal and distancing.

Half a century later Pope Joan returned after a long absence to the London stage when Caryl Churchill's play *Top Girls* was first performed at London's Royal Court Theatre in 1982 with Selina Cadell playing the She-Pope. Later that year the production transferred to Joe Papp's Public Theatre in New York.

The first of the three acts features the central character, Marlene, a modern working woman who struggles to survive and maintain her principles of equal opportunity in a man's world, dining with a group of mould-breaking women from history – Isabella Bird, a late-nineteenth-century Scottish traveller; Lady Nijo (born 1258), a courtesan at the Japanese imperial court who later became a wandering Buddhist nun; Dull Gret, the apron-and-armour-clad heroine of a Brueghel painting who charges through hell, fighting off devils; Patient Griselda, the obedient wife in 'The Clerk's Tale' in Chaucer's *Canterbury Tales*; and Pope Joan.

Churchill's Joan is a rather solemn, unforgiving, masculine creature of unspecified age, drinking a little too much and dwelling on the past with the benefit of hindsight. Asked what inspired her to seek an education as a young girl, she replies: 'Because angels are without matter, they are not individuals. Every angel is a species.' But, tucking in to canneloni and salad, she relaxes a little, mixing theological arguments with light-heartedly labelling herself a walking heresy. Her downfall, she relates to the other women, came because 'I forgot I was pretending'. When she was elected pope, she was carried away with the importance of the office – 'I would know God. I would know everything' – but soon she realised God knew that she was a fraud.

Like the other historical characters summoned up by Marlene in Churchill's play, Joan is shown to be a poor role model, a sad, disappointed woman who denies her gender and who ends up drunk, vomiting into a bucket.

By contrast, Christopher Moore's musical *Pope Joan* was an out-and-out celebration of the She-Pope. First performed by the Bailiwick Repertory Company in Chicago in March 1995, it was picked up by Michael Butler, the Broadway producer of such hits as *Hair*, who staged a larger-scale production in Chicago and who now has plans to transfer it to New York. Bailiwick's production won a clutch of Jeff Awards in 1995 – the city's version of an Oscar – including best director for David Zak.

Zak saw the appeal of the She-Pope as her contemporary parallels. 'I see her as the equivalent of a woman in business who finds her career blocked by the glass ceiling,' he says.[26] 'A thousand years after Pope Joan women are still not taken seriously for the top spots because of their sex, particularly in the Catholic church.'

The musical followed the Martin Polonus account, though like many of its predecessors it did weave in a love story – with Joan falling for King Louis of France, as hinted at in the much-amended Paris version of the *Book of Popes* that Joan Morris had discovered. Zak was convinced of the historical reality of Pope Joan, but admitted that the side of the musical which presented her as a social revolutionary – giving the Church's wealth to the poor – was imaginary: 'I see her as someone defeated by the forces of power and wealth in the Church. And I think that struck a chord in our audiences. We had everyone from feminists to nuns to representatives of the local Catholic archbishop. It was first produced during a pre-election period and I think this theme of challenging the establishment made a special impact.'

The musical score was a first in Pope Joan's long history in the theatre. 'The number that I believe will one day become famous', says Zak, 'is the closing song, a great ballad called "A Thousand Years From Now". The chorus is about progress one step at a time, one day at a time, and how Joan fits in to that evolution.'

There have been other celebratory theatrical versions of Pope Joan's life, including Bruce Stewart's 1978 *Pope Joan Lives* for the BBC, which made the She-Pope an icon for modern-day campaigners for women's ordination in the Catholic church. However, perhaps the best-known recent version of her life was Anglo-Canadian director Michael Anderson's 1972 film, *Pope Joan*, starring Ingmar Bergman's muse, the Norwegian actress Liv Ullman.

Based on Emmanuel Royidis's novel, augmented by screenwriter John Briley – later an Oscar-winner on *Gandhi* – it amended to themes of sex and violence that of a battle with powers of darkness. Joan is gang-raped by monks, witnesses pagan ceremonies and oversees a series of costumed blood-lettings. The most interesting aspect was the part played by Franco Nero as the Holy Roman emperor who had fathered Joan. The film suggests that his genetic legacy to Joan was to make her a natural leader.

The British and European version of Anderson's film made no use of a modern-day sub-plot, with a young woman who believes herself to be the reincarnation of Joan, but the extra material was included in the film's American release under a new title *The Devil's Impostor*. One reviewer noted that 'it could have been a gem of a subject if handled by a woman director'.[27]

Subsequent efforts to raise funding for another film version of Joan's story – including one in 1996 by a young Polish-born New York female producer and another by a German couple with impeccable art-house, independent cinema credentials – have so far failed,[28] though with the Meryl Streeps and Jessica Langes complaining of the dearth of strong female leads, the history of Pope Joan has a definite Hollywood appeal.

Pope Joan may have played many parts, but her most enduring role has been as one of the stars of the tarot trumps. Some hold that they date back to the ancient Egyptian Book of Wisdom, but more realistically the tarot trail has been followed back to Renaissance Italy and the Visconti-Sforza family.[29] In the fifteenth century they commissioned Bonifacio Bembo to design what remains the standard tarot pack. Influenced by a love of Greek and Roman legends and a passion for ancient pagan myths, the Visconti-Sforzas came up with a series of images that encompass much of heaven, earth, hell, this life and life thereafter. The images provided a framework for imagination and fantasy.

The *Penny Catechism* of my Catholic childhood contained stern warnings against tarot cards. No matter how often I passed the 'Gypsy Rose Lee, seer of the future' booth on New Brighton pier on family holidays, I could go no further than temptation because I knew that recourse to the crystal ball was a fast track to hell.

Though it marked a relaxation in some past prohibitions, the updated *Catechism of the Catholic Church*, published in 1994, gave not an inch on divination. Though horoscopes now rival the births, marriages and deaths as the staple of every newspaper and seers even get to sit in on board meetings of major companies where the chairman or chairwoman feels that new-age insight might help with decision making, Pope John Paul remains as steely in his condemnation as the municipal buildings in his native Krakow. 'All forms of divination are to be rejected ... Consulting horoscopes, astrology, palm reading, interpretation of omens and lots, the phenomena of clairvoyance, and recourse to mediums all conceal a desire for power over time, history, and, in the last analysis, other human beings, as well as a wish to conciliate hidden powers. They contradict the honour, respect and loving fear that we owe to God alone.'[30]

With such teaching resounding in my head, going to have my tarot cards read by 'Dillie' was a fretful business. She didn't show any outward sign of being bent on ruling the world, but, superstitious Catholic underneath any veneer of worldliness or reason, I was not so much on my guard as clad in armour. And as if I wasn't suspicious enough, the entrance to Dillie's 'consulting room' conformed to every stereotype of a brothel that I had ever seen in the cinema: a seedy shop in London's Covent Garden; incense and joss sticks just failing to take away the whiff of damp; a steep staircase, lined in badly fitting lavatory-green woodchip; a dingy landing ringed by cubicles.

Inside Dillie's booth the woodchip changed to purple but there was little else to make it homely. A cheap cloth covered a picnic table. She began shuffling her pack of tarot cards. I could hear murmurings and gasps from neighbouring booths.

The Popess card – traditionally a seated woman wearing the papal crown and clerical dress, reading a book – may have been inspired by Joan whose story was celebrated in the fifteenth century. But equally, tarot historians have argued, it may have come from one of the family's scions, Maifreda di Pirovano, a mystic nun at the end of the thirteenth century. Maifreda led a small Milanese sect called the Guglielmites who hoped for a female messiah in 1300. They were disappointed and soon died out, but the image remained a popular one in northern Italy and may indeed have contributed to and later been subsumed into the cult of Joan.[31] (Martin Polonus's account of Joan pre-dates the first records of the Guglielmites by forty or so years.)

The bare historical facts, though, seemed disappointingly insubstantial and Dillie had been recommended as someone who could tell me about the images conjured up in a tarot seer's imagination by the Popess card. Any such consultation, she told me, would have to come as part of a reading of my cards. Making a mental note to go to confession, I agreed, on condition that she didn't tell me anything terrible. She laughed with all the reassurance of Morticia Addams. Dillie had trained in psychology, she said, firmly crushing another of my stereotypes, but realised that she had a gift that was intuitive and not logical. 'I can picture images and feelings with the cards and then put them into words. I am a visionary.'[32] That hint of blasphemy just would not go away.

She started laying the cards in the shape of an 'H', with one leg missing. In the middle were the Queen and Four of Swords. I waited for Pope Joan to put in an appearance. Finally she surfaced, clinging like a limpet to the back of another trump.

For Dillie, the Popess was all about silence and trust, a sign that we could expect no pattern, or a clue if she turned up near the end of a reading that all that had gone before was bogus. Joan was like the joker – the odd one out in the pack, unpredictable, tongue-in-cheek, a keeper of secrets. She was one of the hardest cards to read.

This all had a fairly obvious basis in Joan's story but when Dillie turned to the Popess's darker side the link lost even the illusion of subtlety. I had been asked to reverse four cards at the beginning of the reading and place them back in the pack. If Joan comes out as one of these, Dillie said, it could mean that people were out of touch with themselves, often denying their sexuality. It could be a sign of homosexuality, Dillie thought, or even transvestism.

Sure by now that John Paul II had overestimated the power of tarot, I was already irritably putting on my coat when Dillie asked why I was so hostile. Rather than labour how unenlightening her account of the Pope Joan card had been, I gave her a brief résumé of my Catholic grounding. To my surprise, she told me that she was a convent girl and had once shared the scepticism and fear. But now she saw her two faiths as complementary. I begged to differ and departed.

Chapter Twelve

'Through the intricate metres of their slow advancement, God, through his daughters here, is taking aim.'
Thomas Blackburn '*Luna*' (1975)[1]

The prophets of science and religion have scarcely been on speaking terms since the seventeenth century when the Inquisition forced Galileo to recant his unholy views about the earth moving round the sun. But in recent years a thaw has begun with scientists beginning to study religious phenomena – miracle cures, mystical experiences, supernatural visitations – not from the age-old perspective of ridiculing them, but in an effort to understand the psychological make-up of faith. Academic posts have been created to bridge the gap between science and religion, and surveys showed that four out of ten scientists in the United States believe in God.[2]

This new rapprochement, it occured to me, might be of benefit at this late stage in my investigation in unravelling the riddle of Pope Joan. Psychological profiling offered an alternative avenue to my imagination and the insights of the conventional – *pace* Dillie – experts I had called in. Its strengths, compiling rounded portraits from often disjointed pieces of information, were well matched to the She-Pope's history. A psychological profiler could bring a new, more empirical, dimension. And forensic science is, after all, crucial to all good detectives' success rates. Footprints, blood-traces all give physical clues. Psychological profiling, described by some as 'the detective work of the future', provides the behavioural clues, highlights the tell-tale patterns. Despite reservations in some quarters it has become an important though controversial part of murder investigations in recent years. As police have struggled to get to grips with horrific and seemingly random killings, they have called on the help of psychologists to draw up profiles of the likely perpetrator based on the often few facts known about the crime.

And its remit is increasingly spreading out beyond crime. In the wake of the deaths of sixteen schoolchildren in Dunblane in 1996 at the hands of a crazed gunman, there was even talk among police representative organisations that those wishing to hold gun licences should be forced to undergo psychological profiling.

Could this be applied to historical figures too? Professor David Canter is one of the leading exponents of psychological profiling in Britain. I had seen his name mentioned in the papers as helping with several major police inquiries, so I contracted him at the Department of Psychology at the University of Liverpool. He was, he replied somewhat to my surprise, intrigued by what I told him of Pope Joan and agreed to help.

When we met, Professor Canter admitted that he had almost refused my request. Though he had been one of the first academics in this country to develop the concept of psychological profiling, it was being abused at present, with some high-profile practitioners becoming what he called 'sub-journalists' rather than objective scientists. In seeking headlines they ran the risk of jeopardising dispassionate analysis.

And Pope Joan was after all, he pointed out, no criminal. She may have misled the Vatican, but she could hardly be ranked alongside Myra Hindley or Charles Manson. But just as I and countless writers and travellers had been hooked and hauled in by her story, there was something in Joan's tale that David Canter had found challenging. 'Let's look at what we know about the conditions under which these frauds occur and see first of all whether the facts add up. From that we can draw out the story that the individual is telling themselves, the story they they are living and then build up from that.'[3] It was, he said, better suited to a form of thinking aloud than a rigid academic model.

I had already seen Joan in many lights – female pioneer, mould-breaker, interloper, hidden figure of history, victim of ambitious revisionists, anti-clerical symbol, weapon of the anti-Catholics. But as a fraudster? As David Canter showed, she fitted the pattern in more than one way. 'Firstly, she was a foreigner, always described as "Joan the English" from Germany. And from the beginning she was an outsider. The notion of having to succeed against the odds, of starting with a handicap, of going against the existing prejudices is classic. You are driven by showing that you can make it.' That recurring question as to what had impelled her to aspire so high had been niggling at the back of my mind since I met Father Boyle in the Vatican Library.

Professor Canter put Joan in the same category as contemporary fraudsters like the publishing tycoon Robert Maxwell, another foreigner (born in Czechoslovakia) who forced his way to the top by sleight of hand and disguising his origins. 'They feel that the system deserves to be got at, subverted. That may only be the starting perspective in that once they're caught up in it all they forget what was the rationale or justification for it all.' One strong motivation to continue with her deception, at least in the early stages, would surely have been seeing young women of her age, her childhood playmates, with three or four offspring before twenty, or worse still dead in childbirth.

The second detail that jumped out at Professor Canter from Martin Polonus's brief synopsis of Joan's life was the suggestion that she had a child, possibly by some sort of junior chamberlain. 'That makes an enormous amount of sense,' he said. 'If she had an affair with anybody in any position of authority, they could then weaken her authority. She wouldn't have had a bit on the side with an archbishop or cardinal, because it would have weakened her, whereas someone lowly posed no threat. You can see the risk, the excitement.'

But why take such a risk? Why would someone who had risen to the pinnacle of the Church against all the odds, whose whole life was based on a deception, risk it all on what may have been a fling? 'But that's precisely it,' said David Canter. 'Classic fraudsters enjoy risk-taking. And there comes a point when getting away with it, pulling the trick off, isn't enough. You want to show these people that you've got away with it.'

Joan, then, was a victim of her own success. She got carried away with it, disillusioned almost at how easy it had become, and possibly felt trapped in her disguise. She found release in running risks. 'The point with all these fraudsters', said Professor Canter, 'is that they typically start off with trying to see what they can get away with when they've been denied possibilities and access by other means. It begins in a very reversible way when there is not necessarily a lot to lose. What happens is that they enjoy fooling people, the risk, the excitement involved and then it gets out of control and they have to keep with it. There's a tendency to push it further and further.'

That label of fraudster was still worrying me. Joan had, the chronicles recount, grown up in Germany the child of God-fearing missionaries. She had travelled in disguise to get an education not because she wanted to subvert the whole Christian system. Her triumph – through her learning and erudition – had been achieved not through malice but because in this Dark Age period the leadership of Christendom was largely ignorant and morally bankrupt. She had shone, was popular and admired. Yes, she was tricking people, but there did not seem to be the malevolent calculation that the description con-man or woman seemed to imply.

'People do live with conflicting perspectives,' Professor Canter suggested. 'It's one of the discoveries of present-day psychology. Psychologists in the 1950s and 1960s put a lot of store by looking at the coherence and logic of thought processes and how we distort everything to make them fit together, but modern psychology is beginning to recognise that people can quite happily hold quite contradictory perspectives.'

So Joan could convince herself that she was doing the right thing at the same time as knowing it was wrong. In which case, why didn't she go on for ever?

> Those contradictory perspectives break down in a variety of ways. By being appointed pope, you'd probably believe that you were pretty close to God. One can imagine a thought process whereby someone would say 'well I've been cheating all this time, but now I've ended up as Pope. There must be something right about it, God must be on my side.' We don't know how far her thought processes had gone. She would have had to create an enormously self-convincing justification. You couldn't keep that thing going without believing that you were doing it for a reason, that there was some sort of logic to it. You would have overlaid all your interpretations with justifications of what was going on.

Driven, determined, messianic, even deluded towards the end, this was the picture of Joan's mind-set that emerged from Professor Canter's reading. All were at best neutral, at worst negative qualities. This Joan was not the attractive, romantic figure who has ensnared generations of writers.

Yet, as with every expert I had called in to help with my search for Joan, Professor Canter was beginning to appreciate the romance of her tale. Perhaps it was the bottle of wine we shared oiling our own thought processes and therefore making her seem more benign. More likely it was something intrinsic to the story itself.

> Perhaps it's the romantic in me. I would like to know how malicious she was. Whether in the end she thought she was doing something really worthwhile. That this was an opportunity to contribute. Look at Robert Maxwell – he supported the Labour Party and the state of Israel and clearly believed on one level that the power and authority that he had got through his own domineering intelligence was something that was to the benefit of others. There's a hint that Maxwell wasn't maliciously milking the system.

Some pensioners struggling to make ends meet after Maxwell walked off with their funds might disagree, of course.

So did Joan's story have the ring of truth? 'Yes it rings true psychologically.' Professor Canter's psychological imprimatur, when lined up alongside my own efforts to show that the historical details of her history were credible, and Rosalind Miles's sociological insights, completed in my mind the definitive Pope Joan jigsaw. But before I delivered a verdict there were some outstanding questions I needed to tie up.

On the first Wednesday of each month, a small group of women mount a vigil on the piazza outside Westminster Cathedral, John Bentley's ornate red-brick-and-marble Byzantine extravaganza that is the London headquarters of English Catholicism. They walk in a circle around a big candle with the word 'earth' imprinted on its side. Clutching bowls of oil, they anoint one another, before silently processing to the wall of the cathedral to which they cling for seven minutes. Then they sing hymns and finally disperse.

They are all members of the Catholic Women's Ordination movement, founded in the wake of the decision by the Church of England General Synod in 1992 to allow women priests and dedicated to spreading such enlightenment to Catholicism. Some of the members of CWO referred to it as 'Quo'.

Quo's purpose at the vigils is to draw attention to their own exclusion from the priesthood. They want to break bread as well as make it. As once Pope Joan did, these women feel called by their talents to a leadership role in the Church. They consider, as she did, that their gender is not a drawback but rather a gift to Catholicism.

The symbolism of their monthly ritual is carefully defined. Each protester wears the colour purple as a sign of her own priesthood. Silence is maintained as an act of mourning for the lost gift of women. They assemble in a democratic circle rather than a hierarchical triangle. Their seven minutes of clinging recall the seven sacraments of the Church.

Deeply into symbolism, Quo would, I suspected, appreciate the symbolism of a female pope. It is certainly true that the stories of the women of the early Church – Hilda, Theodora "episcopa", Pelagia – are as well known in these circles as they are overlooked elsewhere. They are the backdrop to Quo's campaign to restore the early Church's openness to women's gifts. And Joan Morris's executor, Ivan May, had told me that her privately published pamphlet on Pope Joan was still in demand with Catholic feminists in the States.

So what did Quo make of Pope Joan? Another name to add to the lengthening list of female pioneers who have been officially lost, an embarrassment to the cause because of her treachery, or an irrelevance?

Strangely, the She-Pope had not yet been scrutinised by Quo but her story did intrigue them. Come and tell us more, they asked. If in the next century there is a heritage body with a brief to erect blue plaques outside houses that have been centres of pre-millennial radical talk, then one property just south of the River Thames, facing out on to London's Southwark Cathedral, has a stronger claim than most in the 'church' section. Home to architect Austin Winkley, his wife Lala, a founding member of Quo, and their two daughters, these four walls have hosted many a meeting of disaffected and reform-minded British and European Christians over the past twenty years. It was here one cold November evening that Quo members gathered to assess the significance for their struggle of Pope Joan.

Seated round the dining-table next to a blazing fire were the leading lights of Quo. They included the nun, former convent school headteacher and now theology student Myra, Ianthe, stalwart of the women's movement, psychotherapist Sue, Lalla and her daughter Emma plus an old friend, Dorothea McEwan of the Warburg Institute.

All confessed to knowing bits of the Pope Joan story, mainly from the film, but only Dorothea, alerted by our previous encounter, had any detailed knowledge. I outlined the basic plot, added a few of the flourishes cooked up by my investigation and left this talkative group to make of it what they would.

Myra was the most enthusiastic. The symbolic value of a woman 'getting one over on the men' amused her. Seemingly battle-scarred from her own dealings with all-male ecclesiastical authorities, she warmed at once to Joan's courage in finding a way round a seemingly immovable object. Even if it were an elaborate myth embroidered on a much simpler but true story, Myra felt the legend of the She-Pope in all its aspects had an enduring importance and a contemporary significance to Quo.

Dorothea was having none of it. She insisted that you could make too much of stories. The fact that Joan's had lasted so long did not give it a special importance. But, protested Myra, if the story was made up of various parts, how did we know which were real and which false?

'Perhaps she made the men so mad because she got away with being pope that they thought afterwards we'll clobber her, we'll discredit her by making up a story about a baby. Then it sends out a message to all women that however high they aim, they will always get found out.' This idea of a woman being brought down because of something that is unique to her sex found a ready echo round the table. As Myra said, the Church had always insisted that women were the weaker sex, and while most of Joan's story might be seen as turning that proposition over, it had a sting in the tail – proof that women were unsuitable leaders. If it had been tacked on to a real story to turn it at the same time into a warning and a fable, then it had been a masterstroke.

In this vein Myra was intrigued by the timing of the first mentions of Joan in early medieval chronicles. 'This was precisely the time when the male and female battle was taking place,' she pointed out. 'Look at Hildegard of Bingen' – the twelfth-century nun and mystic who battled with the ecclesiastical authorities to use her considerable gifts – 'she wanted to preach and they stopped her. It confirms what we know already – that women in medieval times, whatever obstacles were put in their way, had great spirit. Joan broke a bad system.' Yet the system survived for another millennium. Now it was Quo that was trying to break it again. Did they find Joan an inspiration?

Far from seeing the idea that the She-Pope had a child as a clerical diversion added to the story to send out a warning signal, Sue was inspired by it. 'I like the idea of a pope giving birth,' she said. 'It shows men and women in balance even if they are archetypes. Giving birth to a child breaks the masculine side.' Ianthe was of like mind. Perhaps, she wondered aloud, the distortion of the Pope Joan story to include a baby was an early case of womb envy.

Dorothea remained unmoved. 'This story was a joke – and part of the joke was at women's expense. You take the highest political office at the time – emperor or in this case pope – and you give it to a woman as a huge political joke.'

'I'm not convinced by this idea of it as a joke,' confessed Myra. 'Why use it? The joke after all was at the expense of the men who were tricked by Joan.'

As Emma pointed out: 'There's a world of difference between wanting to get an education and wanting to be pope.' But, her mother reflected, 'was her whole story a deliberate act to be pope – or did it just happen? Perhaps it just all got out of control.'

The jury couldn't reach a decision. The symbolic value of Joan's example in beating a bad system had to be weighed against doubts about which parts of her story were true and her real motives in adopting a disguise. Was she a forerunner or a freak aberration? As dinner drew to a close Quo was intrigued, but some way off adopting Pope Joan as its patron saint.

Early on in my investigation, in a rush of the organisational activity that can be a comforting substitute for tackling the big and intractable problems – like whether Joan's story was true – I had started a file on women's ordination. The link with Joan was not direct – especially after my meeting with Quo – but the experience of contemporary women in trying to break down the doors of the all-male Catholic club of celibate clerics might, I reasoned, provide insights into the She-Pope's state of mind, frustrations and motivations.

The *International Herald Tribune*'s headline 'First Women To Be Openly Ordained as Catholic Priests' had been one of those that caught my eye, but the story was not quite what it seemed.[4] In Germany there has been more than one Catholic church for over a century. Unofficially that could be true of many other countries where papal pronouncements often fall on deaf ears among local church-goers but in Germany the division is out in the open and publicly acknowledged. In 1870 a group of Catholics (including the celebrated anti-Joanite, Dollinger) broke with Rome after the First Vatican Council's declaration of papal infallibility. This distinctly Catholic doctrine is of course of relatively recent vintage, though it is often presented as if it were as old as the hills. It falls under the banner of tradition and practice rather than God-given teaching.

In 1878 this splinter church abolished priestly celibacy and latterly its 230,000 members have enjoyed a close relationship with the world-wide Anglican communion. In June 1996 it ordained its first women priests. Both were once mass-going Catholics but had grown disillusioned with Rome. 'Is it not truly painful', asked Bishop Joachim Vobbe, head of the Old Catholic church in Germany, 'that the Church has taken almost 2000 years finally to come to the conclusion that women should be brought into the highest service of the Church, just like men? Does this not show a basic error of the Church, a frightening lack of dynamism?'[5] Whether he meant his own tiddler of a Church or the one-billion-strong 'proper' Catholic church was – perhaps deliberately – unclear.

If it was the latter, then he would have found support in the United

States. A 1995 *New York Times* poll showed 61 per cent of the faithful wanted women priests.[6] And I found another ally for Bishop Vobbe in Congo in Africa. Bishop Ernest Komo of the Catholic diocese of Owando shocked his fellow Catholic bishops, gathered in Rome for the Synod on the Consecrated Life, with his suggestion that women be made lay cardinals and given leading positions in the Church. Their potential to be 'incandescent light illuminating the world' was being held back by rules and regulations, Bishop Komo told delegates.[7]

But the most intriguing item in my file was the story of sixty-six-year-old religious education teacher Ludmilla Javorova, believed to be the first woman in modern times to have been ordained a Catholic priest by a bishop who was in full communion with Rome. As I read her story – and particularly the way she had disguised her priesthood from the communist authorities in her native Czechoslovakia and risen to a central and powerful position as a quasi-bishop – I realised that here potentially was a latter-day Pope Joan. *The Devil's Impostor* had attempted to give a contemporary edge on film to the Pope Joan story. Ludmilla Javorova offered me the same opportunity. I had to meet her.

I arrived in the Czech Republic on Students' Day, 17 November, a time when memories of the tumultuous period of 1989 leading up to the Velvet Revolution are particularly vivid. This was the day when protesting students gathered in Wenceslas Square in central Prague had refused to disperse on the orders of the communist authorities. Such defiance, their resilience to the bullying of threats, sticks and bullets, precipitated the downfall of Moscow's client state.

Tucked in a corner between the new border created by the Czechs' recent divorce from the Slovaks and, on the other side, the long-standing frontier with Austria, Brno is the industrial heartland of the Czech Republic. It was as depressing as only an industrial town can be. Acres of concrete, graffiti, desolation, poverty and deprivation choked its citizens as effectively as the cloud of smog that hung over the roof-tops.

My interpreter and guide, sensibly clad in fur and boots, finally managed to locate block 23, an unlikely and anonymous home to the woman who claims to be the world's first female Catholic priest – or certainly the first in modern times.

Ludmilla Javorova peered out nervously from behind the heavy front door. I managed to explain who I was and remind her that we had an appointment. Her small, thin, pinched face, with hair pulled back severely into an insubstantial bun, was reminiscent of one of the more tragic figures in Maggie Smith's repertoire. After some initial reluctance she guided us into her two-roomed flat. We couldn't stay long, she said, looking nervously away as if she was hiding someone in the next room.

Once I had explained the complications of my journey there she apologised for her cool welcome, but told me that she had had a terrible time with journalists. Since she had given an interview a couple of years ago to an Austrian Catholic paper, *Kirche Intern*,[8] the press had chased her as assiduously as any royal princess. Publicity was the last thing she wanted, she stressed. 'It will damage the Church, me and the memory of Bishop Davidek.'[9] She bobbed her head down in reverence in the direction of a black-and-white picture of a fierce-looking cleric with sunken cheeks and cold eyes that was propped up on the bookshelves. 'I only agreed to see you,' she went on, anticipating my next question, 'because you are writing a book.'

She gestured to a divan where I perched with the interpreter. As I began to question her about her extraordinary life it was immediately clear she was having second thoughts and the distinction between journalists from newspapers and journalists who write books had blurred. She kept glancing around her as if we were about to be interrupted at any minute. She sat in a 1950s-style armchair by the window that covered one wall of the flat.

Dressed in a yellow sleeveless blouse and a thick, straight, browny-purple skirt, she wore a simple religious medal round her neck. Her face alternated between the passivity of a nun and the animation of a politician on a street husting. When the latter became more dominant, I started to notice little touches – earrings, a splash of red dye in her greying hair, bright-red carpet slippers. Unlike Pope Joan she made no attempt to disguise her femininity.

Given her sensitivity, the direct approach was ill-judged. It was only going to make her more defensive. So we sipped tea and talked about the weather, her job as a teacher, the situation in the Czech Republic, my interpreter's family. Did Ludmilla have a family? No. 'The Church is my family.' The local parish? 'No. The underground Church. We remain close. Most do not talk about their experiences with outsiders.' She conjured up the illusion of a core-group, united in the changing times that they were now experiencing. Yet it somehow didn't ring true, for she had the air of a woman who was utterly alone save for her memories and her icon to the dead bishop.

For thirty years before the revolution of 1989 Ludmilla was one of thousands of Catholics who defied the Czechoslovak communist government by clandestinely spreading the gospel, propagating the faith and administering the sacraments. The authorities followed the Marxist Stalinist line of 'scientific atheism'. While they allowed churches to remain open, believers were persecuted and the actions of clerics closely supervised by the STB or secret police. It was a rigidly controlled and narrow public existence for the Church. The government instituted what was in effect a modern equivalent of Henry VIII's dissolution of the monasteries, banning religious orders, seizing Church property, jailing and frequently murdering the clergy, allowing first two and then only one seminary to operate under communist supervision and controlling the issue of priests' 'licences' to operate.

The Vatican's approach to this onslaught was twin-track – ostensibly encouraging greater understanding between the regime and the official Church, turning the other cheek in the face of provocation to ensure that there was still mass and communion on a Sunday if no other Church life. But at the same time Rome was reinforcing a resistance movement. Brno was the main base for this 'silent Church'.

Part of the Vatican's contribution was to grant special rights to priests so that they could secretly ordain other priests. They were called 'Mexican faculties' because their precedent was similar special rights granted during the anti-clerical revolution there earlier in the century. Likewise, bishops could consecrate bishops without the usual recourse to Rome, thereby circumventing the block the authorities had placed on all Church appointments without their approval.

Felix Davidek was a central figure in this covert Church. A curate in Ludmilla's home village near Brno, he was imprisoned between 1948 and 1962 for his beliefs. The Prague Spring of 1968 briefly raised his hopes of greater toleration, but its brutal crushing by Soviet forces forced him to think of alternative and radical ways to ensure the future of the Church as it faced renewed persecution. 'It was an extraordinary time,' Ludmilla recalled, a resistance fighter reflecting on her wartime service. 'You have to understand that.' She looked at me in my comfortable western clothes with my cosy, sympathetic look of concern. 'You cannot understand. For us it was a question of survival. We feared the Church would not survive.'

In 1970, Bishop Davidek – he had been secretly consecrated by Bishop Jan Blaha in 1968 – preached a radical gospel at a secret meeting of the underground Church. His ideas split the gathering. He wanted to ordain those the authorities were least likely to suspect of being priests – married men, and women. The logic was compelling. The communists may have despised the Catholic church but they took it at face value when it said ordination was only for celibate males. For Davidek tradition could be sacrificed for survival.

His proposals created divisions within the underground Church that persist to this day. While most of its members have now come into the open and joined forces with those who had struggled on publicly in the face of communist threats, the married men that Davidek ordained remain a sect apart, locked in a battle with Rome which refuses to legitimise their ministry. Its suggestion is that they join the Uniate church, an eastern branch of Catholicism which allows a married priesthood. They respond that they were willing to give up their lives for Catholicism. While they didn't expect medals and papal knighthoods, being palmed off into another Church seems like a poor reward.

At least they have a choice. For the women – and Ludmilla confirmed that there are others in Slovakia with whom she talks and corresponds, though she would not name them or give an estimate of numbers – the Vatican has simply denied that they were ever priests. There is a hierarchy of truths and traditions at play. The Vatican seems prepared grudgingly to allow the breaking of celibacy by shuffling the married priests into an affiliated sister Church, but under no circumstances will it permit celibate women to be regarded as priests. Bishop Davidek simply did not have the power to break this taboo, Rome contends, whatever the extenuating circumstances.

He died in 1988 and is unable to answer back. The married priests have been fighting their corner publicly, but of the women only Ludmilla has raised her head above the parapet. Hers has become a one-woman crusade to make the Vatican act justly. She was both cowed and angered by the Vatican, half inclined to fight and shout and stamp her feet in rage, but simultaneously retreating within herself, unwilling to entrust what she believes to the judgement of men in Rome who cannot understand what the underground Church has been through. 'We learned to trust no one. If they betrayed us, we faced prison, death. We lead double lives. In the day I would teach and then at nights we would have our meetings. I would have to stay up all night to prepare my school work for the next day in case anyone was suspicious. No one knew details about the other priests except Bishop Davidek.'

Ludmilla's primary role was to visit women prisoners – including nuns. The authorities denied them access to priests and hence the sacraments, but because Ludmilla was a woman they did not suspect and let her come and go freely. So successful was her disguise, that she began to act as go-between with the underground priests and Bishop Davidek. If the bishop held all the information about his network of priests in his head, she knew almost as much. She had the power of life or death over many men.

Her role has been likened by former colleagues to that of a Vicar-General to Bishop Davidek, an assistant bishop, but she firmly resisted such a description. 'I helped Bishop Davidek. I was his assistant.' She described her duties as akin to a secretary. Others – like Father Julius Eyma, by day a tram driver and by night Bishop Davidek's chauffeur on clandestine missions – have described her as his closest associate.[10] And there was undoubtedly a terrible sense of loss in her voice whenever she mentioned him – loss of his charismatic guidance, his courage, his willingness to go it alone. He would have made the current situation right, she seemed to think. He could have made the Pope understand. In his absence, she was taking his place.

She kept coming back to the extraordinary circumstances of the time and I wondered if, however terrifying they were, she felt lost in the open society of the Czech Republic. She resisted such a description. 'Things are different now, but still we have to keep our secrets. The people who persecuted us, they are still here now.' She gestured out towards the desolate strip of grass outside her window.

Did she still consider that she was a priest? 'The Vatican says I am not.' But what does she think? 'The Vatican says I am not, that the times were extraordinary.' She would not be drawn. Friends in the underground Church, however, say that she still says mass privately. Is it that the Vatican does not consider Bishop Davidek to be a proper bishop? She was outraged at such a slander but her desire to protect his reputation helps to explain her uneasy combination of revelation and secrecy. Some now say he was a madman. Others that he was not properly ordained as a bishop, though Bishop Blaha's credentials cannot be faulted as even the Vatican has acknowledged.

At the Synod of 1970 he made his supporters swear never to reveal that women priests had been discussed. Furthermore, Davidek had created an atmosphere of paranoia in the underground Church. He believed that the Vatican had been infiltrated by KGB agents and that Cardinal Casaroli, pioneer of Rome's policy of *Ostpolitik* towards the regimes of the eastern bloc, was a Soviet plant. Such attitudes would have infected Ludmilla as his closest associate and may now have been making it hard for her to distinguish between real, imaginary and past dangers.

Surely now, I probed, there was no need to be frightened? 'I still cannot trust people,' Ludmilla said, looking away. 'I cannot trust you. There are still bad people out there.' She was retreating into her shell. Even some of the men who worked most closely with Javorova and Davidek have noted this fear in her. 'It's very hard for her,' said one. 'She's accepted neither as a priest nor as a woman.'[11]

In the interview with *Kirche Intern* that had so upset her she was reported as saying of her former colleagues: 'Outwardly they recognise me because they know I have been ordained, but they cannot come to terms with this fact inwardly. You cannot change a 2000-year tradition of male priests overnight.'[12] But today she denied saying such a thing. 'We are all still close,' she reaffirmed.

The earlier quotation seemed to fit with all she had told me. Her denial only emphasised her own confusion, while her isolation was almost too painful to watch.

Did she know the figure of Pope Joan, I wondered, changing tack? She looked puzzled. 'You cannot have a woman pope.' I was tempted to say you cannot have a woman priest, but in stilted conversation via a translator such asides can cause problems. And Ludmilla was still visibly twitchy. I outlined the She-Pope's history. 'That is a part of history I have not read,' she said and looked down nervously at the tape recorder. I felt like an interrogator. It was as if she thought I was trying to trap her. I promised to send her more information when I got back to England.

The parallels between the two women were clear; both had broken the rules of the all-male club; both had been hidden women in clerical ranks; both had been shunned and disowned once they were revealed for all the world to see; both had used a calculated element of disguise – Joan of her sex, Ludmilla of her priesthood; both started with modest roles and grew in importance when their sleight of hand gave them a chance to show their true potential; both will occupy a dubious position in the history of the Church – Joan already written out and Ludmilla in the process of being overlooked.

She was getting agitated. She had to visit a friend in hospital, she said. We would have to go. She gave me a book about Bishop Davidek in Czech. It would tell me all I needed to know about him. 'And about you too?' I asked.

'I helped with the book but it is about Bishop Davidek. I'm not important.'[13]

Once she had shut the door behind us there was a rattling of chains and keys. I sat outside in the car listening back to a recording of the interview for twenty minutes, making notes. She did not appear.

Some of those who know of her case hope that Ludmilla will be the means of showing that women make good priests. They point out that it was the case of another woman, ordained by an independent-minded bishop in a time of trial, that had brought the world-wide Anglican communion round to women priests. Florence Tim Oi Li was ordained in war-torn Hong Kong in 1944 by Bishop Ronald Hall who was unable to communicate with Canterbury to get approval for his pioneering move. His move was immediately repudiated once peace broke out.

Yet in the decades that followed, the Revd Tim Oi Li was a persuasive, likeable and always humble advocate of women's ordination on the world stage. She reverted to the traditional submissiveness of Chinese women, telling Bishop Hall in a letter that she was a 'mere worm' in relation to him. Yet she never resigned her orders and determined that her claim to the priesthood would stand or fall by her acts not her words. Her courage – especially as a Christian missionary in communist China – and the quiet dignity with which she defended her position eventually changed minds.[14]

Conclusion

'There's a world of difference between laughing at religion and laughing at those who profane it by their extravagant opinions.'

Pascal, *Lettres provinciales* (1656)

Did she, or didn't she? Could a German woman of English parentage pull off one of the greatest deceptions of all time and rise, disguised as a man, to the pinnacle of the Catholic church in the ninth century? If so, did the Catholic church then achieve a remarkable triumph by putting this embarrassing skeleton back in the cupboard in the post-Reformation period? Or is Pope Joan an empty and malicious legend promoted by generation after generation of anti-Catholics and anti-clerics? Perhaps, though, the truth is less clear-cut. Could Pope Joan be a significant myth or an allegory for some other historical happening? Or a bit of both?

There are three major obstacles to endorsing Pope Joan as an historical reality. The first and least important concerns the extraordinary nature of her demise. The story as told by the chroniclers has, I had felt from the start of my investigation, the instinctive feel of pure invention, the ninth-century equivalent of a 1980s urban myth.

There can be no doubt that even the most august clerics down the ages have suffered from what the Catholic church to this day likes to call 'broken celibacy', so the idea of a pope having a lover need not detain us. And while her giving birth in the street gives her story an air of freakishness, otherwise intelligent women have, particularly as they approach their menopause, mistaken pregnancy for the onset of the change of life and turned up at hospital with stomach pains to be delivered of a baby hours later. (And vice versa in the case of Mary Tudor and the series of tragic delusional pregnancies of her later years.)

Professor David Canter had fitted such total denial into the pattern of Joan's 'outsider' mentality, but Dr Rosalind Miles was for me a particularly effective witness in challenging this crucial part of the prosecution case. 'Joan's story – or at least the ending – could well be a fiction by men, proving the point that for every culture there is a counter-culture. The stronger the culture, the stronger the counter-culture. And in as much as the Church loves and needs the pope, it must also hate and resent the pope because that is the way it works. A strong papacy is bound to throw up a strong counter-culture – in this case Joan.'[1] The very power of the papacy, then, encourages characters like Joan to rebel, but the enduring strength of the institution means that such rebellions get 'normalised' in the end. Joan is, from the institution's point of view, satisfyingly punished, while the men take back their lost control.

If every culture produces an equally strong counter-culture, then the facts of Joan's success could have made those most indicted and threatened by it invent a tale of her fall to negate all that had gone before. A flesh-and-blood example to inspire and liberate women could with a deft turn of the hand be transformed into one that subjugated them and made them prisoners of their bodies and biology. Joan's deception may well have been discovered, and she may have been sent off to a nunnery or even imprisoned, but by making her with child and then depicting her giving birth in the street, she was twisted to fit into the pattern of admonitory literature used to keep its mainly women readers from overreaching themselves.

If the anti-feminist ending was added to a pro-feminist life story, it was a stroke of genius. Catholicism, despite all its traditionalism and exclusion of women from public positions of authority, is after all a women's religion. The nineteenth-century historian W. E. H. Lecky wrote: 'It can hardly, I think, be questioned that in the great religious convulsions of the sixteenth century the feminine type followed Catholicism while Protestantism inclined more to the masculine type.'[2] By balancing out Joan's example, the authors gave women within the Church the chance secretly to rejoice in her initial success, but also the comfort that the *status quo* was restored and justified by her demise. They were not, after all, missing out on anything.

The second and more significant obstacle to belief in the She-Pope concerns the theories of such distinguished historians as Edward Gibbon that mention of an imaginary Pope Joan as some sort of code for damning other disreputable but real popes. The notorious mother and daughter, Theodora and Marozia Theophylact, and their attempts in the tenth century to turn the papacy into a family sinecure, are often mentioned in this context. Yet the accounts of their misdeeds and lustful appetites were seldom suppressed and certainly not at the time when the story of Pope Joan was most widespread. This explanation, and other variations on the same theme concerning effeminate pontiffs and eunuch patriarchs, does not make any sense.

The third and most serious objection raised by those who would deny Joan a life is the gap of 400 years between her pontificate and Martin Polonus's landmark account. Less sophisticated sceptics say that this silence arose because Joan was not spoken of until her story was made up by Protestants after the Reformation and then inserted into pre-Reformation texts by skilled forgers. Such talk of a conspiracy is nonsense as my trip to the Bodleian Library in Oxford had confirmed. Undoctored accounts of her exist from pre-Reformation days.

Joan Morris, the scholarly Catholic feminist whose own incomplete research was privately published in 1985, offered a glimmer of light on the hiatus between Joan's pontificate and Martin Polonus's account with her work on the Paris version of the *Book of Popes*. Ultimately, though, she could do no more than suggest a possible halving of the period of silence. Definitive proof eluded her.

Despite many hours spent in libraries with catalogues and ancient manuscripts following up the clues Morris had left in her papers, I could not make any further progress in turning back the clock. The gap, I am forced to conclude, has to be seen in the context of a strong oral tradition, of visiting preachers, of widespread illiteracy, of very few books and of the unsavoury activities of the librarian Anastasius who was perfectly capable of deleting all mention of Joan, should it suit him for the purposes of his own advancement. The loss of Martin Polonus's source leaves an unfathomable mystery, but his reputation would suggest that he was not the sort of Church writer simply to make something up. He would have had a source, but as with Frederick Spanheim, in his exhaustive seventeenth-century catalogue of mentions of Joan, too many original documents have been lost. The destruction of the library at Fulda where, I discovered on my visit, not a single ancient manuscript now resides, brought home this point.

With these persuasive but inconclusive arguments, failure to bridge the gap between 855 and the latter half of the thirteenth century cannot deliver the prosecution victory. Many of history's most crucial and most accepted events are known of only because of much later writings – the gospels immediately spring to mind. And that 400-year gap is just one part in the puzzle.

It is worth recalling in this context that evidence of many of the officially recognised popes of the Dark Ages on the Church's roll of honour is at best fragmentary and certainly not contemporary. In the case of Pope Lando at the start of the tenth century, for instance, only one fragment of proof survives that he even existed – a record of a benefaction to the cathedral in Siena. Pope John VI at the start of the eighth is a completely unknown quantity. Taken on the merits of the evidence, both deserve to be consigned to limbo. But they are men and so survive. Joan represents more of a challenge to the authorised version of Church history.

Set against what had increasingly over the course of my investigation been exposed as a weak prosecution case are many positive reasons for believing that the She-Pope was more than a made-up story. The evidence of some 500 medieval writers cannot but impress. Senior papal servants, writing in books dedicated to their masters, endorse Joan unambiguously. Academics and inquisitors accept her as fact. Such widespread belief, filtering up to the pinnacle of power in the Catholic church, cannot lightly be dismissed as a Protestant plot, a fable, or a cipher for some other story of papal skullduggery. Why, for example, did Sienese pope after Sienese pope allow Joan's statue to stand in their home cathedral? The logical answer is that they regarded her, however grudgingly, as a predecessor.

These substantial testaments to Joan's life are, of course, circumstantial. They do not prove her existence, only that of her cult. Yet, at the very least, a story can exist because people go on believing it. It endures because people want to listen to it time and again. And it transmutes according to their tastes and needs. In that sense Pope Joan is again undeniably true. She was believed in, and people remain fascinated by her and attracted to her, be they directors, artists, playwrights or novelists. One anonymous sender of floral tributes in Rome would still appear to have faith in her to this day. (Despite my efforts, I never did discover his or her identity, though in the course of my investigation I had my suspicions about correspondents from Europe, the States and Canada, all of them Pope Joan devotees of admirably sane but slightly quirky credentials.)

Despite all attempts to kill her off, Pope Joan keeps cropping up in our own times. People believe in her and go on believing in her because they want her to have happened. They like the inversion at the heart of her story. It's like the boy bishops and the Lord of Misrule of the Elizabethan period, where the most unlikely person becomes king or bishop for the day.

Yet this appeal can distract from the fact that Pope Joan is much more than a wonderful story. She was taken as read not only by chroniclers but by generation after generation from the thirteenth century to at least the seventeenth. The Vicus Papissa, 'the street of the woman pope' where Joan gave birth and met her end, exists with its shrine, although her statue has been lost. The street was avoided because of Joan by papal processions as the Master of Ceremonies, Bishop Burchard, testified in the fifteenth century. Likewise the strange chair for checking the pope's manhood exists and, travellers record, was used. The bust of Joan in Siena existed. And a playful illustration of her labour remains in Saint Peter's at the foot on the *baldacchino* over the main altar to this day.

And there are more immediate historical reasons for suggesting that Joan be restored to her rightful place among the popes. The details told by the chroniclers fit neatly with the middle of the ninth century. There was, for instance, a celebrated colony of English missionaries in Germany then – hence the name 'Joan the English', though she was born in Mainz. And it is undeniably true that Greek-educated figures, as Joan was alleged to be, were prominent and revered in Rome at this time. Some, indeed, went on to be elected to the throne of Saint Peter thanks to the system which then prevailed – an unpredictable popular vote which favoured the deacons collected around the dead pope, and which occasionally threw up a saintly and scholarly outsider.

All these essential details may have been mangled and exaggerated as the history of Joan was passed across medieval dining-rooms and library desks down the ages but, once ironed out and reassembled, make perfect sense in the context of their time. Nothing is out of place.

Moreover, when I had moved beyond verifying the details told in the chronicles, I had discovered that the all-male atmosphere of the Church in the ninth century was of very recent vintage. Women like Cuthburga of Wimborne and Hilda of Whitby had ruled over double monasteries of men and women with quasi-episcopal powers. Some scholars, like the American historian Vern Bullough, hold that the official Church was at pains to promote stories of cross-dressing women saints as role models for clever young girls like Joan. Even if you are cursed with a woman's body, the subliminal message went, for curse it was certainly regarded by the all-male hierarchy, if you take on every masculine attribute, you may just gain admittance to the inner sanctum as an honorary man.

Turning to the basic mechanics of Joan's disguise, I had established a convincing case that her physical sleight of hand was possible. The ninth century was a time when priests were told to shave off their beards. With her fair chin and upper lip, Joan would in previous centuries have been damned. In the ninth she could have thrived.

Moreover, history shows that women have successfully passed themselves off as men to achieve positions of great power. Their bodies, especially in a frugal time like the Dark Ages, have been relatively easy to transform.

The mental leap of imagining herself a man and one entitled to run the Church had caused me to pause. Jan Morris demonstrated that Joan could have made mental sense out of such a change of gender even in her own Dark Age world, but it was Professor David Canter, pioneer of psychological profiling in Britain, who convinced me on her state of mind. Psychology, his distinctly late-twentieth-century discipline, enabled me to move beyond all others who over the centuries had considered the claims of Joan. The professor lent his professional good name to the case for the defence. Stripped of the embellishments of over-eager admirers and exploiters, Pope Joan, he believed, adds up to a real person with recognisable and consistent traits, a character, moreover, with antecedents and descendants down to our own times.

Weighing all this evidence, I am convinced that Pope Joan was an historical figure, though perhaps not all the details about her that have been passed on down the centuries are true.

For a century, since the work of the German anti-Joanite Professor Dollinger, those historians, scholars and believers who have stumbled across Pope Joan in ancient manuscripts or dusty corners of the Vatican Museum have dismissed her as a colourful legend. Talk of her has been deemed anti-Church. Writers who in other circumstances expend considerable energy investigating anything from the Turin Shroud to bleeding statues are content to toe the official line. Yet looking back into this episode in the history of the Church, however troubled and inglorious, is not anti-Church *per se*. In my own case knowledge has not put any distance between me, my church and my faith. Quite the opposite, whatever the omens of all those hearses. If I had relied on the official explanations I would long ago have given up on the Church in frustration.

With such an uncomfortable slice of history as Joan – comprising equal measures of fact, distorted fact and the subsequent embroidery of well-natured but unsatisfactory fiction – chronology cannot be all. A dancer to different tunes down the ages, Joan has fitted the mood of many periods, be they anti-clerical, anti-Catholic, feminist, romantic or erotic. She has even, I was told by one who should know, become something of an icon for religiously minded transvestites.

I accept, of course, that some who have reached this stage of the investigation may pull up short of my qualified conclusion. I would ask them at least to admire Pope Joan's extraordinary tenacity down the centuries. Her story has survived all attempts to bury it because it has proved greater and longer lasting than any of the ways in which it has been communicated, the causes to which it has been annexed, or the groups who have chanced upon it. That has been its ultimate danger, and one specially relevant at a time when Catholic women, like Ludmilla Javorova, are determined to have their claims to the priesthood recognised.

Having accepted that Pope Joan is based in part on fact and a real person, the final question is where to draw the line between taking on every detail and discounting most. A starting point at this lower end of the scale is the prophetess of Moguntia – another name for Mainz – who succeeded, according to a sixteenth-century edition of the chronicle of Sigebert, in persuading her archbishop to ordain her to the priesthood. That story may have been overblown and fictionalised into Joan.

My own inclination, having lived and breathed Joan for six months, is to go for a medium point – that she achieved the papacy at a time when the office was hopelessly debased and corrupt, was moderately successful but that her triumph was short-lived. She was uncovered, not in dramatic fashion in the Vicus Papissa, but when her 'outsider' mentality, as outlined by Professor Canter, made her careless. The drawbacks of her secret achievement may even have outweighed the benefits and she could have voluntarily given herself up to life in a convent, a vow of silence and the rewriting of history to exclude her.

Such a scenario is speculation, based on the facts with undeniable historical validity that I have laid out. Speculating, though, is one of the rewards of surviving a long investigation and is part of the pull the She-Pope continues to exert.

In a more general sense, if this search serves any purpose at all, it will be, in ascending order of priority, to see Joan's name mentioned at sites like Fulda, Siena and Wimborne; for her example to be treated with a little more seriousness by historians and all sides in the gender debates that continue to divide the Catholic church; and for the 'official' Church to show a little more humility when dictating from on high which episodes of history – usually those that reflect well on it – are worthy of respect and which can be swept under an already lumpy carpet.

Significant Dates: An Overview

715   Boniface sails from England for Germany
750   Rome breaks its links with Constantinople
755   Boniface buried at Fulda
800   Pope Leo III crowns Charlemagne Emperor
846   Saracen raid on Rome wrecks Saint Peter's
847   Pope Leo IV elected
853   Pope Leo dies. Joan elected
855   Pope Joan discovered and deposed. Benedict III elected
858   Pope Benedict dies. Nicholas I elected
1225   Jean de Mailly's *Chronica universalis* appears with unequivocal endorsement of Joan
1265   Martin Polonus's chronicle, principal source on Joan, first appears
1484   Papal Master of Ceremonies confirms that popes avoid the Vicus Papissa
1565   Last sighting of Pope Joan statue in Rome
1691   Frederick Spanheim's survey of 500 sources on Pope Joan published late 1600s
      Joan removed from papal busts in Siena Cathedral

Bibliography

Accessible works on Pope Joan include:

Non-fiction:
Boureau, Alain, *La Papesse Jeanne* (Paris, 1988)
D'Onofrio, Cesare, *La Papessa Giovanna* (Rome, 1979)
Morris, Joan, *Pope John VIII, an English Woman, Alias Pope Joan* (London, 1985)
Pardoe, Rosemary and Darroll, *The Female Pope* (Wellingborough, 1988)
Royidis, Emmanuel, *Pope Joan – A Historical Survey* (translated by Charles Hastings Collette, London, 1886)
Thurston, Father Herbert, *Pope Joan* (London, 1929)

Fiction:
Borodin, George, *The Book of Joanna* (London, 1947)
Dunan, Renée, *Pope Joan* (London, 1931)
Ince, Richard, *When Joan Was Pope* (London, 1931)
Maitland, Sara, *Telling Tales* (London, 1983)
Pasteur, Claude, *La Papesse* (Paris, 1983)
Royidis, Emmanuel, *Pope Joan* (translated by Lawrence Durrell, London, 1954)
Wood, Clement, *The Woman Who Was Pope* (New York, 1931)
Woolfolk Cross, Donna, *Pope Joan* (New York, 1996)

Other excellent background sources include:

Bullough, Vern, *Sex, Society and History* (New York, 1976)
Duffy, Eamon, *Saints and Sinners: A History of the Papacy* (London, 1997)
Garber, Marjorie, *Vested Interests: Cross-Dressing and Cultural Anxiety* (New York, 1992)
Hibbert, Christopher, *Rome: The Biography of a City* (London, 1985)
Hughes-Hallett, Lucy, *Cleopatra* (London, 1990)
Llewellyn, Peter, *Rome in the Dark Ages* (London, 1971)
Miles, Rosalind, *The Women's History of the World* (London, 1988)

Morris, Jan, *Conundrum: An Extraordinary Narrative of Transsexualism* (New York, 1974)

Morris, Joan, *The Lady Was a Bishop* (New York, 1973)

Torjesen, Karen Jo, *When Women Were Priests* (San Francisco, 1993)

Warner, Marina, *Joan of Arc: The Image of Female Heroism* (London, 1981)

Notes

Chapter One

1 Traditional summary of words found in *Sermons* (Antwerp, 1702)
2 *The Companion Guide to Rome* by Georgina Masson (London, 1972)
3 Pope Hadrian IV (1154–9)
4 *The Oxford Dictionary of Popes* by J. N. D. Kelly (Oxford, 1986)
5 Father John Owen's article was published in the *Catholic Herald* on 8 October 1989
6 *Saint Clement's, Rome* by Leonard Boyle OP (Rome, 1989)
7 *The Name of the Rose* by Umberto Eco (London, 1983)

Chapter Two

1 Figure quoted by Frederick Spanheim in *Histoire de La Papesse Jeanne*, vols 1 and 2 (Paris, 1720). See later in chapter for more detail
2 *Berlin Lat. qu. 70*, folio 196r in the Staatsbibliothek. See also *MGH Scriptorum* edited by G. H. Pertz (Basle, 1872)
3 See note 1 above
4 See Dollinger's *Fables Respecting Popes of the Middle Ages* translated by Alfred Plummer (London, 1871)
5 See Leonardi Claudio's *Anastasio Bibliotecario* (Studii Medievali, 1967)
6 See chapter 1, note 4
7 See L. Wallach, 'The Genuine and the Forged Oath of Leo III' in *Traditio* (vol. 11, 1955)
8 Joan Morris includes a whole section on historians' views on the relationship between Joan and Anastasius in her *Pope John VIII, an English Woman, Alias Pope Joan* (London, 1985)
9 *Marianus Scotus Chronica*; Heroldt edition (Basle, 1559)
10 *Dictionary of the Middle Ages* edited by Joseph Strayer (New York, 1985)

11 Sigebert's *Chronicon* is in *Germanicarum Rerum Quator Celebriores Vetusque* edited by Lamberti (Frankfurt, 1566)

12 See note 10 above

13 Otto of Freising's *Chronica* edited by A. Hofmeister (Hanover, 1912)

14 Godfrey of Viterbo's *Pantheon* in *Rerum Germanicarum Scriptores aliquot insignes* edited by J. Pistorius (1726)

15 Gervase of Tilbury's *Otiis Imperialis* can be found in Rolls Series no. 66 edited by W. H. Stevenson (London, 1875)

16 Jean de Mailly's *Chronica universalis* was translated into French by A. Dondaine (Paris, 1947)

17 *La Papessa Giovanna* by Cesare D'Onofrio (Rome, 1979)

18 See note 16 above

19 Stephen de Bourbon's *De Diversis materiis praedicabilibus* is found in *Scriptores Ordinis Praedicatorium* edited by J. Eccard (Lipsae, 1723)

20 See Peter Stanford's *The Devil: A Biography* (London and New York, 1996)

21 Found in the collection *Monumenta Germaniae Historica: Scriptores*

22 See note 21 above

23 Manuscript 179 in the Bodleian Library, Oxford

24 Manuscript 452(A) in the Bodleian Library, Oxford

25 Bernardino Coreo, *Historia continente la storia di Milano* (Milan, 1503)

26 *The Chronicle of Adam of Usk* edited by Edward Maunde Thompson (London, 1876)

27 Lawrence Banck, *Roma triumphans seu actus inaugurationum* (Frankfurt, 1645)

28 Platina, *Storia delle vite di pontifici* (Venice, 1761)

Chapter Three

1 For example Dollinger – see chapter 2, note 4

2 See *Making Saints* by Kenneth Woodward (New York, 1990)

3 *A Woman in the Chair of Saint Peter* by Professor N. C. Kist (Leyden, 1843)

4 *A Thief in the Night* by John Cornwell (London, 1989)

5 In Matthew 8:14 Peter's mother-in-law is mentioned

6 See *Dear Dodie: The Life of Dodie Smith* by Valerie Grove (London, 1996)

7 *The Lady Was a Bishop* by Joan Morris (New York, 1973). Published in Britain as *Against Nature and God*

8 See chapter 2, note 8

9 Author interview

10 There is a full account in Joan Morris's book – see chapter 2, note 8

11 *Le Liber Pontificalis* by Louis Duchesne (Paris, 1886). Re-edited by C. Vogel in 1955 and 1957

12 See Lucy Hughes-Hallett, *Cleopatra* (London, 1990)

13 Ibid.

14 See Marina Warner, *Joan of Arc: The Image of Female Heroism* (London, 1981)

15 See Lucinda Coxon's play, *The Three Graces*, first performed 1995 at the Lakeside Theatre, Colchester.

Chapter Four

1 Louisa May Alcott, *Little Women* (New York, 1868)

2 Felix Haemerlein, *De Nobilitate et Rusticitate Dialogus* (1447)

3 See chapter 2, note 21

4 Paul Johnson, *A History of Christianity* (London, 1976)

5 *Saint Benedict's Rule* (various imprints)

6 See G. W. Greenaway, *Saint Boniface* (London, 1955)

7 See C. H. Talbot, *The Anglo-Saxon Missionaries in Germany* (London, 1954)

8 Rudolphius was referred to by Spanheim – see chapter 2

9 See chapter 3, note 7

10 Lina Eckenstein, *Women Under Monasticism* (London, 1896)

Chapter Five

1 From Freud's *New Introductory Lectures on Psycho-Analysis* (1933), collected in the standard edition of *The Complete Psychological Works of Sigmund Freud* edited by James Strachey (London, 1964)

2 Part of her contribution to *The Hidden Tradition*, a BBC1 film broadcast in 1992 and directed by Angela Tilby

3 Pliny, *Natural History* edited and translated by H. Rackham, ten volumes (London, 1938–63)

4 See Luke 8:1–3

5 *When Women Were Priests* by Karen Jo Torjesen (San Francisco, 1993) is the most recent update on the work of feminist historians on these issues

6 See note 2 above

7   See chapter 3, note 7

8   See note 2 above

9   The Infancy Gospels are intelligently covered in Marina Warner, *Alone of All Her Sex* (London, 1976)

10 See chapter 3, note 7

11 *Saint Thomas Aquinas Summa Theologiae: A Concise Translation* edited by Timothy McDermott (London, 1989)

12 Saint John Chrysostom, 'To the fallen monk Theodore', quoted by Marina Warner, see note 9 above

13 *Saint Augustine Confessions* translated by Henry Chadwick (London, 1991)

14 Alban Butler, *Lives of the Saints*, revised edition edited by Thurston and Attwater (London, 1926–8)

15 Eusebius, *The History of the Church*, written in the early part of the fourth century and now published as a Penguin Classic

16 Hippolyte Delehaye, *The Legends of the Saints* (Brussels, 1905) translated by Donald Attwater (London, 1962)

17 See Julie Wheelwright, *Amazons and Military Maids* (London, 1989)

18 Author interview

19 See Michael de la Bedoyere, *Life of Catherine of Siena* (London, 1947)

20 Quoted in Vern Bullough, *Sex, Society and History* (New York, 1976)

21 Quoted in Marjorie Garber, *Vested Interests: Cross-Dressing and Cultural Anxiety* (New York, 1992)

22 See note 21 above

23 See note 20 above

24 *Jerome: His Life and Writings* by J. N. D. Kelly (London, 1973)

25 *Ambrose: His Life and Times* by A. Paredi (London, 1964)

Chapter Six

1   *Conundrum: An Extraordinary Narrative of Transsexualism* by Jan Morris (New York, 1974)

2   'Yentl: The Yeshiva Boy' by Isaac Bashevis Singer in *The Collected Stories* (New York, 1982)

3   Blessed Mary Ward (1585–1645)

4   Author interview

5   See Jacques de Vitry, *The Life of Maries d'Oignies*, translated by Margot H. King (Saskatoon, 1986)

6 Jo Ann Kay McNamara, *Sisters in Arms: Catholic Nuns Through Two Millennia* (Harvard, 1996)

7 See note 6 above

8 Quoted in Lady Holland, *Memoir* (London, 1855)

9 Reported to the author by one of those present

10 Quoted in Marjorie Garber – see chapter 5, note 21

11 First recited by Bishop Baumgartner in *Christian Century* magazine and subsequently cited in Janet Mayo, *A History of Ecclesiastical Dress* (London, 1984)

12 See note 10 above

13 Janet Mayo, *A History of Ecclesiastical Dress* (London, 1984)

14 Laonici Chalcocondylas, *De origine rebus gestis turcorum* edited by Conrad Clausero (Basle, 1556)

15 Author interview and see Dr Rosalind Miles, *The Women's History of the World* (London, 1988)

16 See note 1 above

Chapter Seven

1 Caesar Baronius, 'Annales Ecclesiastici' in *Monumenta Germaniae Historica* vols III and XIV, edited by A. Theiner (Rome, 1868)

2 F. Gregorovius, *History of the City of Rome in the Middle Ages* translated by A. Hamilton (London, 1884)

3 See chapter 2, note 1

4 Notably in Claude Pasteur's novel *La Papesse* (Paris, 1983)

5 *Pope Joan* by Emmanuel Royidis (1886) translated in 1954 by Lawrence Durrell

6 Christopher Hibbert, *Rome: The Biography of a City* (London, 1985)

7 See chapter one

8 See note 6 above

9 The founding father of eastern monasticism

10 Peter Llewellyn, *Rome in the Dark Ages* (London, 1971)

11 Theodore de Niem, *de Iuris* edited by Thomas Guarini (Basle, 1573)

12 See Walter Ullman, *A Short History of the Papacy in the Middle Ages* (London, 1972)

13 Nicolas Cheetham, *Keepers of the Keys: The Pope in History* (London, 1982)

14 See note 11 above

15 See chapter 5, note 15

16 See chapter 1, note 4

17 Author interview

18 See note 1 above

19 See chapter 3

20 *Saints and Sinners: A History of the Papacy* by Eamon Duffy (London, 1997)

21 See note 1 above

22 John Potter, *A History of Christianity* (London, 1875)

23 See note 1 above

Chapter Eight

1 Henri Perrodo-Le Moyne and C. Caillet, *Un Pape Nomme Jeanne* (Paris, 1972)

2 David Yallop, *In God's Name* (London, 1984)

3 See chapter 3, note 4

4 *Mirabilia Urbis Romae* edited by E. Parthey (Berolini, 1869)

5 *Mirabilia Urbis Romae of 1375* in an 1889 edition

6 Bernard Montfaucon, *Diarius Italicum* (Paris, 1702), published as *The Travels of the Learned Father Montfaucon from Paris through Italy* (London, 1712)

7 Quoted by Joan Morris – see chapter 2, note 8

8 See Eugene Muntz, 'La Legende de la Papesse Jeanne' in *La Bibliofilia*, II (1907)

9 John Burchard, *Liber notarum* edited by E. Celani (Citta di Castello, 1907)

10 See chapter 7, note 11

11 J. C. von Orelli, *Inscriptionum Latinarum* (Rome, 1828)

12 G. Tomassetti, 'La Statua Della Papessa Giovanna' in *Bulletino Della Commissione Archeologica Comunale de Roma* (1907)

13 Robert Bellarmine, *de Romana Pontifici* edited by I. T. Roccaberti (Rome, 1698)

14 Elias Hasenmuller, *Historica Iesuitici Ordinis* (Frankfurt, 1593)

15 Thomas Harding, *A Confutation of a Booke Intituled An Apologie of the Church of England* (London, 1565)

Chapter Nine

1 Interviewed in the *Empire News and Chronicle*, 19 February 1956

2 Bishop Burnet, *Some Letters containing an account of what seemed remarkable in Switzerland and Italy* (Rotterdam, 1686)

3 Jean Launoy, *Epistolarum* (Paris, 1665)

4 See chapter 2, note 4

5 Antoine Pagi, *Critico Historico-chronologico in universos annales ecclesiastici Cardinal Baronii* (1727)

6 See chapter 7, note 1

7 Alexander Cooke, *Pope Joan: A Dialogue between a Protestant and a Papist* (London, 1625). Collected in *The Harleian Miscellany – a collection of pamphlets and tracts selected from the library of the Second Earl of Oxford*, vol. 4 (London, 1809)

8 Jean Mabillon, *Itineria Italia* (Paris, 1887)

9 In *Archeologia dell'Opera del Duono memorie IV*, folio 49

10 See chapter 8, note 9

11 See chapter 2

12 See chapter 2, note 17

13 See chapter 7, note 6

14 See chapter 8, notes 4 and 5

Chapter Ten

1 Quoted in Richard Ellman, *Oscar Wilde* (London, 1987)

2 *Pastoral Care of Homosexuals*, issued by the Sacred Congregation for the Doctrine of the Faith in 1986

3 *Guardian*, 22 June 1996

4 See chapter 8, note 8

5 See chapter 2, note 28

6 See chapter 2, note 1

7 See chapter 5, note 9

8 Petrarch, *Libro degli imperador et pontifici* (Florence, 1470)

9 See chapter 2, note 8

10 Boccaccio, *de Claribus Mulieribus* (Augsburg, 1545) containing wood engravings; translated by G. A. Guarino as *Concerning Famous Women* (London, 1964)

11 See chapter 6, note 15

12 Alain Boureau, 'La Papesse Jeanne: formes et fonctions d'une légende au moyen age' in *Des Inscriptions et Belles-Lettres* (Paris, 1984)

13 *Historia et Monumenta Joannis Hus* (Norimbergensem, 1715)

14 Quoted in *Pope Joan – A Historical Survey* by Emmanuel Royidis translated by Charles Hastings Collette (London, 1886)

15 See chapter 8, note 15

16 Bishop John Jewel, 'Defence of the Apology of the Church of England' in *The Works of John Jewel* (London, 1850)

17 See chapter 9, note 7

18 A summary of this period of persecution of English Catholics can

be found in *The Catholics and Their Houses* by Peter Stanford and Leanda de Lisle (London, 1996)

19 Blondel, *de Ioanna Papissa* (Amsterdam, 1657)
20 Pierre Bayle, *Dictionnaire Historique* (Paris, 1720)
21 See note 14 above
22 Alan Cope, *Dialogi Sex Contra Summi Pontificatos* (Antwerp, 1566)
23 *The History of Pope Joan and the Whores of Rome* (London, 1687)
24 Sabine Baring-Gould, *Curious Myths of the Middle Ages* (London, 1877)
25 See chapter 3, note 3
26 J. H. Wensing, *De verhandeling van N. C. Kist* (The Hague, 1845)
27 Antonio Bianchi-Giovani, *Esame critico degli attie documenti relativi alla favola della papessa Giovanna* (Milan, 1844)
28 See chapter 2, note 1
29 See chapter 7, note 1
30 See chapter 2, note 4
31 Father Herbert Thurston, *Pope Joan* (London, 1929)
32 Richard Ince, *When Joan Was Pope* (London, 1931)
33 Clement Wood, *The Woman Who Was Pope* (New York, 1931)
34 Note in the Joan Morris archive in the Fawcett Library at London Guildhall University
35 See chapter 7, note 1
36 Ulla Westerbergh, *Chronicon Salernitanum A Critical Study* (Stockholm, 1950)
37 Edward Gibbon, *Decline and Fall* (London, 1776 and 1778)
38 The Theophylact tale is told in E. R. Chamberlin, *The Bad Popes* (London, 1969)
39 See chapter 7, note 1
40 *The Works of Liudprand of Cremona* translated by F. A. Wright (London, 1930)
41 See note 38 above
42 See chapter 2, note 4
43 See note 12 above
44 See chapter 2, note 4

Chapter Eleven
1 Virginia Woolf, *Orlando* (London, 1928)
2 *Pope Joan* by Donna Woolfolk Cross (New York, 1996)
3 *Telling Tales* by Sara Maitland (London, 1983)

4   See chapter 3, note 12

5   Philip Henslowe, *Diary* edited by Walter Greg (London, 1908)

6   Elkanah Settle, *The Female Prelate* (London, 1680)

7   Alain Boureau's account of this whole revolutionary period is definitive. See his *La Papesse Jeanne*, an enlarged account of his earlier paper (Paris, 1988)

8   See chapter 5, note 17

9   See note 7 above

10   In Durrell's introduction – see chapter 7, note 5

11   Stendhal, 'Promenades dans Rome' in his *Œuvres completes* (Geneva, 1974)

12   G. W. M. Reynolds, *Pope Joan* (London, 1888)

13   See a fuller treatment of this period in Peter Stanford's *Cardinal Hume and the Changing Face of English Catholicism* (London, 1993)

14   Author interview

15   See any of the various collections of G. K. Chesterton, *Stories of Father Brown*

16   See chapter 10, note 32

17   *I Crowley* by Snoo Wilson (Oxford, 1997)

18   See chapter 10, note 33

19   Renée Dunan, *Pope Joan* (London, 1931)

20   George Borodin, *The Book of Joanna* (London, 1947)

21   See chapter 7, note 4

22   See note 2 above

23   Bertolt Brecht, *Letters 1913–1956* translated by Raplh Manheim, edited and with notes by John Willett (London, 1990)

24   Bertolt Brecht, *Diaries 1920–22* edited by Herta Ramthun, essay by John Willett (London, 1979)

25   Ibid.

26   Author interview

27   Critic Verina Glaessner, writing in *Time Out*

28   New York producer Silas Shabelwska and German-Greek-Swiss couple Cristina Kallas and Luciano Glooer have both circulated funding proposals which, at the time of writing, have not got off the ground

29   John Shephard, *The Tarot Trumps* (Wellingborough, 1985)

30   *Catechism of the Catholic Church* (London, 1994)

31   See Henry Charles Lea, *A History of the Inquisition of the Middle Ages* (London, 1888)

32 Author interview

Chapter Twelve
1 Quoted in Lavinia Byrne, *The Hidden Voice* (London, 1995)
2 Quoted in the *Guardian*, 3 April 1997
3 Author interview
4 *International Herald Tribune*, 28 May 1996
5 See note 4 above
6 *New York Times*, 20 September 1995
7 *Catholic Herald*, 14 October 1994
8 *Kirche Intern*, November 1995
9 Author interview
10 Quoted in the *Guardian*, 2 November 1996
11 See note 10 above
12 See note 8 above
13 Petr Fiala and Jiri Hanus, *Koinotes: Felix M. Davidek* (Prague, 1994)
14 See Jonathan Petre, *By Sex Divided* (London, 1995)

Conclusion
1 Author interview
2 W. E. H. Lecky, *History of European Morals* (London, 1869)

Index

alternative theories 136–44,
180
and child 24–5
and education 7–13
as a challenge to contemporary
Catholicism 7, 168–71
Athens 84–6
beard 80, 81, 183
black magic 155–6
card game 154–5
classical literature 76–7
contemporary Joan 172–8
deacons 96–7
devil's disciple 28–9, 76,
122–3, 149
double monasteries 48–50, 183
edicola or shrine 5–8, 102–9
effeminate patriarch 136–7
English roots 44–50, 85
eroticism 155–7
female myths 42–3, 147–8,
158–9
feminist icon 99, 168–71
film 160–1
first 'biographer' 18–20
French revolution 127–8,
149–52
Fulda's role 22–3, 47–8, 55–6,
65–9, 181
gay icon 127
German folklore 73–7
hermaphrodite 133–4
hidden in St Peter's 119–124,
183
in Bologna 110
in fiction 85–6, 134, 145–157
in Siena 110–115, 182
influenced by cross-dressing
saints 57–64, 73, 80, 183

inspired by tales of women
priests 51–6, 183
Jewish myths 70–7, 155
Leo's widow 35–6
medieval chronicles 18–34
misogyny 129
Ostia 25, 103–4
parentage 72–3, 160
physical disguise 77–82, 183–4
'pierced chair' 7–8, 9–12,
33–4, 115–8
'Pope Books' 21–2, 24, 38–42,
93–8
post-Reformation rhetoric
148–9
prophetess of Moguntia 25,
185
Protestant forgery 16–34, 182
psychological aspect 81–3,
165–8, 179–80, 184
Reformation 128–9, 132–4,
181
Renaissance view 130–1
role of Dominicans 14, 28–9,
141–4
Rome 86–98
silent gap in churches 35–42,
180–2
statue in Rome 107–9
tarot 161–3
theatre 157–160
transvestite icon 184
Vatican-Lateran conflict 118
'Vicus Papissa' 102–9, 118–9,
128, 179–80, 182–3, 185
Joan of Arc 42–3, 130, 146–7,
153
John VI, Pope 87, 94, 182
John VII, Pope 87
John X, Pope 139

204